Praise for *Mastering the Future of Finance Michelle Beyo*

"At the heart of Michelle's book is the critical issue of trust. Her exploration of how the fintech ecosystem must acquire and scale that trust should be central to all organizational thinking. Without trust, we simply cannot unlock the true potential of the new technologies reshaping financial services."

—**David Birch,** *Forbes* Contributor and Global Author on Digital Identity and Money

"Michelle Beyo has captured something truly essential about the future of finance: that every technological advancement, no matter how complex, ultimately converges on trust. In *Mastering the Future of Finance*, Michelle does the heavy lifting for the reader, breaking down the rapidly evolving landscape of fintech, digital identity, and AI. By grounding these immense shifts in the three pillars that matter most—trust, data, and technology—she provides a clarity that is rare in today's market. This is not just a perspective piece; it is a vital roadmap for anyone building in this space. It is clear, insightful, and, above all, highly actionable for the modern commerce leader."

—**Carol Grunberg,** Fortune 100 Global Speaker and Chief Partnerships Officer at AU10TIX

"The transformation of our financial infrastructure is occurring at a staggering pace. In *Mastering the Future of Finance*, Michelle Beyo brilliantly simplifies the simultaneous shifts in AI, embedded payments, and security. She provides a vital roadmap for the road ahead, reminding us that while technology evolves, trust remains the ultimate guide to our future. A must-read for anyone looking to stay ahead."

—**OB Rawls,** Executive Director at Wellesley Hills Financial and CEO of Vult Security

"In an era of unprecedented digital transformation, Michelle Beyo reminds us that innovation without trust is unsustainable. *Mastering the Future of Finance* highlights the fundamental need for Privacy by Design in the next generation of finance, illustrating how we can build a financial ecosystem that is both technologically advanced and deeply respectful of what Michelle calls human data rights. This is an essential guide for anyone seeking to navigate the complexity of the future without forfeiting privacy."

—**Dr. Ann Cavoukian,** Executive Director of the Global Privacy & Security by Design Centre and Three-Term Privacy Commissioner of Ontario

"With years of experience scaling payment infrastructure, I've seen that data empowerment is the next great frontier. Michelle Beyo's book breaks down how open finance can bridge the gap between legacy constraints and innovative, user-centric solutions. It is an indispensable resource for any leader building the future of our industry."

—**James Neville,** CEO of Yaspa

"The transition to a digital-first economy requires a fundamental understanding of the infrastructure beneath it. In *Mastering the Future of Finance*, Michelle Beyo navigates the complexities of AI, digital currencies, and blockchain, showing how these technologies are not just trends but the core foundation of global value exchange. A vital resource for anyone navigating the next frontier of money."

—**Jaime Leverton,** CEO of ReserveOne

"Michelle Beyo has written a one-stop guide to the digitalization of finance that all professionals concerned with the future of finance need to read. This book synthesizes a remarkable array of topics providing insights on technology, innovation, decentralization, and regulation. She's been at the forefront of the open banking movement, advocating tirelessly for fintech and consumers. With this book, she lays out a vision of a decentralized financial system that is efficient, inclusive, and democratic."

—**Dr. Michael R. King,** Professor at UVic Business School

"With the precision of a strategist and the heart of an advocate, Michelle argues that the 'Internet of Value' must be built on a foundation of consumer data rights. She deconstructs the shift from passive data collection to active data ownership, proving that privacy is not a barrier to innovation; it is the ultimate catalyst for it. For any leader or policymaker, this book is a definitive manifesto on building a financial world that is inclusive, secure, and powered by the unwavering sovereignty of the individual."

—**Jane Barratt,** Chief Advocacy Officer at MX

"For 80 years, financial services focused on consolidation and globalization. Today, that trend is reversing as decentralized technologies and AI turn the industry upside down. Michelle Beyo's insights are indispensable for navigating this shift. She masterfully deconstructs the nine key elements driving the future of finance, offering a practical foundation for the next generation of innovators."

—**Sanjib Kalita,** Fintech Thought Leader and CEO of Guppy

"Beyo distills the complexity of modern finance into clarity. Just as the telecom industry connected the world to share information, she explains how the new 'Internet of Value' connects us to move money, making the future of finance both understandable and actionable."

—**Mellie Chow,** Venture Capitalist, Angel Investor, and Product Innovation Executive

MASTERING THE FUTURE OF FINANCE

MASTERING THE FUTURE OF FINANCE

HOW DATA, TRUST, AND TECH ARE RESHAPING THE GLOBAL ECONOMY

MICHELLE BEYO

WILEY

Published by John Wiley & Sons, Inc., Hoboken, New Jersey.

Library of Congress Cataloging-in-Publication Data is Available:

ISBN 9781394402076 (Cloth)
ISBN 9781394402083 (ePub)
ISBN 9781394402090 (ePDF)

Cover Design: Wiley
Cover Image: davstudio/stock.adobe.com
Author Photo: Courtesy of the Author

Printed and bound by CPI Group (UK) Ltd, Croydon, CR0 4YY
C9781394402076_270726

Disclaimer

AI Disclosure.

In researching and creating infographics in this book, AI tools such as Google AI Studio, ChatGPT, and Figma's AI-enhanced design suite were used to assist with data research, synthesis, and conceptual design. All data points, statistics, and sources have been manually verified by the author, who retains full responsibility for the final content.

I am deeply grateful to my loving family, my supportive husband, my incredible kids, and my entrepreneurial parents. Thank you for being my sanctuary and my inspiration. Your patience and belief in me made this book possible. I am also thankful for my friends and global professional network for your unwavering support and shared wisdom. To those who strive to make the future of finance better for everyone, this work is dedicated to you.

Contents

Foreword

When Michelle asked me to write this foreword, I hesitated, not because of the huge privilege of being able to add my grain of sand to the work of someone as accomplished as her but as I wondered if I'd be able to add something meaningful to *Mastering the Future of Finance*.

Michelle and I go back more than 10 years, and I've had the pleasure of being on countless fascinating panels with her at events including Money 20/20, Open Banking Expo, and Payments Canada Summit.

Payments and finance are ubiquitous; pretty much everything we do in life carries a payment consideration, either directly or indirectly. It impacts those who make or receive payments and even more so those who are, unfortunately, excluded from our financial systems.

Fintech, open banking, and real-time payment systems have revolutionized financial inclusion for people like the hundreds of millions of Africans who have a mobile wallet but perhaps not a traditional bank account and the 60 million Brazilians who use Pix but don't have a credit card.

And it's about both: serving the unserved and the underserved, for example, by giving consumers and small businesses choice and far more competitive rates. This has been the case for remittances, but also for travelers and students on exchange, who can now use global e-wallets to dramatically reduce foreign exchange conversion spreads and control the timing of conversions.

As Michelle crisply describes, "Trust is the new currency," and bulletproof ID is the cornerstone of any e-wallet, regardless of the consumer credentials, funds, and/or data it holds. When done flawlessly, this removes friction for users. Emerging technologies, such as stablecoins and agentic commerce, can further enhance the user experience: (a) stablecoins as a sort of global alternate payment method, instant, cost-effective and irreversible, and denominated in the currency that minimized foreign exchange costs, and (b) agentic commerce as a way for consumers to delegate the task of curating and analyzing market data to make the optimal purchasing decision. In other words, they save time and pay less for the things they buy.

The richness of Michelle's journey has put her in a unique position to articulate and share with us her vision of the future of finance, a vision that ties together her pioneering work in open banking, open finance, and open data.

These are not just buzzwords; McKinsey estimates that for some countries, open data may increase GDP by up to 5%. This is a significant uplift, not just in microeconomics but also in the real impact these services will have on consumers and small businesses. Reduced friction means consumers can access competitive interest rates on their investments, foreign exchange rates, loans, and insurance, thanks to increased competition. Small businesses can also apply for loans and insurance across multiple institutions with minimal effort, freeing up their time to focus on what matters most: growing their businesses.

There's an additional angle: countries that create an environment conducive to innovation will reap the benefits of job creation and a critical mass of fintech expertise, which will spur economic growth and value creation. India, with Aadhaar (biometry) and UPI (real-time rails), and Brazil, with Pix (real-time rails), are case studies on how regulators can become catalysts for growth and innovation. Conversely, those who are slow to move decisively into the future will lose a magnificent growth opportunity.

I'll now let you dive into Michelle's writing, which is bound to become the new fintech page-turner, full of her generous and insightful perspectives on the future of finance.

—Daniel Kornitzer

Head of Global Partnerships at EBANX

Author's Note

This book reflects my professional experience, interviews with global leaders, and extensive research to provide insight into the rapidly evolving world of finance. The goal is not only to educate but to inspire curiosity, critical thinking, and forward-looking exploration. While it is impossible to predict every future development, I have focused on nine elements—fintech, baas, embedded finance, open data, cybersecurity, digital trust, AI, blockchain, and digital currencies—that I believe will significantly shape the financial industry over the next decade.

All content, statistics, and sources have been carefully verified, and this book is intended to serve as a launchpad for learning, discussion, and innovation. Readers are encouraged to navigate the future of finance responsibly, creatively, and ethically, combining technological literacy, regulatory awareness, and ethical considerations to help build a financial ecosystem that is innovative, inclusive, and resilient.

I hope you enjoy stepping into the future of finance with me and that this journey inspires curiosity, sparks conversation, and opens new ways of thinking. Financial technology rules, standards, and practices can differ quite a bit from one country or region to another. Because of that, some of the information in this book may not apply where you live or do business. For guidance that's specific to your location, it's a good idea to check with your local regulators and consult a qualified legal professional.

Introduction

Mastering the future of finance has been a lifelong journey, marked by a multitude of twists and turns. I have faced three major challenges on this path: finding my voice, stepping into knowledge, and learning to stand in confidence.

Over the last 20 years, I have asked hundreds (maybe thousands) of questions, soaked up insights, taken risks, failed forward, thought differently, learned to challenge the status quo, and even built my own company called Finavator. Just like fintech, my journey continues to evolve and grow. Come along this winding road with me and step into the future of finance.

Finance has always been about more than the transfer of value; it is about the ability of individuals and businesses to participate fully in the opportunities society offers. The future of finance, at its core, is about empowerment, personalization, and convenience. Going forward, we must also incorporate what I call "human data rights" and "privacy-by-design." What we are marching toward is not just the digitization of money but the creation of an entirely new financial fabric, one that is instant, intelligent, and deeply personalized.

My career journey has not followed a typical path, but it has followed a common theme: emerging technology. My path began in 1999, when I started my first technology role at the head office for a telecom store, while still in high school. For the next six years, I helped this franchisee open five locations. I was intrigued by the new phones, from flip phones to smartphones, and enjoyed teaching myself how to use all the features. This is when I began mastering the skill of simplifying the complex. I pushed to complete high school a year early to make up for being held back a year when switching from French immersion to English school in fourth grade and to work full-time. Eventually, it became part of my job to train the team, sell to customers, and help them set up their new phones. I fell in love with the power of technology!

Next, I spent eight years in online shopping, focused on helping United, Delta, Alaska, and Lufthansa airlines offer their customers ways to earn loyalty points, not just by flying but also by shopping online. This international marketing company had a mostly male executive team and board. Luckily, I had the pleasure of having the only female leader as my boss, and she was a rockstar. Kelly Lee Smith studied computer science in the 80s, which was not typical for the time, and she was an impressive innovator. She was my first mentor and taught me important lessons about the corporate world, from the art of client management to building relationships with IT teams and driving innovation. I am forever grateful.

I then took my first step into the world of payments and spent three years working at the international head office of a leading prepaid company on a 50/50 Canadian executive team of three men and three women. This team was created by a forward-thinking Brazilian leader, Felipe Papaleo. Felipe's vision was clear: to drive innovation through planning and the development of strong structures. I learned the art of setting purpose-driven KPIs, creating project dashboards, and applying Six Sigma. All of these skills have helped me become the leader I am today. It is true that having an amazing boss motivates you to go the extra mile. In addition, we had a powerful team that pushed itself to achieve its goals.

I was leading three departments and helping to drive innovation. I spent time learning from colleagues in 30 countries and helped launch one of the first digital B2B prepaid card shopping malls, where businesses could buy bulk gift cards from Nike, Amazon, Home Depot, and others for employee or customer incentives. One of the most challenging projects was creating a retail-sold, reloadable Mastercard while ensuring compliance with regulations across the country. This meant spending hours with legal teams, simplifying product details, and training major retailers on what reloadable prepaid cards were and the steps for the reload function online. Both products promote digital access and financial inclusion and are enabled by prepaid technology. Those benefits are why I am still so passionate about sharing how fintech innovated now and continues to do so with prepaid and BaaS technologies in today's ecosystem.

My curiosity about each aspect of fintech has continued to push me forward, even at times when months of work resulted in a false start or required a complete restart. I learned to enjoy the challenges, the lessons, and especially the wins.

In 2017, I had the chance to collaborate with InComm's global team on a 7-Eleven pilot in British Columbia, integrating WeChat Pay for QR-based top-ups. I quickly learned about the "Super App" model, which was impressive. This proof of concept (POC) was a small test allowing their consumers at the time, including international students and travelers, to fund their digital wallets at the pilot locations. Although the Canadian project was an exploratory test and did not reach a full rollout with InComm, it provided a front-row seat to the innovative QR code payment technology. This work ran parallel to the successful InComm Japan rollout in April 2017, and the insights I gained into QR code integration and cross-border digital wallets remain foundational to my understanding of the global payment ecosystem.[1]

This led me to take the first Ivey Business School program focused on fintech, digital identity, and blockchain in 2017, taught by Professor Michael King. This involved an 80-hour pre-read and a 3-day executive in-person course where I met like-minded individuals. It was an insightful experience that gave me the confidence to say "yes" when, only months later, I was offered a role as chief client officer at a digital identity start-up focused on consent in blockchain use.

As someone new to both blockchain and digital identity, I found this not an easy decision to make. It was truly a risk-on-risk opportunity. I was honored to be offered the role by Bruce Silcoff, a CEO whom I had known for years in the loyalty and payments industry. He not only offered me a role; he offered me my first C-suite position. I was concerned about leaving my 50/50 executive team and told Bruce. To my surprise, he quickly replied and formed a very balanced team of executives, which definitely helped. I was so thankful to have a supportive husband and two amazing young kids who believed in me. I had the support I needed to make the hard decision to transition from my corporate life into the start-up world. This experience shaped me in many ways, first by learning how to live in the fast-paced, ever-changing start-up world, as well as taking a deep dive into the inner workings of blockchain, and how it could empower the future of finance, and then simplifying my learnings into short presentations that unlocked global speaking opportunities.

The following chapters lay the foundation for simplifying complex innovations and technologies destined to change the world of finance. Having spent more than two decades at the intersection of online platforms, telecommunications, digital identity, and finance, I have had a front-row seat to the evolution of the modern economy. My goal in these pages is to use that perspective to simplify the global world of finance for my readers. In an environment as vast and rapidly changing as this, my desire is to act as a navigator, distilling 20 years of enlightenment and interviews with leading experts into clear insights that can inspire innovation. This book serves as a guide to the history, current state, and rapid transformations as of early 2026, rather than a definitive prediction of what lies ahead.

I have purposely separated the information about the evolution toward the future of finance into three parts titled "Financial Innovation," "Trust Is the New Currency," and, finally, "Groundbreaking Technology." The content in each part has made a powerful impact on the financial world. When learning about the future of finance, it's necessary to understand hundreds of terms and acronyms. I have created a glossary, available for free download at www.finavator.com, to help you on your journey of understanding.

I have learned over the years as an entrepreneur that having freedom is true success. I write those words at the beginning of every new notebook as a reminder that no matter how hard the day is, I am free to dream big and focus on innovation. This book is me dreaming big and I hope it will help you do the same.

Part I: Financial Innovation

In this part, we begin with a high-level review of 4,000 years of banking history, the foundation on which we are building today. We then dive into the "Rise of Fintech," which is set to reach close to $882 billion globally by 2030, and the infrastructure that has unlocked these incredible solutions, including prepaid payment technologies and banking as a service (BaaS).[2] I can't wait to share how embedded finance is simplifying how we pay for coffee and secure our mortgages. I will also explain emerging new technologies, including agentic and QR code payments, and how they are making money movement seamless while also adding financial capability directly into the flow of life.

Many people come into this field thinking fintech is all about coding or apps. The real "aha" moment is realizing that fintech is ultimately about solving human problems. It has always been about access, empowerment, and trust. Once you start thinking in terms of ecosystems and behavior rather than just technology, your whole approach shifts.

Part II: Trust Is the New Currency

In this part, we are going to explore how data is the new oil powering the digital economy, why it should be protected, and how it helps all of us to unlock choice and freedom with open finance and trusted identity. Trust has become an important new currency. It is vital in the digital economy to connect with our daily lives, from simply unlocking our phones with Face ID to signing up for a mortgage from the palm of our hands to sending earned money to our kids' digital wallets with a few clicks. We rely on trust to ensure we move money safely through our banking app and when logging in to virtual business calls. We need our financial ecosystems to set a high bar for trust, with strong compliance and security to help combat fraud. Also, empowering consumers by embedding privacy-by-design and content-driven data sharing into their foundations. Resilient systems are not just technical; they are principled, ensuring that inclusion and protection go hand in hand.

Part III: Groundbreaking Technology

In this part, we will dive into the groundbreaking technologies that are transforming the future of finance. One of the biggest innovations of the current generation, with a global impact, is the worldwide adoption of the Internet, which has helped to unlock innovation that has become essential for our everyday lives. Many of us have had a front-row seat for this change. The next groundbreaking technologies include how agentic agents and artificial intelligence (AI) could enable the next level of productivity, as well as the power of blockchain, the empowerment that tokenized assets can unlock, and the freedom that digital currencies and stablecoins are bringing to consumers. They are all redefining how we store, move, and use money. The interactions we have with platforms and with each other are no longer isolated; they are nodes in a global network of interoperability and interconnectedness. Each transaction, each connection, strengthens the foundation of trust and possibility. The future of finance is, therefore, not only faster and more secure but also more integrated into who we are and how we relate to one another. Modern finance can connect you to the world while focusing on your personal needs, using smart technology backed by a combination of human and AI support.

Considering the mindset needed to embrace this tidal wave of transformation, I think back to a similar time in 1997 to the iconic Apple ad campaign celebrating those who "Think Different." A poem was written for all the rebels in history who helped change the world, from the genius of Albert Einstein to the pioneering efforts of Amelia Earhart, and even to the generation-defining music of Bob Dylan. This campaign raised my awareness of the power of thought and how individuals can truly make a difference. The impact of that ad still carries weight in my mind today as I learn from and commune with industry experts who are shaping the future of the world through technology. You will read quotes I agree with from leading industry voices at the beginning of each chapter, and you will learn from several of them, as they agreed to share their thoughts in interviews on their areas of expertise.

The Apple ad campaign made me think about my own strengths and the impact I want to make in my lifetime. Back then, as I focused on determining how I could "think different" in the wonderful world of technology, I discovered that my strength wasn't what I expected it to be. Like others before me, I was afraid of public speaking, yet after reading Angela Duckworth's book *Grit*, I wrote it down as a goal for 2017. When I was offered an opportunity to speak later that year, I said "yes" even though I was terrified.

There was an audience of 200-plus people, including regulators, at Opal Group's conference in Newport, Rhode Island. I had prepared for hours and, as you might imagine, could barely sleep the night before. When it came time to share my insights on prepaid technologies and how they enabled the pilot launch of QR top-up functionality to help consumers load WeChat wallets at a major retailer in Canada, I not only simplified this complex new technology but also realized that doing so came almost naturally. I still remember the feeling after stepping off at that first stage. I could see that I had sparked interest and excitement in the room; the audience wanted to learn more about how to enable a similar offering across North America.

This was a light bulb moment for me; I had identified this new skill of simplifying the complex, and it was helping turn the fear of change into excitement for stepping into the future of finance. Since then, I have spoken more than 100 times on virtual and in-person stages around the world, including TEDx, Money2020 (USA, Europe), Fintech Meetup, Finovate, Fintech South, Fintech Retreat, Open Banking Expo Payments Canada Summit, TechSki, and many others.

What you are reading is both a roadmap to the future and an invitation to imagine finance not as infrastructure alone but as a living system, one that empowers billions, bridges cultures, and evolves with us as our identities, technologies, and societies continue to converge. As the financial industry continues to rapidly evolve, many key technologies will disrupt its ecosystem. It is becoming increasingly clear that we need a new kind of financial literacy to stay at the forefront of this transformation. It is important for any professional working in the financial ecosystem to understand not only the trends and their implications but also how to leverage these new technologies effectively across their organizations. Let's step forward into the future of finance together.

Part I

Financial Innovation

Chapter 1

The Rise of Fintech: Empowering a New Financial Era

"Financial technology can lift communities and empower individuals. That's what makes this work so meaningful."

—Sebastien Taveau, author of *The Deliveryman*

I have found that one of the best ways to begin understanding complex systems is to break them down into their simplest elements. While working on these chapters, my daughter was studying the periodic table, and it clicked with me that this was the perfect way to share the nine key elements of finance, even though science was not my favorite topic in school. This is an important tool that helps to show not only the elements of the future of finance but also how they connect with each other.

I created Figure 1.1 to be your quick-reference guide for the nine influential elements of fintech reshaping our world today. Through this book, we will explore these nine elements together to help build a better picture of the finance of today and the finance of the future, and you can continue to refer to them throughout your journey, whether you're a leader, technologist, regulator, or investor. These are the building-block elements that make up the future of finance, but there are more we are still discovering, just like scientists.

The first element we will cover is "fintech." Fintech, short for, you guessed it, financial technology, is the use of innovative technology (often software) to make

Figure 1.1 Nine influential elements of fintech

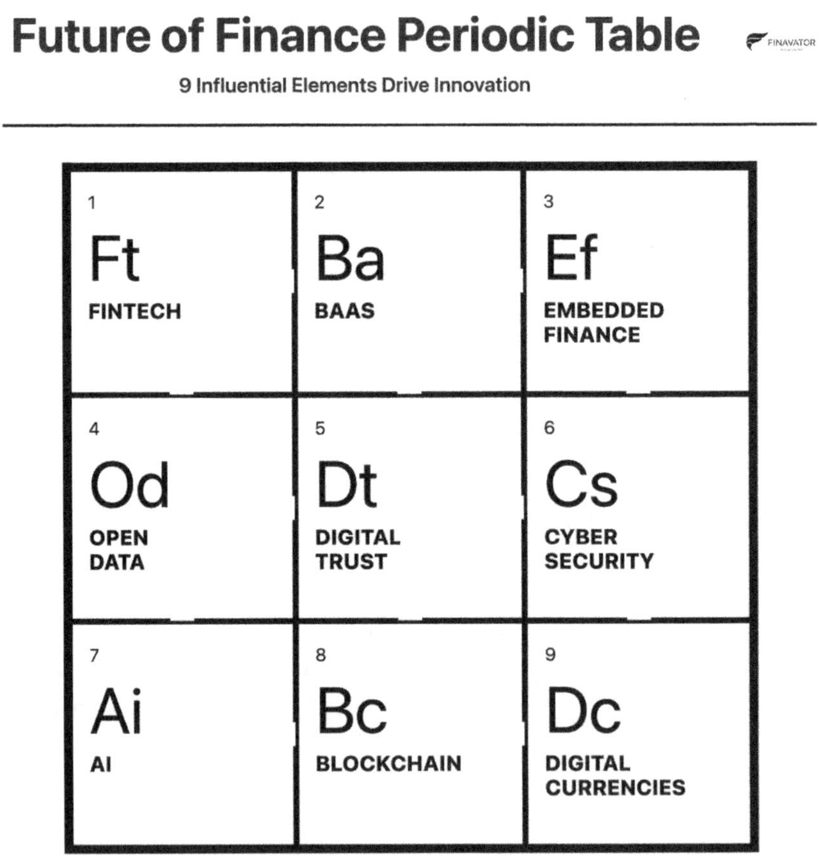

financial services better, faster, more efficient, and accessible. The rise of fintechs worldwide has been impressive. According to Fintech Futures in March 2025, "The market is projected to grow to $882 billion by 2030."[1] This projection has captured the attention not only of investors but also of world leaders, government regulators, and everyday users. What I find interesting is that fintech touches all the other booming sectors of the world economy. These include insurance, healthcare, real estate, investments, lending, transportation, and even travel. Each of those industries has come to rely heavily on fintech to empower and simplify transactions and to increase the speed of business.

To help you master the future of finance, let's begin with the rise of fintech and how fintech is rewiring finance. I've found that fintechs are:

- Changing the game when it comes to offering speed and convenience at a reduced cost
- Hyper-focused on client-centric journeys and use cases such as access to faster, more affordable loans, which can help millions of consumers worldwide
- Offering unique, personalized financial services that empower everyone from consumers to small businesses, even underbanked and underserved

While these are some of the most visible changes fintech is driving, the deeper foundation is revealed in the quote from Sebastien Taveau that opens this chapter, where he notes that "it's necessary that financial technology can lift communities and empower individuals." Sebastien is a global fintech innovator, speaker, and author of *The Delivery Man*, with decades of experience building and advising payment and financial technology platforms worldwide. Over the years, we have had several interesting discussions about the future of finance, and the consistent theme is our shared belief that the core bottom line of financial innovation is not efficiency or scale, but the empowerment technology can enable for consumers. Technology expands access, strengthens agency, and creates opportunities. That shared mission is why I chose his quote to open this discussion.

One of the first modern fintechs of our generation, PayPal, launched in the United States in 1999. It is an online payment system that allows people to send and receive money securely worldwide by linking their credit card, debit card, or bank account. Its impact has been felt globally, with more than 434 million active users across 200 markets and a total payment volume in 2024 of more than $1.68 trillion, a 10% year-over-year increase.[1] The company's ability to simplify online payments, allowing money to change hands at a speed previously unimaginable, led the way in this arena. By thinking differently, they inspired a generation to disrupt the entire financial ecosystem.

With the pace of change in fintech, it's understandable that consumers constantly feel they're playing catch-up to learn what's new, while innovators feel they can't innovate fast enough to keep up with technological advancements and global demands. It's easy to get caught up in the excitement of this whirlwind of progress. I sure have.

Bob Dylan wrote the words to "The Times They Are a-Changin" as a reflection of societal changes in the 1960s. I find the same phrase as an appropriate representation of our need to embrace the ever-evolving financial landscape of current times. Unfortunately for some, the speed of change can be overwhelming, even paralyzing; for others, it can provide a positive push in an entirely different direction.

I experienced one of those paralyzing moments myself, and it sent my corporate career in a completely different direction. It happened almost eight years ago, yet it still feels like yesterday. At the time, I had a secure job, two incredible young kids, a loving husband, and a life that looked exactly as I had planned it. I was steadily climbing the corporate ladder with a healthy, safe paycheck that had a small annual increase. In reality, I was working 9–10 hours a day, running three departments for a global fintech enabler, and traveling often for client meetings and conferences. I did everything I could to protect family time, but there was very little space left for myself, let alone friends. Then, in 2018, everything shifted. I was devastated by the death of my best friend, Shannon Phair, from colon cancer at age 36. She had been my childhood neighbor, my rep soccer teammate, and my best friend since the age of six; she was the first person I called with all good news, after my husband.

Shannon often asked me why I worked so much and why I was always striving for the next promotion. Her passing at such an early age forced me to rethink every aspect of my own life. With her diagnosis, four years before her passing, I watched her finally step into her passion as an artist, even having a full art gallery show in our hometown. Her art impacted me greatly. The first piece I purchased sits on my Finavator desk to this day. The background is a starry night sky with a solitary star shining very brightly. Over it are the words "There is a quiet security in knowing you are part of something bigger." As she faced death, Shannon's passion and love for every day gave me the gift of understanding that we have only one chance to make a difference in life and not to wait until it is too late to step into our passion.

Thanks to her wisdom and presence, everything from my sense of who I am and how I spend my time to my mission to leave my mark on the world changed. Her influence gave me the courage to leave the corporate world and start my own business, Finavator, knowing that if I failed, I would find a way to fail forward, and, thankfully, though my journey as an entrepreneur has had its ups and downs, I feel like I have found my calling. Today, as part of the fintech community, I feel like a rebel *with* a cause. I am fortunate to help both banks and fintechs develop strategies that unlock new growth opportunities, drawing on my industry expertise and ecosystem connections. I get to be at the forefront of the times that "are a-changin" every single day, and I wouldn't trade it for anything.

My Fintech Journey

To understand my excitement about fintech and why I see it as an important part of the financial ecosystem, I want to share some of my personal experiences. Let's begin with my parents. Both of my parents were entrepreneurs. As I grew up, I realized their approach to money and financial independence was quite different from that of my friends' families. This was demonstrated vividly in my teen years. When I was 14, they helped me get my first debit card. I still remember how empowered I felt to have my own card, my own access, my own responsibility, my own sense of agency. It was a small moment, but it planted the seed for everything that would come later.

When I was 16 and old enough to drive, like any typical teen, I had great expectations for the new freedoms a driver's license could bring. Also, like most teens, I asked my parents for a car. To my surprise, instead of discussing when I could borrow their car, my parents went ahead and applied for a job at McDonald's on my behalf and told me I had an interview the following Monday. Their expectation was clear that I would work to save money to buy my own car. The added requirement to park it at their house was that it needed to be either a Volkswagen or an Audi due to their reliability and high safety ratings.

So, off I went on a mission in my first year of high school to work nights and weekends to afford my first car. It was a beautiful, navy blue 1983 Volkswagen Cabriolet convertible. My parents got a loan for it, but I was expected to pay for it. I worked hard and saved enough to pay it off by the following spring. I loved that car and learned an important lesson about setting goals and how good it felt to achieve them with a little hard work and dedication.

Another of my parents' lessons was to be myself and spend my non-school time as I wanted. I'll warn you now that I was not your typical teenager. Instead of hanging out with friends, I often chose to work. I had multiple part-time jobs throughout high school. After working at McDonald's, I worked as a hostess and then a waitress at a local steakhouse. In eleventh grade, I became the office store manager at a cell phone company. That might sound crazy, but I found work to be both satisfying and financially rewarding. So, I worked hard and enjoyed earning my own money. I even set new financial goals each year.

Back then, banking was a time-consuming process with a lot of room for improvement. I remember standing in line at my bank to deposit multiple bi-weekly checks. Methods for automatic deposits, as well as online and mobile banking options, were still only being dreamt about. I even had to request a paper copy of my bank balance from the teller each time I made a deposit or payment. Looking back, fintech advancements from the likes of Chime, Revolut, and Wise would have saved me so much time and money. Even though I was learning a lot about managing my finances and taking positive steps toward adulthood, how I managed my money was based on the limited options available at the time. Banks just didn't offer the conveniences of remote deposit, real-time balance viewing, savings goal setting, and alerts that we rely on today or the ability to manage everything from a phone.

When I turned 18, my parents sat down and explained why I needed a credit card. They also cautioned me not to use it if I couldn't pay it off each month. They had me pay my cell phone bill on that card to begin building my credit score. These lessons are not provided to enough young adults early enough in life, as quite a few of my friends struggled with credit issues at a young age. I tried to help them by sharing what I had learned. Doing so set the tone for my mindset on money management early in life.

Credit card debt is a major problem, especially in the United States, reaching $1.209 trillion as of June,[2] the highest level recorded since the New York Fed began tracking it in 1999. Financial education, unfortunately, is not as commonly taught as it needs to be. Some of the best advice I received early in life about credit was to:

- Use less than 30% of your credit limit
- Pay with credit cards in full and on time every month
- Set up autopay for your bills to avoid missed payments
- Keep old accounts open to have a long credit history
- Limit new credit card applications to avoid the negative impact of hard inquiries

I love that many fintech offerings take the mystery out of banking by providing examples of their solutions with simple descriptions. They're not just providing tools; they're helping educate consumers while also helping them save money.

The Path to Modern Banking 2000 BCE–2000 CE

The evolution of the types and availability of today's financial services fascinates me, as I recognize the changes in consumer needs and the technological advancements that deliver each new level of service.

We have come a long way in the 4,000 years of recorded banking, with far more developments than I could explain in this chapter alone. So, I will take you through a quick recap of the key highlights.

In Figure 1.2, I've broken down this journey into four eras, highlighting more than 20 major banking milestones. To help you understand the path from the earliest financial systems to today, I've outlined what I believe are the four most important eras of banking innovation. Ideally, some of these developments will sound familiar from both your ancient and recent history studies, each one a stepping stone to the financial world we know today.

Figure 1.2 Banking and fintech timeline

Banking Innovation Timeline

1750 BC to Present

ERA 1 ANCIENT/MEDIEVAL (1750 BC–1400 AD)	ERA 2 EARLY MODERN (1400–1800)	ERA 3 INDUSTRIAL/MODERN (1800–1980)	ERA 4 DIGITAL/FINTECH (1980–2026)
Foundation of Banking Systems	**Central Banking & Paper Money**	**Mass Banking & Technology**	**Digital Banking Revolution**
1750 BC First banks in Babylon temples under Code of Hammurabi	**1472** Monte di Pietà establishes Italian public banking	**1913** Federal Reserve System created in the US	**1980** First US home banking via American Bank and RadioShack TRS-80
600 BC Lydia issues first standardized gold and silver coins	**1609** Bank of Amsterdam creates standardized currency exchange	**1933** Glass-Steagall Act passed; FDIC created	**1995** EMV chip and PIN secures card payments worldwide
1157 First state-operated Venetian Bank established	**1694** Bank of England founded as official note issuer	**1944** Bretton Woods establishes global monetary system	**1998** PayPal mainstreams digital peer-to-peer payments
1200s Bills of Exchange enable trade without physical gold	**1750s** Letters of credit standardized for global trade	**1950–1970** Credit cards (Diners Club, Visa), first ATM (1967), Mastercard	**2008** Global Financial Crisis hits, Bitcoin whitepaper published
1397 Medici Bank pioneers double-entry bookkeeping	**1791** First Bank of the United States established	**1974** Equal Credit Opportunity Act grants women credit access	**2011** WeChat redefines embedded finance and QR payments in China
	1792 New York Stock Exchange established	**1975–1978** SWIFT launched, debit cards introduced, EFT regulation enacted	**2014** Apple Pay launches, mobile-first payments accelerate globally
			2016 PSD2 and Open Banking APIs open financial data access
			2020 COVID accelerates digital banking, DeFi emerges, BNPL surges
			2023 ChatGPT sparks AI race, banks adopt AI across service and risk
			2025 GENIUS Act passes, agentic payments scale globally

Era 1: Ancient/Medieval (1750 BCE–1400 CE)

Banking originated with the first standardized gold and silver coins from the Babylonian temples and the Kingdom of Lydia. This period saw the rise of state-operated banks and the introduction of bills of exchange by Italian merchants. It concluded with the Medici Bank pioneering modern banking through the adoption of double-entry bookkeeping.

Era 2: Early Modern (1400–1800)

This era marked the birth of central banking and standardized currency exchange through institutions like the Bank of Amsterdam and the Bank of England. The introduction of letters of credit revolutionized global trade by enabling merchants to transact without physically transporting gold. The period ended with the early foundations of the US financial system and the establishment of the New York Stock Exchange.

Era 3: Industrial/Modern (1800–1980)

Mass banking and global monetary systems emerged through the creation of institutions such as the Federal Reserve, the Federal Deposit Insurance Corporation (FDIC), and the Bretton Woods agreement. Technological innovation also transformed the consumer experience with the launch of the first credit cards, ATMs, and interbank networks like Mastercard. The era closed with the expansion of electronic infrastructure, including the SWIFT network and the introduction of debit cards.

It is important to note that with the accelerated pace of change in the last 25 years, there have been as many, if not more, advancements during this time than there have been since 2000 BCE. In the last 10 years alone, we have seen a wave of innovation that is reshaping consumer engagement across fintech, embedded finance, open banking, and digital currencies. And the projections for the future are that the best is yet to come.

Era 4: Digital Banking (1980–Present)

The last 25 years of banking innovation began with the rise of digital peer-to-peer payments through PayPal in 1999 and expanded greatly during the 2007 revolution of mobile money for the unbanked via M-Pesa. Following the 2008 Global Financial Crisis, the industry saw both major regulatory reforms and the birth of decentralized finance with the creation of Bitcoin in 2009. By the mid-2010s, the landscape shifted toward super apps such as WeChat Pay and the emergence of mobile-only challenger banks, while Open Banking APIs began to integrate financial services directly into consumer apps.

The COVID-19 pandemic then served as a major catalyst, accelerating the global adoption of contactless payments and making digital-only interactions standard for everyone. During that time, the rise of digital platforms demonstrated how banking could be seamlessly embedded into social and commercial interactions, further blurring the lines between finance and everyday life.

Looking ahead, the focus is shifting toward AI-driven fraud detection and hyper-personalized financial management that anticipates customer needs in real-time. The signing of the US GENIUS Act in 2025 represented an important milestone in formalizing the crossroads of traditional banking and digital innovation.

The timeline shows a clear trajectory. Banking has changed from solely handling physical assets (gold/temples) to institutional trust (central banks) to consumer convenience (cards/ATMs) and finally to digital autonomy (AI/open banking). Throughout this evolution, fintechs have played a significant role in driving innovation and expanding the depth and accessibility of financial services worldwide.

Today, we are living in the world's fastest-moving era of financial innovation, and this is only the beginning. We are already on the cusp of a fifth era, in which we will see the progression of everything, from biometric and agentic payments to blockchain, cloud computing, artificial intelligence, cryptocurrencies, and stablecoins for starters. Fintech is not one thing; it is all things. Most importantly, it continues the long tradition of expanding access and making financial tools available to more people than ever before.

Fintechs Are Changing the Game

In our current consumer-first world, fintech is giving individuals control over tools once reserved for banks. Although it's a relatively new term, combining the two terms *financial* and *technology*, fintech is more than 150 years old, dating back to the first use of telecommunication in 1860, when financial institutions in Europe and the United States used it to enable financial transactions.

Historically, financial institutions set the standard for who they would and would not serve, primarily courting the wealthy. In our lifetimes, Internet accessibility, combined with the universal adoption of devices like smartphones and tablets, has made financial transactions practically instantaneous for anyone, anywhere. In today's world, where the real value in the banking arena is serving the masses, fintechs are helping banks open a whole new, massive, global market.

According to a McKinsey report from October 2024, global retail banking revenue surpassed US$3 trillion, reflecting the sector's size, profitability, and central role in the global economy.[3] Commercial banks in the United States account for a sizable portion of this revenue, highlighting the dominance of established financial institutions and their broad customer base. Fintechs can drive growth by offering more affordable, flexible, and user-friendly products, either as partners to banks, embedding innovative services within traditional infrastructure, or as competitors, providing alternatives that challenge legacy banking models and meet evolving customer expectations.

For consumers around the world, think of gig workers who deliver food or offer ride services, needing quick access to the money they're generating. Fintech has enabled funds to be transferred directly from the business to a digital prepaid card, with many drivers receiving same-day payment. This service eliminates the need for underserved or underbanked drivers to wait for physical checks and possibly use check-cashing services, where they pay a large percentage of their funds in service fees. This fintech service has helped the gig economy on a mass scale.

Fintechs are serving traditional financial institutions by offering new, meaningful ways to improve consumer experience. An example is how consumers using fintech with AI-powered fraud detection receive instant alerts when a suspicious transaction is detected. These faster, more convenient, and often cheaper alternatives greatly enhance the consumer's trust and provide a wide range of services literally at their fingertips. Fintechs can do this by leveraging cutting-edge technologies such as blockchain, cloud computing, and artificial intelligence.

These technologies enable fintechs to streamline processes, secure transactions, analyze data, reduce costs, and provide personalized services for customers' banking, lending, and investing needs. In some cases, fintechs even partner with banks to help elevate the bank's consumer experience. It is also powerful for businesses, including retailers, to partner with a fintech by white labeling its services to expand how its customers handle transactions and increase revenue.

For example, Walmart has been working with the fintech Affirm since 2019 to offer a buy now, pay later (BNPL) option at checkout. One of the leading UK fintechs, Revolut, offers multicurrency banking, payments, investing, and travel services all in one app. They report having enabled 65 million customers globally in 2025, to manage money seamlessly across borders and reached $4 billion in revenue in 2024.[4]

Fintechs can also work directly with consumers, as in the case of PayPal, which is available in more than 200 countries worldwide. Another example is Robinhood, a mobile app and web platform that allows users to buy and sell stocks, ETFs, options, and cryptocurrencies with no commission fees. It's aimed at making investing accessible to everyday consumers, especially beginners. Partnering with fintechs can enhance a company's reputation by empowering customers to make smarter, cost-saving financial decisions, ultimately strengthening trust.

Fintech vs. Traditional Banks

Today, fintech refers to the use of advanced technology to improve the delivery of financial services worldwide. They are overcoming barriers, and their innovative models offer unique, more affordable, and personalized services that also help the underserved. Fintechs are becoming known as somewhat more inclusive than banks, with a focus on trying to serve consumers, even those with lower credit ratings who are often underbanked or unbanked.

Banks differ from fintech companies in that they hold government-issued licenses and operate under strict regulatory frameworks. Banks are legally permitted to take deposits, provide loans, and participate in payment systems under regulatory oversight. A few examples are these:

- In the United States, the chief banking oversight bodies include the Federal Reserve (Fed), the Office of the Comptroller of the Currency (OCC), and the Federal Deposit Insurance Corporation (FDIC).
- In Canada, banks are primarily regulated by the Office of the Superintendent of Financial Institutions (OSFI), with deposit insurance provided through the Canada Deposit Insurance Corporation (CDIC).
- In the United Kingdom, oversight is shared between the Prudential Regulation Authority (PRA) and the Financial Conduct Authority (FCA), with deposit protection through the Financial Services Compensation Scheme (FSCS).

A traditional bank activity and that of a fintech company both belong to the same industry: providing financial services to consumers or businesses. The difference is that fintechs are primarily digital first, hyper focused on solving specific pain points using technology such as BaaS and Prepaid to offer financial services often in partnership with BIN sponsor banks with largely digital support only, whereas banks are traditional institutions that offer multiple financial service offerings using both digital and physical infrastructures (such as branches) and a mix of digital and human support.

It can be challenging for banks to focus on single use cases, like fintechs do, as they typically offer multiple services to a wide range of customers. This can make the partnership between banks and fintechs highly impactful, as banks have a loyal, larger client base, and fintechs offer new, innovative, personalized product offerings. Paired together, they can drive value for both banks and fintechs and provide a better consumer experience. It's a true win-win situation.

Because of their long-standing reputations, big banks have earned tremendous brand recognition and maintain deep relationships with their customers. Most of their customers will use the same bank for checking and savings accounts, credit cards, business accounts, and even investing services. Something to consider regarding innovation and technological advances is that traditional banks have multiple systems to maintain and, as a result, are not as nimble as fintechs.

Also important to note, traditional banks are highly regulated and bound by legal obligations that do not apply directly to fintechs. Having added flexibility than banks allows fintechs to innovate with additional ease. Faced with an increasingly competitive landscape, banks are collaborating and partnering with fintechs more often to provide specialized services for both small businesses and consumers that fall outside their core offerings.

Fintechs benefit from banks' scale, creating opportunities to collaborate on the creation of even more products and services. The list continues to grow at a fast rate. The anticipation is that there are many additional services in the ideation stage of development as you read this. Some fintech companies eventually secure a banking license that helps them expand into other areas. For example, Revolut achieved official recognition as a bank as of March 2026 in the United Kingdom and some other markets.

When I started Finavator in 2019, I used several fintechs to help my business get off the ground. One of the first I used was QuickBooks, an accounting software company that many use to run accounting systems. I linked it to my core traditional business bank account as there weren't a lot of fintechs focused on small and medium sized business (SMBs) banking at the time. I also used the pay tech company, PayPal, to open a business account for cross-border payments from clients in other countries. I secured my business insurance with an Insurtech company similar to NextInsurance and FoxQuilt.

On a personal level, I have used quite a few fintech products, including micro-investing platforms similar to Robinhood and Wealthsimple. Over the years, I have purchased a couple of expensive items with BNPL providers such as Klarna and Affirm, and as you will read later, I also use youth apps such as Greenlight, GoHenry, and Mydoh to help my kids with allowance payments and budgeting.

In my mind, the more partnerships that exist between traditional banks and fintechs, the better the consumer experience. It's a win for both institutions in that banks can offer additional customizable services, and fintechs get to scale while operating within the compliance and security infrastructures of the banks. I believe that the opportunities for layering services between the two create exponential opportunities for innovation.

The Power of Fintech Partnerships

By bringing together the innovation and speed of start-ups with the experience and scale of established banks, these collaborations create solutions that are smarter, faster, and more customer focused. Partnerships like these allow companies to build seamless digital experiences, expand access to financial services, and deliver products that truly meet the needs of people and businesses. When thoughtfully brought together, fintech partnerships are about more than technology. They are about creating opportunities, driving inclusion, and shaping the future of finance in ways that put people first.

As you see in Figure 1.3, when partnering with a fintech company, the advantages are plentiful, including not having to secure regulatory licenses directly and a faster time-to-market with new products and services in as little as six months. There is a reduced initial investment, potential reductions in ongoing maintenance costs, and new revenue opportunities. White-label fintech solutions enable businesses to launch sophisticated financial services in weeks instead of years, at a fraction of the cost of building in-house. Partnering with a fintech company offers many advantages, including not having to secure regulatory licenses directly and leveraging proven platforms with built-in compliance, security, and scalability. Companies can focus on customer acquisition and brand differentiation while experienced providers handle complex financial infrastructure. The white-label model has become the preferred path for companies seeking to add financial services without becoming fintech companies themselves.

Figure 1.3 Why businesses white label

The Impact of Fintech

By unlocking the full range of financial services that cut across use cases, fintech has carved out an important space for itself in the daily lives of consumers. In January 2025, Plaid reported that half of US consumers use its technology daily. Daily! Take a moment to take in the sheer volume of transactions that could be. It represents a whole lot of trust in technology.

Fintech companies are helping to foster financial freedom by offering millions of underbanked consumers around the world access to financial products, such as savings accounts and investment services, many for the first time. Fintech is helping consumers change habits and gain a better understanding of their financial circumstances and available options, giving them more confidence to act and achieve better outcomes. It's paving the way for a more financially free and equitable future. Here are the most common uses:

PayTech refers to digital payment processing and money transfer services that enable electronic transactions across a wide range of channels. These companies facilitate payments between consumers, businesses, and financial institutions through mobile apps, online platforms, and point-of-sale systems. Their solutions make sending, receiving, and managing money faster, safer, and more convenient than ever before.

Examples: PayPal, Stripe, Square, Venmo, Zelle, Paysafe

Micro-investing platforms broaden access to investments through user-friendly apps and low-cost trading. These services often feature commission-free trading, fractional shares, robo-advisors, and educational resources to make investing accessible to retail investors.

Examples: Robinhood, ETRADE, Wealthfront, Betterment, Acorns, WealthSimple

InsureTech involves technology-driven insurance companies that streamline policy management, claims processing, and risk assessment. They use data analytics, AI, and digital platforms to offer more personalized coverage and faster service than traditional insurers.

Examples: Lemonade, Root Insurance, Oscar Health, Metromile, Next Insurance

Neobanks are digital-only banks that operate without physical branches, offering banking services through mobile apps and online platforms. They typically offer checking, savings, and payment cards with lower fees and enhanced user experiences.

Examples: Chime, Revolut, N26, Monzo, Current, Nubank

Budgeting offerings include personal finance management tools that help users track spending, create budgets, and achieve financial goals. These apps aggregate financial accounts to provide insights into spending patterns and to automate savings.

Examples: Mint, YNAB (You Need a Budget), Personal Capital, PocketGuard, Goodbudget

Digital lending platforms provide various types of loans in the palm of your hand, including personal loans, business loans, and peer-to-peer lending. They use alternative data and algorithms to assess creditworthiness and often offer faster approval processes than traditional banks.

Examples: SoFi, LendingClub, Prosper, Kiva, OnDeck

Buy Now, Pay Later (BNPL) is a service that allows consumers to purchase items immediately and split payment for the items into installments, typically "four payments over four weeks," and is often interest-free. This is not a new offering; "Buy Now, Pay Later" was offered in the early 1900s to consumers who did not have the funds to buy expensive goods outright (e.g., furniture, pianos, and farm equipment). What is new about BNPL is that the process is seamless. With a click of a button, you can buy your next vacation or latest Nikes before you have the funds to pay for them or to help spread the payments over time to suit your budget.

Examples: Klarna, Affirm, Afterpay, Sezzle

Crypto exchanges and digital asset platforms are technology-driven financial services that allow individuals and businesses to buy, sell, store, and transfer cryptocurrencies and other tokenized digital assets. These platforms act as marketplaces where users can trade assets like Bitcoin, Ethereum, and stablecoins. These platforms often provide additional services, such as secure custodial wallets, staking, payments, and blockchain-based financial tools. A lot of them also offer education, compliance features, and fraud monitoring to help users navigate the emerging digital asset ecosystem. By simplifying access to crypto markets, these platforms help broaden participation in digital finance and support innovation across Web3, payments, and tokenized value.

Examples: Coinbase, Binance US, Kraken, Bitstamp, Gemini

Accounting and SMB finance tech are software and platforms designed to help SMBs manage core financial tasks, including bookkeeping, invoicing, payroll, tax preparation, expense tracking, and cash flow forecasting. These tools automate manual processes, integrate with banks and payment systems, and provide real-time visibility into a company's financial health. By reducing the administrative burden and improving accuracy, accounting tech enables business owners to focus on growth while maintaining compliance and financial control.

Examples: QuickBooks (Intuit), Xero, FreshBooks, Wave Accounting, Zoho Books

RegTech (regulatory technology) includes software and platforms that help financial institutions, fintechs, and regulated businesses manage regulatory compliance, risk, and reporting. Processes such as regulatory monitoring, identity verification, anti-money laundering (AML), fraud detection, and compliance reporting can be automated through RegTech using AI, machine learning, and data analytics. RegTech integrates with core banking and fintech systems to reduce manual compliance costs and meet evolving regulatory requirements. It reduces operational risk while increasing trust, transparency, and regulatory alignment in the financial ecosystem.

Examples: ComplyAdvantage, Trulioo, Onfido, Chainalysis, Fenergo

Overall, fintech growth and innovation are bringing more personalized financial services to consumers, including those who have been underbanked or underserved. Fintech democratizes financial services by making them more available to a wide range of consumers.

Fintech lending uses APIs to make it easy to obtain small loans without the hassle of in-person meetings and the cost of multiple documents, offering a fast, easy online application process with quick turnarounds. They also use additional datasets in their decision-making, which often results in a high approval rate.

A few examples of these are:

- **Peer-to-peer lending:** A fintech company connects borrowers with willing investors, in turn collecting a small fee for the service. Prosper is a US fintech known for this service.
- **Investor loans:** Fintechs like better source loans and sell them to banks, like a mortgage broker but without the high consumer fees.
- **Mortgages:** Some fintechs, such as Rocket Mortgage, offer loans and mortgages, like traditional banks, using advanced technologies to speed up processing and reduce costs.
- **Business loans:** Companies like BlueVine help small businesses access capital using advanced technology to better assess risk, which is difficult through traditional banks, as small businesses are perceived as being high risk.

With fintech and now many banks, consumers can quickly open a digital account on their phones through a diverse range of apps. It's fairly common for fintech offers to include no-fee checking, interest on deposits, overdraft protection, and sometime even early access to paychecks. By democratizing access to financial services, fintech has created additional options for consumers to improve their financial health and lives. It's no wonder that everyone is focused on where fintech is headed next. Just imagine how their partnerships will develop, and with whom. What impact will it have on the future of finance?

The Fintech Investment Ecosystem

If there's one thing I've learned in more than 20 years in this industry, it's that even the most brilliant fintech idea needs the right fuel to truly take flight. Through my work at Finavator, I've seen firsthand how a diverse network of financial leaders provides the essential resources to scale these innovations across borders.

The future of finance relies on capital and investment partnerships around the world. A few examples of venture capital providers in this space include Grit Capital Partners (US), Ribbit Capital (US), Luge Capital (Canada), Canavan Capital (Canada), Index Ventures (UK), and Seedcamp (UK). Investment banking and M&A firms include FT Partners (US), Wellesley Hills Financial (US), Canaccord Genuity (Canada), and Barclays (UK).

Technology That Makes Fintech Apps Work

Fintech is enabling innovation and unlocking global growth. What is needed to enable fintech is a combination of technologies that often begin with a prepaid infrastructure to get to the market. Once growth has fully occurred, the next step may be to add banking-as-a-service (BaaS) infrastructure to enhance functionality and even a move to apply for a banking license.

Just like a kitchen faucet isn't much use until it's attached to the sink itself and to the pipes to access water supply, fintech apps need connectors to work properly. Some of those connectors include:

- **Application programming interfaces (APIs):** Financial APIs define the contract of what, when, where, and how data owned by a system can be accessed, and who can access it. Well-designed APIs are the solution for real-time, secure data transfer in the digital world.
- **Mobile apps:** Mobile applications provide additional security through on-device authentication, such as Face ID, and local storage, so data doesn't need to go to the cloud.
- **Web-based:** While a mobile app can be more secure and faster for short-term everyday tasks, for complicated financial needs and longer user sessions, like filing taxes or applying for a mortgage, fintechs often offer a browser version of their service.
- **Prepaid technologies:** Prepaid enables fintechs to create virtual, preloaded Visa, Mastercard, or Discover accounts that power everything from BNPL and teen cards to corporate expense solutions, delivering secure, real-time funding and flexible speed controls. Experts in the industry often refer to prepaid as the "innovation rail" as the technology powering it is fueling so many fintechs globally. It's used by well-known fintechs such as Greendot, Payoneer, and GoHenry.
- **Banking as a service:** BaaS creates the opportunity for licensed banks to offer their digital banking services directly into products of nonbank businesses through a B2B offering. They often use a combination of embedded, white-labeled user interfaces, out-of-the-box compliance modules, and APIs. BaaS is a key to unlocking the fintech superpowers of companies like Revolut, Chime, N26, Brex, and thousands more.

I can't wait to share more about the power of this type of plumbing in Chapter 2, where we will break down how prepaid and BaaS and infrastructures work, enabling the fintech ecosystem.

The Fintech Revolution is Global

All in all, fintechs are reshaping the future of finance. By embracing innovation and technology, they are helping to enable financial inclusion and literacy, simplifying financial options for consumers, improving internal efficiency, and driving competition in the industry. Whether you are a consumer or a financial professional, understanding fintechs is essential to navigating the evolving financial landscape.

Fintech has expanded financial access globally. In 2025, the global fintech market was valued at approximately $395 billion, reflecting broad adoption of digital financial services and revenue growth across payments, embedded finance, and related sectors. Global fintech investment also rebounded, with about $53 billion raised in 2025 across nearly 6,000 deals, signaling renewed investor confidence. Meanwhile, digital wallets have become ubiquitous, with around 5.2 billion users worldwide, and the total number of fintech companies has grown to more than 31,000.[5] Also, the world has reached 397 fintech unicorns, according to a Fintechlabs 2025 report.[6] These are companies with a value of more than $1 billion. Fintech is not just a passing trend. It's an everyone, everywhere, all-the-time opportunity. The potential for innovation is unlimited and expands with every new idea.

To help you fully understand the global fintech ecosystem, Figure 1.4 summarizes the top 10 fintech countries' 2025 market size, leading companies, number of fintechs, and key use cases. The US fintech market is currently the largest with more than 10,000 fintechs and a market of more than $67 billion, with leading use cases focused on payments and digital banking with leading companies Robinhood, Stripe, and PayPal to name a few.

The global fintech industry continues to scale rapidly, reshaping how consumers and businesses interact with money. This growth will be driven by digital payments, embedded finance, AI innovation, and wealth tech adoption across regions. The United States, China, and Europe remain the largest individual markets, while emerging regions in Africa, South America, and Southeast Asia are accelerating growth through mobile-first solutions and financial inclusion. Let's break down five of these regions and their future potential.

Figure 1.4 Top 10 global fintech markets, 2025

Top 10 Global Fintech Markets 2025

FINAVATOR

Market Size, Leading Companies & Innovation Metrics

Top 10 Fintech Markets by Market Size

1 United States
Market: $67B | Global fintech leader
Top: Visa, Mastercard, Stripe, PayPal, Block
Ecosystem: 10,755+ fintechs
Strengths: Payments, capital markets, digital banking

2 China
Market: $51B+ | Asia's largest market
Top: Ant Group (Alipay), Tencent (WeChat Pay)
Ecosystem: 5,000+ fintechs | 450M+ active users
Strengths: Mobile payments, super-apps, platform scale

3 India
Market: $51B+ | Fastest-growing major market
Top: PhonePe, Paytm, Razorpay, CRED
Ecosystem: 9,000+ fintechs | 24 unicorns
Strengths: UPI real-time payments, digital infrastructure

4 United Kingdom
Market: $18.5B+ | Europe's fintech leader
Top: Revolut, Wise, Monzo, Starling Bank
Ecosystem: 2,500+ fintechs
Strengths: Open banking, cross-border finance

5 Germany
Market: $16.7B+ | European BaaS hub
Top: N26, Trade Republic, Solaris
Ecosystem: 900+ fintechs
Strengths: Banking-as-a-Service, challenger banks

6 Brazil
Market: $5.5B+ | Latin America leader
Top: Nubank, PagSeguro, Stone, Mercado Pago
Ecosystem: 1,300+ fintechs
Strengths: Pix instant payments, financial inclusion

7 Singapore
Market: $4.8B+ | Southeast Asia gateway
Top: Grab Financial, Nium, Funding Societies
Ecosystem: 1,100+ fintechs
Strengths: Digital banking, cross-border payments

8 Australia
Market: $4.5B+ | Oceania leader
Top: Afterpay, Tyro Payments, Up Bank
Ecosystem: 750+ fintechs
Strengths: BNPL innovation, Consumer Data Right

9 France
Market: $4.2B+ | European innovation hub
Top: Lydia, Qonto, PayFit, Luko
Ecosystem: 700+ fintechs
Strengths: SME banking, payroll fintech

10 Canada
Market: $4B+ | North American challenger
Top: Wealthsimple, Nuvei, Shopify Capital
Ecosystem: 650+ fintechs
Strengths: Wealthtech, e-commerce payments, BaaS

The United States

The United States remains the largest single fintech ecosystem, currently at $67 billion and projected to reach roughly $181 billion by 2033.[7]

It has become a hub for fintech start-ups, dominating in the ranking of the largest fintech companies, with San Francisco, New York, and the Los Angeles area as geographic leaders of innovation. Top use cases include digital payments, embedded finance, and API-driven banking integration. I am sure you have heard of several of their top fintechs: PayPal, Stripe, and Chime.

When I think of fintech, I first think of the US market, where more than 200 unicorns have changed the lives of millions around the world. As you can see from my LinkedIn feed, I am often in the United States, attending conferences such as Money2020, Fintech Retreat, Fintech Meet Up, Finovate, Fintech South, and more. This is a key market to follow and lean into if you are interested in the world of fintech.

Canada

Since I am a proud Canadian, I feel compelled to include my country's contributions to the fintech revolution, with Toronto and Montreal among the top cities for fintechs to launch here. Canada's fintech market is growing, with estimates rising from $4 billion in 2025 to around $18 billion by 2033.[8]

Exciting moves were found in the Canadian government's 2025 budget, which outlined moves toward open banking called "consumer-driven banking," enabling real-time rails and even a push toward stablecoins. Some of the top fintechs are Wealthsimple, EQ Bank, and Nuvei, with key use cases ranging from wealth management to digital banking and payment solutions. Canada is starting to catch up to global ecosystem changes.

United Kingdom

Across the United Kingdom, from Belfast to Durham, Edinburgh to Cardiff, and Bristol to Birmingham, there is significant fintech activity that is positively impacting job growth. According to a 2024 Farm Search report, the government estimated that approximately 76,500 people were working in the UK fintech industry.[9] Industry Today reports a market growth projection from $18.5 billion in 2025 to almost $43 billion by 2031.[10] The top three fintechs in the United Kingdom are Revolut, Checkout.com, and Monzo. Key use cases include digital banking, payments infrastructure, and credit innovation.

When I first started to get excited about fintech, the United Kingdom was one of my favorite markets, as there was such a buzz around the empowerment Revolut was enabling for consumers.

Brazil

South America has emerged as one of the fastest-growing fintech regions globally, driven by high mobile penetration, a large underbanked population, and proactive regulation. Millions of consumers are leapfrogging traditional banking and adopting digital wallets, mobile banking, and alternative lending platforms as their primary financial tools. Brazil is the top market in Latin America, estimated at $5.5 billion in 2025 and projected to reach $17+ billion in 2033.[11]

The top three fintechs are Nubank, PIX, and Ebanx, with key market use cases including neobanking, payments, and embedded finance. I really enjoy learning about the mass growth and inclusion fintechs and open finance have enabled in Brazil, and I follow this marketing very closely.

China

Asia has emerged as a global fintech leader, driven by rapid digital adoption, supportive regulatory environments, and a large, underserved population. The top Asian market is China, with around $51 billion in 2025 and estimated to reach $123 billion in 2031.[12] It could take the lead globally as early as 2033. Their top fintech cities are Shanghai and Beijing. The three standouts for Chinese fintechs are Ant Group, Tencent (WeBank), and Lufax, with key use cases of digital payments, super apps, and embedded finance solutions. This is a market to watch for growth and added innovation.

From both a personal and business perspective, I find the global growth of fintech thrilling and eye-opening. For like-minded individuals in the fintech arena, recognizing how to spur innovation through opportunity is key. I am excited about what the future holds for all of us, with both business growth and greater ease in handling our financial matters.

Looking to the Future

The fintech global ecosystem is helping to reshape both consumer and business finance. Here's why and what we all need to be paying attention to:

- Developed markets (United States, Europe, United Kingdom, Australia, Canada): Driven by payments modernization, open banking, and embedded finance
- China and Singapore: Scale from super-app ecosystems and regional hub roles
- Emerging markets (Brazil, Africa): Growth from mobile-first models and financial inclusion

Fintech is elevating and expanding financial services worldwide. The potential for innovative products or services and new liaisons is unlimited. The trick to achieving great success in the fintech industry is to keep focus on consumers at all costs. The goal is to light that fire of how fintech is helping to enhance consumers' lives, through speed, access to high-interest saving accounts, and low-cost lending with often reduced costs, which can lead to increased adoption rates.

Expert Interview with Sebastien Taveau

I have had the pleasure of meeting Sebastien Taveau at quite a few fintech conferences over the years, including a sit-down discussion at Fintech Fest in California. Sebastien is a global fintech innovator, speaker, and author. He brings experience from Zelle, PayPal, MasterCard, and Yodlee, and he has been a well-respected voice on multiple stages worldwide. His work spans payments, digital identity, open banking, and fintech infrastructure, with a consistent focus on using technology to empower consumers globally.

When we discussed his journey and passion for financial technology, Sebastien shared how his career evolved from semiconductors and smart chip cards to mobile payments and proximity solutions. "This early exposure to consumer-facing technology led me to PayPal," he explained. We both agree that identity and authentication are the true foundations of fintech. Sebastien noted, "It's not just about what you pay with; it's about knowing who you are dealing with." This focus led him to explore biometrics and stronger authentication methods, eventually influencing global standards through the FIDO Alliance.

We discussed his time at MasterCard, where he worked to open networks and APIs to developers. Sebastien emphasized that collaboration is the primary driver of innovation. He states, "Fintechs, banks, developers, and platforms each bring unique capabilities. By partnering, we can combine strengths, experiment faster, and deliver solutions that reach more people." We both agree that fintech plays a vital role in advancing financial inclusion through systems like Brazil's Pix and India's UPI. "These innovations lift people into the financial ecosystem, providing access where traditional banks could not," he said.

Looking ahead, we discussed the rise of AI and agentic commerce. Sebastien views AI as a partner rather than just a tool. "AI is not something you simply use; it is a coworker or partner that enables smarter, faster, and adaptive financial solutions," he explained. We both agree that businesses must remain curious and ready to integrate emerging technologies to enhance customer experiences.

Sebastien's insights on the rise of fintech and the creation of a new financial era can be summarized in three key takeaways:

- User-centric global financial inclusion
- The importance of partnerships and adaptability
- Having a mindset of curiosity and experimentation

Sebastien concluded by reflecting on the broader purpose of fintech innovation. We both agree that it is about creating solutions that improve lives and expand opportunities. "Financial technology can lift communities and empower individuals. That's what makes this work so meaningful," he noted. Sitting down with Sebastien reinforced the idea that collaboration among fintechs, banks, and platforms is the key to ensuring no one is left behind.

Fintech's Alignment to the Future of Finance

Fintech is financial technology that is changing the way we operate in the world and leading us to the future of finance. Every single day, fintechs like Nubank, Stripe, Shopify, Chime, Coinbase, QuickBooks, Wealthsimple, and AfterPay are positively impacting humanity. They are changing the way we make purchases, pay loans, and invest. And there's so much more that it can be done!

Being part of the fintech ecosystem for more than 10 years has been like being part of a family of rebels with a cause *for good*. There's this passion and understanding that you can profoundly affect the future of finance by innovating today. I have seen firsthand how partnerships between banks and fintechs have changed consumers' lives by enabling faster, cheaper, and more accessible financial services to the underserved and unbanked. When a fintech company offers a unique solution that can really change consumers' lives by solving problems, reducing friction, and lowering costs when sending invoices, making payments, or accessing lending, this drives financial inclusion.

After four consecutive years of decline, global fintech funding rebounded in 2025, rising to approximately $52.7 billion and marking the highest annual total since 2022, driven in part by strong investment activity in the fourth quarter.[13]

Therefore, fintech is still capturing both attention and funding from VCs. Fintech is expected to remain a major driver of this growth, fueled by innovations in payments, insure-tech, and financial infrastructure.

To you, as a student, leader, founder, or as a big thinker, I encourage you to keep dreaming, building, and taking the risk to innovate and sometime simply fail forward. We all need to continue stepping toward the future of finance, as I stated at the opening this chapter, fintechs are set to reach $882 billion by 2030, which is supporting the current careers professionals around the world and will also foster new opportunities for many more all while creating better lives for hundreds of millions more.

Chapter 1 Key Takeaways

1. Beyond technology, fintech's true power lies in its ability to solve human problems and to help reduce friction across diverse sectors such as banking, healthcare, insurance, and real-estate to name a few.
2. Fintechs are changing the game by giving individuals access to tools once reserved only for banks, helping drive financial inclusion.
3. The global fintech industry continues to scale rapidly, reshaping how consumers and businesses interact with money, from how they are paid, to how they save, and access loans.
4. **Personal lesson:** We have only one chance to make a difference in life, so don't wait until it is too late to step into your passion.

Chapter 2

Supercharging Financial Access: The Power of Prepaid and BaaS Infrastructures

"The way to think about BaaS and prepaid is that they make it easier for any business, whether a start-up, fintech, or established enterprise, to embed financial services traditionally offered by banks."

—Elena Litani, Head of Value-Added Services at Visa Canada

In this chapter, we will explore the elements of prepaid and BaaS and how their infrastructure is important as backend technologies for fintechs, helping to innovate the financial sector. Some might wonder why I am covering these two infrastructures in the same chapter. It is because I've seen many fintechs start by using prepaid and evolve to adding BaaS as they mature. They both provide services that help to solve consumer and business problems and are often used together. Revolut launched in July 2015 as a fintech challenger bank offering a prepaid debit card that allowed users to spend abroad with real-time exchange rates and lower fees than traditional banks. This initial prepaid card product helped Revolut attract early users and build a platform that later expanded into broader financial services such as multicurrency accounts, investing, business accounts, and credit products.

Using prepaid and/or BaaS, fintechs can empower consumers and businesses worldwide, enabling them to benefit from faster, more affordable, and more convenient financial services. Ease and convenience are two key attributes of what fintechs provides in this area. To open this important chapter on prepaid and BaaS, I invited Elena Litani, head of Value Added Services at Visa, to share her perspective. I fully agree with her that while the end products of fintechs are financial services traditionally offered by banks, fintech has enabled any business to embed those elements.

Simply put, these two powerhouse infrastructures allow fintechs to supercharge financial access for the masses. They provide these incredible opportunities by offering unique and often personalized financial services. Fintechs that are making a difference include neobanks; challenger banks; micro-investing services; budgeting tools; instant loans; buy now, pay later purchasing options; gift cards; and even employee rewards. Fintechs around the world continue to inspire me to keep learning and leaning in, just as the stories of CEOs had sparked my attention in my younger years.

When I received a call from an employment recruiter about an interview for a senior director role at a payments company, I was excited yet concerned, as my knowledge of the inner workings of the payments' world was limited. I was a loyalty and rewards expert at that time and, in my mind, wasn't sure I was qualified for the position.

I connected with my boss for advice as I trusted her and saw her as my mentor. Kelly Lee said, "You can do anything you set your mind to," which was extremely helpful. I took time to think about what I should do. I felt the professional and personal support around me and decided to step into the unknown. I realized that when the industry is moving faster than textbooks, we may just have to learn as we go.

Career opportunities that arise, especially in a fast-moving, innovative industry such as fintech, might require a step into the unknown to participate, even though there may not be a strong foundation of historical knowledge readily available to support us. When taking on something new, I believe asking a lot of questions is fundamental to learning, as doing so can help us build the courage to lean into risk with a mindset of "if I'm going to fail, I'm going to fail forward."

My Path to Prepaid

I joined the team at InComm in 2015 that is a global payments technology company offering both physical and virtual prepaid gift cards. I still remember my first day officially as the head of three departments: Marketing, Sales, and Distribution. The day was filled with introductions and so many acronyms that my head was spinning. I had walked into a whole new world of technology; it was exciting and a little intimidating. Every day, I grew more confident in the innovation we could enable as I was surrounded by an incredible team with the same mission. It was like an extended family filled with payments experts. I quickly felt at home.

Since it is not possible to drive successful marketing when you don't understand the product, I jumped onto a learning curve that felt more like a roller coaster filled with a whole new language of acronyms and terminologies. I had to rely on my inherent curiosity not only to understand the flows and functionalities of the prepaid payments system but also to develop expertise in it. An important aspect of my position was training my team about the inner workings of the prepaid infrastructure. As a marketer and salesperson, I understood how powerful we would be when it could be explained on one page. As with much of fintech, this was no small task but a worthy mission. I invested hundreds of hours and asked countless questions in my quest to understand this complex prepaid ecosystem. As a result, my team was able to create a clean, clear one-page summary that we used often to explain how prepaid worked. This lesson of simplifying the complex into one page has become my go-to when helping clients.

Within my first year, we launched one of the first reloadable prepaid cards sold at retailers nationwide. Leading up to the launch, I had many days when I was stressed with the amount of backend details, tight timelines, and major frustrations. It was not an easy project and required not only teamwork but a lot of grit, a little Six Sigma training, and some powerful key performance indicator (KPI) planning.

My favorite aspect of prepaid is that it drives digital inclusion. Imagine being new to a country without a credit card and needing to pay for an Uber ride. They can go to a retail store and buy an Uber gift card with cash or a reloadable prepaid Visa card, allowing underserved or unbanked people to use the service. The same use applies to global travelers. Prepaid cards carry none of your personal data, often offer the best currency exchange rates, and can be registered to protect your funds in the event of loss of the card. Over the years, I came to see prepaid as an innovation rail, enabling access to the digital economy for all without traditional credit cards.

The global market for prepaid cards is expected to grow at a compound annual growth rate (CAGR) of 10+% between 2022 and 2030, when the prepaid card market is estimated to reach $4.1 trillion.[1] In 2023, the FDIC revealed that 4.2% of American households, representing 5.6 million people, operate without a bank account. There are also 19 million underbanked households, of which 21.6% have used prepaid cards. The use cases vary: 73% use prepaid to pay online bills, 53% to receive gig work payments or income, and 43% say they use prepaid as a savings tool.[2]

What I find exciting about prepaid is how I use it in real life. I currently buy physical and digital gift cards for friends' birthdays, to reward employees after a major project, and to make my next purchase at Starbucks by preloading my wallet in their app. Many of us don't even notice when we are using prepaid infrastructure. All we know is that our transactions are easy, fast, and convenient. They have become part of our daily lives.

I have also signed up for my kids for a prepaid digital spending management app created by MBA students in 2018, now owned by RBC. It's called Mydoh and is similar to Greenlight or GoHenry. It's a reloadable Visa card that allows me to transfer money to my kids for their weekly allowance or as a reward for achieving a goal. It enables my kids to see their money grow and to save for their goals, like a Madrid soccer jersey or a car. They can also allocate a set amount each month to regular savings or charitable donation accounts. This app helps them learn good saving and spending habits.

I used a different fintech savings app for the kids before this one, so they have been exposed to digital savings tools from a young age. I appreciated how easy it was to sign up from my phone and set up their phones with tap-to-pay. With no need to carry the physical card, this helped eliminate the risk that my young kids might lose a cash allowance or a physical gift card. As a bonus, I can see how they spend their money and guide them toward wise choices. This is an excellent example of how prepaid can be an empowerment tool.

I currently use the personal account offered by Equitable Bank (EQ Bank). EQ Bank is a Canadian challenger bank with nearly 800,000 customers and more than $1 billion in revenue as of 2025.[3] Through its digital bank, EQ Bank is known for paying customers high interest on balances while charging them low or no fees for everyday transactions, seeking to change the high-fee and low-interest often prevalent in the traditional banking landscape. My account is also eligible for CDIC insurance for up to $100,000, like an FDIC-insured account in the United States. It's obvious to me why EQ Bank has grown so quickly within the Canadian ecosystem: they are the first "Schedule I Bank" to move their core system fully to the cloud, which makes it easier and faster to enable innovation and respond rapidly to shifting consumer behavior.

I had the privilege of working with EQ Bank in early 2020 as the prepaid expert within a group of consultants on their consumer prepaid reloadable Mastercard. This was one of my first Finavator projects alongside industry experts, and it was an important one as I was also able to share my expertise on BIN sponsorship banks and the potential growth opportunity to support the fintech ecosystem. It was a great honor to contribute to the launch of the EQ Bank Card, which recently surpassed $1 billion in reloads as of 2025.[4]

The impact of using prepaid and BaaS on my family and me is tiny compared to their impact on the fintech ecosystem as a whole and on how we rely on them every day. Anyone with an interest in the fintech industry, whether as an innovator, investor, or technologist, will benefit from understanding how it works and its future potential.

What Is Prepaid, and How Does It Work?

I have had a front-row seat to the impact prepaid payment technology has had over the last 10 years. In my opinion, prepaid has helped transform the fintech industry, fuel growth, and add to financial inclusion. By loading funds to a physical or virtual branded card in advance of a purchase, it:

- Enables fintechs and corporations to launch financial products, such as prepaid cards and wallets, quickly without requiring their own full banking license

- Operates under a sponsor's bank license through a bank identification number (BIN), minimizing compliance and capital requirements for fintech
- Serves the masses as it is ideal for digital challenger bank offerings, gift cards, gig worker payouts, travel cards, youth banking, and loyalty programs

There are two types of prepaid cards.

- **Prepaid closed-loop cards** are gift cards from all the brands you love, such as Starbucks, Uber, Nike, or your local grocer. These cards allow users to spend only the amount preloaded on them, making them a great gift or a helpful budgeting tool. There are also prepaid reloadable cards that let you reload your Starbucks card at any time.
- **Prepaid open-loop cards** can be single-load or reloadable. They can be used anywhere credit cards are accepted, including online and in stores, as they are built in partnership with a BIN sponsor bank and major networks such as Visa, Mastercard, Discover, and American Express.

Even though most consumers do not know the technical difference between them, they know what type of card to purchase for their needs. For example, my brother likes to purchase closed-loop branded cards for birthday gifts, specifically for Sephora or Nike, since my kids like to shop for those brands, and they get a shopping experience as part of the gift.

I use closed-loop gift cards. As the president of the Open Finance Network, I write a handwritten thank-you note to each board member at the end of the year, along with a $50 Visa gift card. We always have a holiday lunch, and as a small token of thanks for their time and effort, the prepaid card allows them to shop wherever they want, in person or online.

With prepaid technology, users can preload funds into a digital wallet accessible via a mobile app, allowing them to pay bills, purchase goods, or receive direct deposits from employers securely and efficiently. There are not only benefits for consumers. Businesses can enable prepaid payment offerings that open new possibilities for engaging a broader customer base, provide meaningful insights, and create additional revenue streams by offering tailored financial products that meet the specific needs of these communities.

Fintechs make money from prepaid products mainly through interchange revenue, gift card merchant margins, and float income. With open-loop prepaid cards such as Mastercard or Visa, issuers earn a small slice of interchange on each purchase, typically 0.5–2% of the transaction value, shared among the BIN, the bank, the issuer, the network, and the processor. Closed-loop programs, such as gift cards, rely on merchant discounts or margins, which can range from 2% for groceries and gas to 10–15% for restaurants and gaming. In some partnerships, fintech can also earn float income, where funds earn short-term interest while remaining accessible to users. Sustainable fintech's combine interchange, margin, and float with some secondary revenue lines to diversify income and smooth volatility across market cycles.

Prepaid has a wide range of uses, including:

- **Microloans:** Small, short-term loans designed to give users quick access to credit, often with simplified approval processes. An example of this is Buy Now, Pay Later (BNPL). This is an innovative solution that allows customers to make immediate purchases by extending instant credit for the exact purchase price. They then pay it back in small installments, typically as a "pay in four installments" option, where the consumer is billed for equal amounts every few weeks. It is, in essence, a line of credit from a financing institution, not the merchant, with no interest or additional fees. When a customer selects BNPL at checkout, the approved amount is instantly loaded onto a prepaid, virtual Visa or Mastercard. That card is used to complete the purchase with the merchant.
- **Trust builder (proxy credit score):** Prepaid is now being used as a tool to help underserved and unbanked build creditworthiness through alternative data such as payment history and account activity.
- **Personal financial management:** Prepaid can be used with a personal finance manager to enable insights that empower consumers, from a digital dashboard of spending to budget-building tools, to improve their overall financial health.
- **Loyalty and rewards:** Loyalty programs are evolving, and prepaid cards are becoming one of the most powerful tools to connect rewards with real financial empowerment. When customers spend reloadable prepaid cards, they not only earn meaningful points and cashbacks but also gain a

more inclusive, accessible way to participate in the digital economy. By allowing points to be redeemed for prepaid Visa, Mastercard, or branded cards, programs transform loyalty into everyday financial utility. And as businesses use prepaid reward cards for promotions and rebates, they're creating smarter, more human-centered engagement models that meet people where they are. This is exactly the direction our industry needs to be moving!

- **Employee incentives:** Prepaid drives solutions for employers and employees, such as:
  - **Expense cards:** These are used to provide employees, such as drivers, with a prepaid reloadable corporate gas card, or sales teams with expense account funds for entertaining clients.
  - **Benefits cards:** These might be prepaid cards for a medical flexible spending account (FSA) or a health savings account (HSA). These funds are heavily regulated, are corporate-owned, and can be used by employees for state- or province-approved healthcare expenses. For example, I give my employees a $500 HSA in January of every year that they can use for dental services, registered massage therapy, and other provincially approved healthcare expenses.
- **Insurance payments:** A prepaid insurance card issued by the insurance company can streamline the payment of insurance claims. In addition to speeding up the claims process, prepaid cards offer benefits for both the insurer and the insured, including reduced costs and improved fraud protection.
- **Gig economy/instant payroll:** Employers can set up reloadable prepaid cards to pay wages, even on the same day. The employee can use or withdraw the funds immediately without waiting for a designated payroll period or accounts payable schedule. Companies like DailyPay, Branch, Rain, and KOHO Financial use prepaid rails to push funds in real time.

The bottom line is that prepaid programs act as a bridge between fintech services and traditional payment infrastructure, enabling modern solutions to be faster, more flexible, and more widely accepted. I expect even wider widespread use of them and exponential industry growth moving forward. Looking ahead, I believe we will see continued innovation and partnerships across the ecosystem.

The Prepaid Technology Stack

The ecosystem powering prepaid transactions consists of five distinct players often coordinated by a program management company. Many fintechs choose to work with a program manager to ensure they have a partner that can connect them to a bank identification number (BIN) sponsor bank, a processor, a card network, and a card manufacturer.

- **Program manager:** Program managers assist with the management of operations and all essential partners. Their role includes customer onboarding, card fulfillment, financial reconciliation, settlement, risk, fraud, data management, and customer support. In today's competitive and complex markets, program managers help companies sustain and grow. Some examples of program managers include Brim Financial, InComm, Green Dot, Marqeta, Netspend, and Berkeley Payments to name a few.
- **Sponsor bank (BIN):** A licensed bank that becomes a BIN sponsor plays a vital role in the issuing process. They provide the BIN and the expertise to ensure regulatory compliance. Benefits of this partnership include enhanced payment processing, reduced compliance burden, and access to advanced analytics. This is often the most affordable and fastest route to launch a payments product. Many do not realize that credit card products require significantly more capital, higher compliance, and a much longer time to market. Some examples of US and Canadian sponsor banks include Cross River Bank, Pathward, Sunrise Bank, Sutton Bank, EQ Bank, and Peoples Group.
- **Card network:** The payment networks that work with prepaid include Visa, Mastercard, Discover, and American Express. These networks route transactions between merchants, banks, and processors globally to ensure the seamless movement of funds. Examples included Visa, Mastercard, Discover, and American Express.
- **Processor:** The processor is a technology platform that manages card transactions, authorizations, and balances. It acts as the vital link between the card network and the program management system to ensure every transaction is valid and funded. Examples of processors include Galileo, Marqeta, i2c Inc., FIS, and Episode Six to name a few.
- **Card manufacturer:** This vendor personalizes and manufactures physical prepaid cards with security features and branding. Examples of card

manufacturers include CPI Card Group, Entrust, Giesecke and Devrient, and ABCorp. These partners ensure that the physical product meets the high security standards required for global commerce.

So you can visualize how these complex layers work together, Figure 2.1 maps out a summary of some stakeholders, illustrating the prepaid card technology ecosystem and the essential flow of data and value between the key players.

Figure 2.1 Prepaid card technology ecosystem

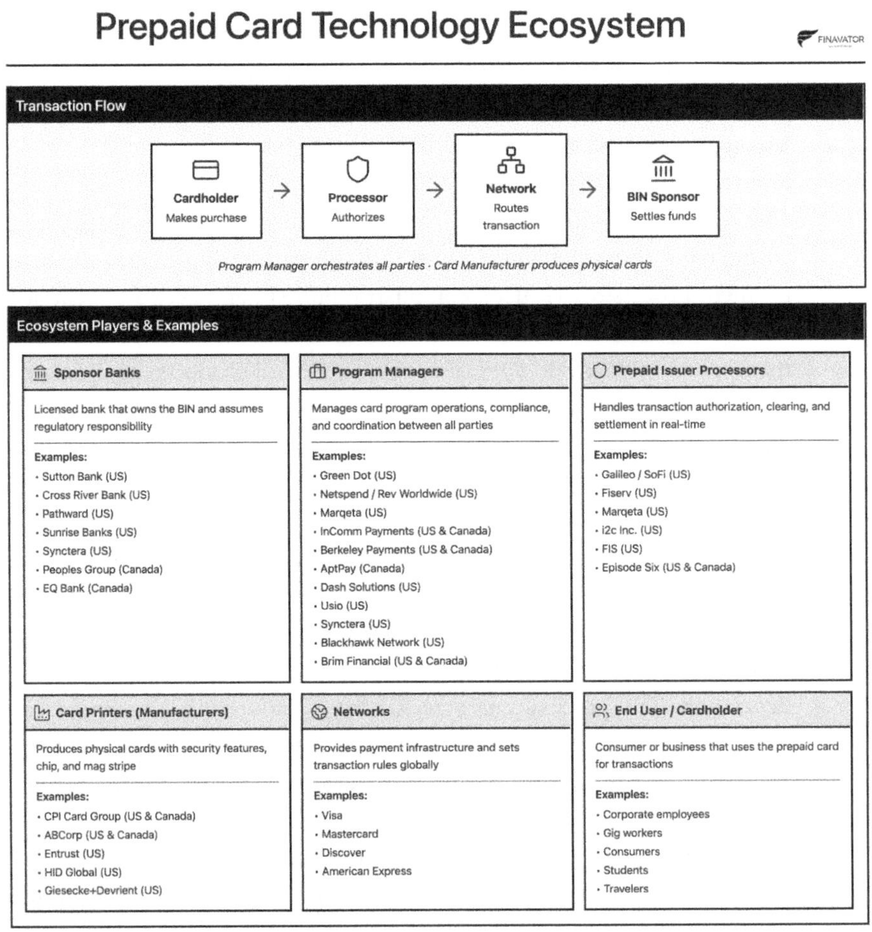

Commercial Users of Prepaid

While prepaid serves a tremendous need for consumers, it also delivers commercial benefits to a wide variety of businesses. Prepaid technology is commonly used by many of the following:

- **Neobanks:** These are digital-only banks that primarily operate through mobile apps and online banking. They need to partner with licensed BIN sponsor banks to offer prepaid cards with digital checking and savings accounts. They are often used by the underbanked and underserved as they are easily accessible without a credit check. Great examples of Neobanks included Chime (US), Revolut (UK), EQ Bank (Canada), WeBank (Tencent/WeChat) (China), and NuBank (Brazil).
- **Challenger banks:** These are chartered banks that operate almost exclusively online but may have some physical locations. These banks are dedicated to challenging traditional banks by putting customer experience at the forefront of their model, for example, through faster account-opening processes. Challenger banks leverage technologies that often also include prepaid offerings, such as travel and expense prepaid cards. They often have lower fees, have more user-friendly interfaces, and offer personalized financial solutions. By harnessing the power of technology, these banks gained popularity and reshaped the financial industry. Examples included Starling Bank (UK), N26 (Germany), and SoFi (USA), all of which use prepaid products alongside additional solutions.

The Future of Prepaid

The market for prepaid cards continues to expand as consumer demand for flexibility, security, and budgeting tools grows. Building a prepaid card is often chosen as there is still healthy interchange revenue in North America, without the heavy liability that offering credit cards would bring to an organization, and the interchange revenue is close to the same. Also, offering prepaid cards rather than debit cards is an advantage, as prepaid cards work worldwide, whereas VISA, Mastercard, and Discover are accepted only in certain countries. This is particularly clear in sectors like retail and healthcare, where it creates a more inclusive and interconnected financial ecosystem.

Regulatory support that standardizes prepaid products as payment methods is helping to increase confidence among both providers and users. AI is only going to accelerate the pace of innovation, and I see fintechs leaning into capturing additional insights to ensure their products are even more personalized for each consumer. Fintechs are bound to continue to capitalize on these trends by offering instant card issuance, app-based account management, and value-added services such as analytics, loyalty, and rewards.

What Is Banking as a Service (BaaS)?

In today's financial landscape, consumers are using multiple services rather than relying on a single bank. Through BaaS, companies of all sizes can embed powerful financial tools directly into their products without the need to have their own banking license. This shift is transforming the way consumers and businesses interact with money, making financial services more accessible, seamless, and personalized than ever before.

What I love about BaaS is that it offers versatile nonbank platforms, such as fintechs, retailers, and tech platforms, access to licensed banking infrastructure through secure APIs, rather than obtaining their own banking license. This can be a game changer for both the companies that implement it and their customers who take advantage of it, as it enables faster innovation, greater competition, and better user experiences. The shift toward BaaS is reshaping the landscape across various industries, including retail, healthcare, and technology, by bridging the gap between traditional banking services and modern consumer demands. In short, while prepaid equals speed and simplicity, BaaS brings depth and scalability. Both serve the same customer, just at different levels.

In our society, banking is necessary for healthcare. We may not think much about it until we have a specific need. However, when we do have that need, we want to use it quickly and simply. When I think about BaaS, it's a way to incorporate everyday banking services into people's lives by meeting them where they are, versus being a separate aspect of life. Here are the key beneficial aspects of BaaS:

- Bring full banking capabilities, embedded finance everywhere. It allows fintechs to offer deposit accounts, payments, lending, and more, all through APIs.
- It has a scalable infrastructure. It provides the backend foundation for embedded finance, enabling long-term product expansion.
- It allows greater control and differentiation than prepaid plans. It supports deeper product integration and customization, enhancing customer experience.

My BaaS Experience

As for BaaS, I have had the privilege of assisting multiple fintechs to enable both prepaid and BaaS offerings. I understand that it is never a simple process, as it requires negotiating with many key partners to ensure the product includes all the elements needed to engage new customers. It is important to consider the overall goals and plan for a clear go-to-market strategy and marketing budget. As previously discussed, prepaid can help with quick market entry, serving gig workers, expense programs, and rewards cards. However, if the goal is to have full banking capabilities, including checking, savings, interest offers, and integrated credit, BaaS is the right platform.

I always enjoy hearing founders explain why they are building their fintechs and helping them find the right partners to build the product they have in mind to solve the consumer's pain points. The path to helping my clients decide between prepaid and BaaS is filled with questions around features and regulatory compliance.

It is important for any financial product offering to have a simple onboarding process on both phones and computers, with know your customer (KYC) as an important part of the first steps. It is crucial to offer features and tools that entice new users and keep them engaged, such as free ATM access or deposit interest, as it is always a mindshare game when launching new products. BaaS provides everything from deposits and a customer dashboard to view all transactions to budgeting tools, balance alerts, and ways to pay bills. The advantage of launching BaaS services is that it allows for a holistic product without the mass lift of obtaining a full bank license and can incorporate additional partnerships, such as rewards and loyalty systems, accounting platforms, and other product-specific integrations.

I moderated a panel on how do you scale a business without breaking the founder at Techskis in early 2026. Joined by three incredible CEOs, we dived deep into the realities of the founder's journey and what it takes to drive innovation and drive real change. A major takeaway from our discussion was just how chronically underserved small business owners remain, and how platforms like Loop Financial, similar to Mercury in the US, are working to bridge that gap. By leveraging Banking as a Service (BaaS) and embedded financial infrastructure, they can offer the compliant cross border, multicurrency, and high interest savings tools that legacy banking systems are not built to provide. Today, more companies are using these robust BaaS rails to deliver the exact, flexible, and real time financial services that our modern entrepreneurs need to scale successfully. These underlying financial rails are quietly transforming the entire global fintech ecosystem and reshaping how we all rely on financial services every single day.

The impact of using prepaid and BaaS on my family and me is tiny compared to their impact on the fintech ecosystem as a whole and on how we rely on them every day. Anyone with an interest in the fintech industry, whether as an innovator, investor, or technologist, will benefit from understanding how it works and its potential for the future.

Having had the privilege of assisting multiple fintechs to enable both prepaid and BaaS offerings, I understand that it is never a simple process, as it requires negotiating with many key partners to ensure the product includes all the elements needed to engage new customers. It is important to consider the overall goals and plan for a clear go-to-market strategy and marketing budget. As previously discussed, prepaid can help with quick market entry, serving gig workers, expense programs, and rewards cards. However, if the goal is to have full banking capabilities, including checking, savings, interest offers, and integrated credit, BaaS is the right platform.

I always enjoy hearing founders explain why they are building their fintechs and helping them find the right partners to build the product they have in mind to solve the consumer's pain points. The path to helping my clients decide between prepaid and BaaS is filled with questions around features and regulatory compliance.

It is important for any financial product offering to have a simple onboarding process on both phones and computers, with KYC as an important part of the first steps. It is crucial to offer features and tools that entice new users and keep them engaged, such as free ATM access or deposit interest, as it is always a mindshare game when launching new products. BaaS provides everything from deposits and a customer dashboard to view all transactions to budgeting tools, balance alerts, and ways to pay bills. The advantage of launching BaaS services is that it allows for a holistic product without the mass lift of obtaining a full bank license and can incorporate additional partnerships, such as rewards and loyalty systems, accounting platforms, and other product-specific integrations.

The Emergence of BaaS

The BaaS model is relatively new to the finance stage. It began to take shape in the late 2010s, when fintechs began partnering with banks to offer financial products, bypassing the need for their own banking licenses. Banks wanted to capitalize on digital innovations without having to create them. Fintechs were seeking ways to scale quickly. The development of BaaS created a win-win situation.

According to Grandview Research, the global BaaS market is on an aggressive growth trajectory, projected to reach a top valuation of $74.55 billion by 2030.[5] This sits at the high end of the industry consensus, which typically ranges from $60 billion to $74.5 billion. While this growth is aggressive, increased regulatory scrutiny, particularly concerning US "Sponsor Bank" relationships, as well as rising cybersecurity overhead, remain primary risks that could dampen these projections.

Fintechs are poised to fuel BaaS growth with full-stack digital banking solutions, API-driven banking platforms, and more. Demands are coming from a range of businesses, including neobanks, payment processors, credit providers, and more. Demand for these products and services is global, but especially strong in North America and Europe. Even though BaaS is relatively new to the marketplace, it is already a proven powerhouse, with even greater innovations expected.

How BaaS Works

BaaS works by providing companies with access to licensed banking infrastructure via secure APIs. This means a retailer, marketplace, or fintech start-up can launch financial products such as accounts, cards, lending, or payments in a matter of weeks, not years, as was the case in the past. By offloading the heavy regulatory and technical burden to BaaS providers, businesses can focus on creating accelerated growth and great user experiences.

A clear example of this in action is through Shopify. "Through its BaaS partnerships, Shopify offers Shopify Balance, a full suite of business banking tools built into its platform. Merchants can receive payouts, access funds, and use cards, all without ever having to walk into a bank. This is the power of BaaS: enabling companies to turn banking into a feature, not a business model."[6]

Through API connections to a licensed bank, BaaS can help businesses embed financial services such as payment processing, lending, and account management into their existing ecosystems, enabling them to enhance the customer experience while streamlining operations. For example, an e-commerce platform can offer instant credit options at checkout, or a gig economy app can provide real-time payments to its workers. Adopting BaaS not only improves operational efficiency but also opens up new revenue streams and competitive advantages.

BaaS Creating New Revenue Streams

BaaS enables companies to embed financial services directly into their products, opening new monetization opportunities. For example, Uber uses BaaS to offer drivers instant payouts through embedded banking features, creating additional value while monetizing financial transactions. Insights available through BaaS from customer financial data can also help cross-sell targeted products, such as insurance or premium account services.

A 2024 report from S&P Global Market Intelligence highlights that community banks offering BaaS experienced an average 18% increase in deposits in Q1 of 2023, compared with flat deposit growth among other US banks with assets less than $10 billion. This growth was achieved without incurring customer acquisition costs, as these banks did not maintain direct customer relationships.[7]

Any ecosystem of value is likely to have multiple components. There are five key components of the BaaS ecosystem. Figure 2.2 shows what they are and how they work. In this example, a Rideshare app acts as the BaaS client by partnering

Figure 2.2 BaaS model explained

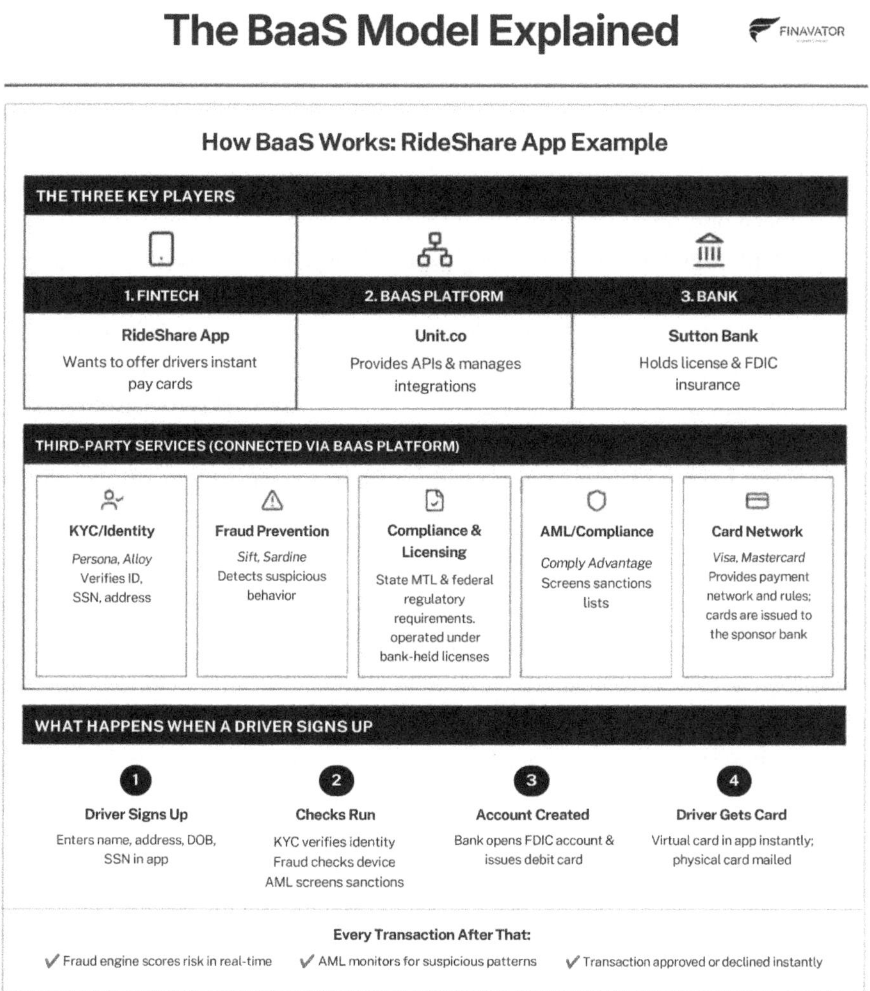

with a fintech BaaS provider to offer prepaid cards to its drivers. The BaaS provider manages technical integrations and third-party services like fraud monitoring while a partner bank provides the essential regulatory framework. When a driver signs up as the end user, the platform orchestrates identity and compliance checks to instantly issue a prepaid card. This collaborative model allows the Rideshare app to deliver integrated financial services without needing a direct banking license.

- **BaaS providers:** These are tech companies or fintechs that create platforms for accessing banking services. They integrate not just issuer, processor, and banking functionalities but also a suite of third-party services necessary for a comprehensive financial offering, i.e., fraud monitoring tools.
- **Banks:** These provide the regulatory framework and the foundational financial services. They are essential for the legal and secure operation of BaaS offerings.
- **Regulators:** Government or independent bodies oversee banking and financial services to ensure compliance with legal and financial standards.
- **Businesses (BaaS clients):** Nonbank companies of all sizes and across various industries integrate banking services into their products or platforms via BaaS. Businesses use BaaS to offer financial products directly to their customers without becoming banks themselves.
- **End users:** Businesses or consumers interact with the financial services integrated into various applications, benefiting from a seamless and enriched service experience.

BaaS can improve operational efficiency by leveraging its platforms. Companies gain access to ready-made banking infrastructure, reducing the time, cost, and complexity of launching financial services. For instance, Chime and Uber Pro Card use BaaS providers to handle payments, KYC/AML compliance, and account management, lowering operational overhead. They can gain a competitive advantage by enabling businesses to differentiate themselves through seamless, integrated financial experiences that enhance customer engagement and loyalty.

Starbucks, for example, integrates a digital wallet and rewards program, strengthening customer retention while collecting valuable spending data. Access to financial insights supports better decision-making and product innovation, while the agility of BaaS platforms enables companies to quickly launch features like buy now, pay later, or embedded insurance, creating a distinct edge over competitors.

BaaS is a powerful infrastructure that enables everything from embedded finance, neobanks, payments apps, lending, BNPL, wealth and investment platforms, and super apps. I am fascinated with super apps, as they are dominating in Asia. They bring together multiple services, such as payments, banking, shopping, mobility, communication, and more, into a single ecosystem. Some examples include WeChat, Grab, Paytm, Revolut, and Gojek, each evolving from a single core service into a multifunctional digital hub. These all-in-one platforms, especially prominent in Asia, integrate various services such as messaging, social media, e-commerce, and financial transactions.

When looking at the current regulatory environment for financial services, it is both extensive and complex. BaaS offers a streamlined pathway for companies to navigate this landscape by leveraging the chartered capabilities, infrastructure, and regulatory expertise of partner banks and BaaS platforms. Companies can use BaaS to collect valuable consumer data, tailor financial products to specific customer needs, and foster greater loyalty and engagement.

Benefits of BaaS

BaaS is allowing the transformation of industries by making financial tools more accessible and customizable for everyone involved. As digital demands grow, BaaS is becoming a key driver of innovation in the financial ecosystem.

- Businesses can benefit from rapid innovation, improved customer experience, cost efficiency, and added revenues. Compliant banking products can be launched in weeks, while avoiding the massive capital requirements of obtaining banking licenses that might take years or building infrastructure from scratch. This helps them to rapidly scale to millions of users through a proven banking infrastructure.
- Banks can generate new revenue streams through fintech partnerships, offering additional banking services while maintaining customer relationships and brand identity. They can also expand their market reach to the underserved and innovate without disrupting existing services.

- Consumers can gain seamless access to financial services through familiar platforms and enjoy the benefits of more personalized financial products tailored to individual needs.

As fintech continues to help drive financial inclusion, I see BaaS as an important infrastructure that will enable access to financial services.

The growth of new technology can bring challenges. One example is Evolve Bank (US), a BIN sponsor bank that works with a BaaS provider. In June 2024, the US Federal Reserve Board issued "an enforcement action against Evolve Bancorp, Inc., and Evolve Bank & Trust for deficiencies in the bank's anti-money laundering, risk management, and consumer compliance programs."[8]

Staying abreast of the latest developments in monetary policy and regulations is vital to the continued success of any fintech that uses BaaS providers. The providers, of course, need to remain compliant. However, fintechs need to remain diligent when sourcing partners.

Core BaaS Service Offerings

Embedded finance and BaaS are helping reshape how financial services are delivered across industries. These solutions come in various forms, ranging from white-labeled banking platforms to API-based services that enable payments, lending, digital wallets, and even full-service bank accounts within non-financial apps and platforms. Companies can choose from a spectrum of BaaS providers, depending on their needs, whether they require end-to-end banking infrastructure or specific financial features. Embedded finance takes this step further by seamlessly integrating these services into everyday customer experiences, such as ride-sharing apps offering insurance or e-commerce platforms providing instant credit.

- **Deposit embedded banking and digital accounts:** Neobanks use BaaS to offer online-only banking accounts with features tailored for digitally savvy customers.
  - **Uber:** Uber introduced Mastercard prepaid cards for its drivers in 2019 that facilitate instant earnings access for drivers, along with entry to a suite of additional financial services.

- **Payment processing:** BaaS providers power hundreds of payment-processing use cases by providing plug-ins to banking services through APIs.
  - **Shopify** has joined forces with Stripe to provide its merchants with comprehensive payment processing capabilities. This collaboration allows merchants to seamlessly accept payments within their online storefronts.
- **Lending services:** BaaS platforms enable businesses to integrate lending services directly into their offerings, facilitating credit products such as loans and credit lines.
  - **Square Loans:** This company offers working capital loans to small merchants using embedded lending infrastructure.

The Future of BaaS

While watching the market for BaaS and speaking with other fintech experts, I believe the next evolution will be defined by even deeper embedding of services under greater regulatory scrutiny. AI is likely to be incorporated into BaaS as well. (More on that in Chapter 7.) Top BaaS trends at the time of this writing include:

- **API-driven banking:** The adoption of application programming interfaces (APIs) has skyrocketed, opening new opportunities for banks to partner with fintech companies and offer integrated services to their customers.
- **Digital-only banks:** More digital banks are emerging, with no physical branches, offering competitive financial products and enhanced user experiences.
- **Open banking:** Financial institutions are increasingly adopting open banking policies, allowing third parties to access customer data and build applications that offer improved financial services and management tools.

BaaS represents a transformative shift in the financial services industry, fostering collaboration between tech companies and banks to create more accessible, efficient, and personalized financial solutions. It's important to stay up-to-date with the current use of top fintechs. Figure 2.3 highlights the 10 leading fintechs in

Figure 2.3 Top fintechs leveraging prepaid and BaaS

Top Fintechs Leveraging Prepaid Technologies & BaaS Infrastructure (2026)

FINAVATOR

#	Fintech	Type	Primary Use of Prepaid	BaaS Layer	Why Both?
1	Chime	Neobank	Debit & spending accounts	Partner banks provide full BaaS	Prepaid powers fast card issuance; BaaS enables banking features
2	Revolut	Neobank	Travel cards, wallets	In-house + partner BaaS	Started with prepaid, expanded to full banking license
3	Cash App	Fintech	P2P + debit cards	Partner banks	Prepaid cards for payments, BaaS for account infrastructure
4	GoHenry	Fintech	Youth prepaid cards	Partner bank integrations	Card + account management for parents/kids
5	Brex	Fintech	Corporate prepaid	Embedded BaaS partners	Manage spend with prepaid, offer treasury & accounts
6	Affirm	Fintech	Merchant checkout cards	Partner banks	BNPL prepaid rails + account funding
7	Green Dot Corporation	Bank	Prepaid debit	BaaS provider itself	Powers many brands like Apple Cash
8	Payoneer	Fintech	Cross-border prepaid	Banking partners	Prepaid cards for payouts, BaaS for accounts
9	Klarna	Neobank	BNPL card rails	Embedded banking	Prepaid issuance + payment accounts
10	PayPal	Fintech	Digital wallet & prepaid debit cards	Partner banks	Prepaid cards enable wallet spending; BaaS supports account storage, compliance, and settlement

2025 leveraging both prepaid and BaaS including Chime, Revolut, Cash App, GoHenry, Brex, Affirm, Greendot, Payoneer, Klarna, and PayPal, each commanding massive user bases and reshaping global finance through innovation. These platforms demonstrate how digital ecosystems are scaling rapidly by combining prepaid solutions for accessibility with BaaS infrastructure for flexibility and reach. Together, they represent the core technologies driving today's financial transformation.

Prepaid systems enable instant digital access to funds without traditional bank accounts, making them vital for onboarding unbanked and underbanked populations. BaaS, meanwhile, provides the technical and regulatory foundation that allows fintechs and nonbanks to embed financial products, such as payments, accounts, and lending, directly into apps and services. By merging these technologies, fintechs delivers seamless, low-cost, and inclusive financial experiences at scale.

This dual approach is fueling both the future of finance and the future of inclusion. Prepaid expands financial participation, while BaaS accelerates innovation and reaches together, creating ecosystems where anyone, anywhere, can access modern financial tools. As Figure 2.3 illustrates, the most successful fintechs aren't just competing in finance; they're building a more connected, inclusive, and digital global economy. Together, these leading fintechs illustrate the scale, diversification, and growing influence of digital financial platforms worldwide.

Expert Interview with Elena Litani

I have had the pleasure of knowing Elena Litani for many years. We first met in 2018 at Money20/20 in Las Vegas and later discovered we lived just 10 minutes apart in Toronto. Elena is a strategic leader with more than two decades of experience driving transformation across financial services and technology. She has held leadership roles at Synctera, TD, and IBM, and currently serves as the head of Value-Added Services at Visa Canada. Elena is also a winner of the Women in Payments Innovation Award.

When we discussed how current financial services are shaping a new era, Elena focused on BaaS and prepaid infrastructure. We both agree that these tools drive innovation and inclusivity. She explains, "The way to think about banking as a service and prepaid is that they make it easier for any business to embed financial services traditionally offered by banks." For companies, it allows them to attract and retain customers with innovative offerings. Elena noted, "For banks, it creates new revenue streams. And for providers, it opens a new market category."

Another key benefit we discussed is speed to market. Elena highlighted that modern platforms are API driven and cloud-based, allowing for rapid deployment. "BaaS allows fintechs and other companies to launch solutions much faster than traditional or legacy banking models," she says. We both agree that this enables companies to deliver value to their clients more efficiently. Elena emphasized that the result is better customer experiences and increased cost efficiency for providers.

We discussed the collaborative nature of the industry today and how integration drives true innovation. Elena noted, "Fintechs, banks, and providers are no longer operating in silos. Each player brings unique value, and the integration of these capabilities is what drives true innovation." We both agree that fintech is about creating an ecosystem that empowers everyone involved, from businesses to banks to consumers.

Elena's perspective on how infrastructure is reshaping the landscape can be summarized in three key takeaways:

- Seamless financial integration via BaaS
- Democratized infrastructure drives financial inclusion
- API collaboration drives rapid innovation

Elena's perspective reinforces that the future of finance is built on accessibility and breaking down traditional barriers to entry. Sitting down with Elena highlights that when we empower partners to innovate, we create a more dynamic and inclusive financial world.

Financial Access's Alignment to the Future of Finance

When I think about the future of finance, I still see prepaid technology as a transformative tool that delivers essential financial services to those who may not have access to traditional banking. Prepaid services can help enable financial services for the masses, including those underbanked or unbanked, as they do not require a credit check. With a global estimated volume reaching more than $4.1 trillion by 2030,[9] BaaS technology is powering embedded finance around the world and is set to reach $60.35 billion by 2030.[10]

This can help remove many barriers, as they are very user-friendly. Any user can simply purchase a gift card at a local retailer with cash or sign up on their phone with a fintech company such as Chime, Green Dot, or Netspend. The future of BaaS is closely linked to the adoption of open banking. By enabling secure data sharing and third-party integrations, open banking is reshaping how BaaS providers operate, driving new business models, partnerships, and revenue streams.

Chapter 2 Key Takeaways

1. The growth of prepaid and BaaS has redefined financial access; while prepaid provides the speed and simplicity needed for rapid inclusion, BaaS offers the deep infrastructure required to scale banking services globally.
2. Prepaid technology is fueling everything from Challenger Banks, BNPL, and corporate expenses to reward cards, and is becoming known as the innovation rail.
3. **Personal lesson:** Asking a lot of questions is foundational to learning, as doing so helps us develop the courage to lean into risk with a mindset of "If I'm going to fail, I'm going to fail forward."

Chapter 3

Enabling New Ways to Pay: From Embedded Finance to Agentic Payments

"Payments are where innovation is most visible and where finance meets everyday life. They have moved from being transactional to experiential."
—Panagiotis Kriaris, FinTech Top Voice on LinkedIn

In this chapter, we will explore rapidly growing elements of the embedded finance landscape and how they are enabling both fintechs and nonfinancial companies to integrate financial services into their platforms in innovative ways. Embedded finance is helping consumers access financial services like new ways to pay, send and receive money, lend, borrow, and save directly in the apps and websites they already use. The clearest example of this is e-commerce where websites and apps like Amazon allow users to pay with their wallets, save their payment preferences for easier checkout, buy now, pay later, or even get a business credit line.

The payments space is one of my favorites, as it is an ever-changing ecosystem that has unlocked financial inclusion in many ways. Since I have spent many hours at conferences, on stages moderating discussions, and listening to webinars and podcasts over the past decade, I consider myself and many experts featured in the book as official "payments geeks."

The chapter-opening quote is from Panagiotis Kriaris, a prominent fintech leader and one of the most influential voices in the payments industry across Europe. Historically, the value of payments has been purely transactional, a functional utility designed to complete a specific task. However, we are now witnessing a fundamental shift toward experiential payments. Through innovative fintech products, payments are no longer just a backend process; they are a front-end experience that creates deeper value and fosters emotional connections, such as brand loyalty and trust. In this new era, the payment is not just the end of a journey but a critical touchpoint in the customer relationship.

As the world of payments continues to evolve, we enjoy the benefits of innovations such as biometric payment, where our faces or fingers become our payment method without the need for a physical card or phone. Another emerging experience is agentic payments, in which an AI agent (bot) makes payments on our behalf with express consent for each purchase. For example, if I wanted to secure tickets to the next Metallica concert for my husband, I could ask an agent through a chat interface to purchase two tickets within a specified price range, date, and location. My agent would then secure the tickets for me and handle the transaction in a tokenized manner without further intervention. My agent does the research, makes the choices within my preset parameters, and completes the transaction, saving me a lot of time.

My goal now is to increase your interest and curiosity about how payments can ignite innovations and provide additional empowerment in a trustworthy manner.

Leaning into Grit

Touching new technology can be exciting as well as a bit scary, especially when there aren't historical resources from which to learn. We need to become more comfortable with learning as we go. I have come to realize that it is normal to have moments of imposter syndrome as we step into something new and complex. There have been many times when I have faced self-doubt and questioned whether I belonged at the table, even after years of gaining knowledge and many accomplishments under my belt.

I've learned that my nerves are tempered by a healthy dose of grit, a skill I developed as a competitive soccer player for 10 years. I am determined to take risks, to make the unknown known, and to grow in both my knowledge and confidence. When we learn to trust ourselves, take time to do the research, and ask questions, we might even become experts on a topic. I could never have imagined in 2015, as I took my first step into payments, that I would not only be speaking on stages all over the world but writing a book about the future of finance.

Helping with a 2017 pilot for 7-Eleven to test QR code wallet top-ups first showcased the impressive fintech growth in Asia and sparked a lasting curiosity about the impact of QR technology on the global payment ecosystem. The completion of this test pilot was a pivotal moment in my career, as it not only gave me confidence that I could help test complex new technology but also pushed me to learn more about what was happening in fintech globally. Once I understood the full functionality of super apps, I realized that the future of finance was already alive and growing in Asia. It inspired me to take the IVEY course focused on fintechs, digital identity, and blockchain, which led me to take the leap into the start-up world.

What Are Embedded Payments?

Embedded payments seamlessly incorporate payment processing within a product or application, simplifying the checkout experience for users. This encompasses a range of payment choices, such as one-click checkout via digital wallets or direct integration with banking services facilitated by open banking frameworks. Embedded finance is part of the flow of consumer transactions. Merchants using it are engaging customers within their sites rather than having to click away to another site before completing a transaction. The key element for the merchants is to work with fintechs that are compliant and trustworthy to manage transactions as it is the brand's name that the customer sees.

When we talk about embedded payments, we talk about organizations that don't normally touch payments. As an example, Starbucks, a coffee company, has embraced a variety of embedded financial experiences. These products range from mobile payments, stored-value cards, and gift cards to reward programs, wearable payments, bitcoin payments, and digital collectibles.

Through the Starbucks app, customers can save their customized orders, preload their Starbucks wallet with a credit card, PayPal, or Apple Pay, and even earn travel miles. According to a post by FINBOLD in May 2024, if Starbucks were a bank, which it is not, "it would be ranked in the top 10% of largest banks in the US. With $1.8 billion in prepaid coffees uploaded by customers, Starbucks possesses a substantial financial presence."[1] Though Starbucks might be one of the largest success stories of embedded finance, it's only one story out of millions.

As you can see in Figure 3.1, the global embedded payments market in total was already set to reach $125 B in 2025. It is being driven by the shift to digital-first commerce, modern payment APIs, and regulatory support for financial innovation. Platforms across e-commerce, software as a service (SaaS), and ride-sharing are leveraging these tools to diversify revenue and streamline

Figure 3.1 Global embedded payments market

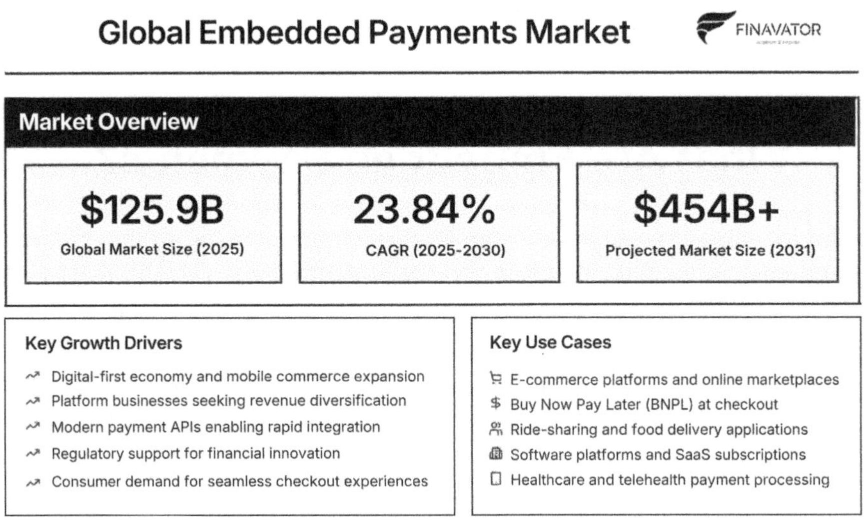

transactions. Consumer demand for seamless checkout experiences is further accelerating adoption across sectors like BNPL and telehealth.

Examples of embedded products include:

- **Payment processing services:** E-commerce platforms integrate direct payment solutions, allowing consumers to make purchases without leaving the site or app.
- **Savings and investment products:** Retail companies offering their customers the ability to open savings accounts or invest in mutual funds directly through their apps.
- **Credit and loans:** Online marketplaces provide instant credit or loans at the point of sale, enabling customers to finance purchases immediately.
- **Insurance services:** Travel booking apps that offer travel insurance as an add-on service during the booking process.

There is a vibrant ecosystem of consumer payment enablers, including Stripe, PayPal, Adyen, and Square, legacy embedded enablers such as Global Payments and Worldpay, and start-ups such as Finix, Fortis, and Payrix. Consumer payments account for more than 60% of all embedded finance transactions. Among the key findings of McKinsey's 2023 Digital Payments Consumer Survey, more than 9 out of 10 consumers say they have used some form of digital payment over the course of the year.[2]

The Future of Embedded Payments

With more than 300 million active customers worldwide, many consumers are accustomed to their Amazon experience. Therefore, integrating financial services into everyday apps is already familiar, allowing users to make purchases, access funds, and complete transactions seamlessly without ever leaving the platform. For instance, when shopping online, a consumer can apply for credit at the point of sale, such as getting an Amazon credit card, with just a few clicks. They might also make a payment directly through a mobile app, such as PayPal or Apple Pay, without entering their credit card information or accessing their banking app.

Embedded finance not only enhances customer convenience but also opens significant opportunities for businesses to increase engagement, collect valuable data, and generate additional revenue streams. While embedded finance was already evolving, the COVID-19 pandemic heightened acute awareness of transmission by contact, something to be avoided at all costs. This resulted in the general advancement and acceptance of contactless payments, which are now a normal part of our everyday lives.

Key Types of Payments

Digital payments driving growth. It is important to describe digital payments as they help us move money fast every day, they are fully digital, and they include everything from Internet bank transfers, wire transfers, and e-checks to mobile wallets and digital payment apps like Apple Pay and Google Pay to the growing use of digital currencies on wallets such as Coinbase. The benefits these apps provide are many.

- Digital payments save time and money.
- Alternative methods eliminate the time spent on mailing, processing, and depositing manual checks, as well as the administrative costs and time required to log, process, and deposit checks.
- Mastercard Send, Visa Direct, and Real-Time Payment (RTP) all process at higher speeds.

Real-Time Rail (RTR) is a payment rail system that enables faster, near-real-time transfers of funds to a recipient's account or wallet from banks or financial institutions, facilitating instant payment processing and settlement. According to the *BIS Quarterly Review* in March 2024, "Real-time payments are live in over 80 countries with two leading countries, RTR systems helping to drive finance, including in both India's with the launch of UPI in 2016, with 613 million users in May 2025, and Brazil's PIX system live in 2020 with over 182 million consumers and 19 million businesses.[3] Last year, Colombia launched its national instant payment system called BreB, which began full-scale operations in October 2025 and allows individuals and businesses to send and receive payments instantly, 24/7, across banks and digital wallets. The US launch of RTR payments was in phases, first with the Clearing House in 2017 and then with FedNow in 2023, and according to the US Bank 2024 report, around 51% of US companies are using faster payments." This is a crucial aspect of the future of finance as real-time payments provide key benefits, including instant bill payments, insurance claim disbursements, and enhanced analytics, to name a few.

Before the inception and acceptance of real-time payments, business owners may have had to wait several days for funds to become available. Consumers may have missed opportunities to buy stocks at their lowest prices due to the lag time between funds being transferred to their trading accounts. Real-time payments helped eliminate many inconveniences worldwide.

One additional benefit of moving to use real-time rails is that many countries, including the US FedNow 13, have added an important update into their systems called ISO20022, which enables data-rich payments. It provides added information about everyday payments, which makes reconciliation seamless for business owners. Without it, when you look at your business bank statement, you see only the wire number, the amount, and the date of a transaction, which makes it hard to match client payments. When the ISO20022 standard is added, it can also include the invoice number for business and the item description for the consumer, "Macy's, Blue Dress, $100 USD." This will be a great time-saver for business owners and will allow customers to see their actual purchase details on their credit card and bank statements.

The Power of Contactless Payments

During the pandemic, I remember having a call with my then 70-year-old mom as she shared her fear of touching the payment terminal in stores, and I didn't disagree. I spent time on a call walking her through how to embed her credit card into her Samsung phone. I then told her how she could tap to pay at grocery stores and the pharmacy, which not only saved her time but also gave her peace of mind. This was the beginning of the mass adoption of tap-to-pay worldwide. It allowed consumers to feel confident and safe, with an additional layer of security provided by an NFC chip that enables tap-to-pay on our phones. This ecosystem enabled the phone payment method to send a tokenized payment without a four-digit PIN, eliminating the need to touch the terminal.

Contactless payments are a method of making transactions without physically touching payment terminals or handling cash. It is commonly known as *tap-to-pay*. This mode of payment uses various technologies to facilitate quick, secure, and convenient payments. These technologies include:

- **Near Field Communication (NFC)** allows two devices, such as a smartphone and a payment terminal, to communicate when they are close together (typically within a few centimeters). Tap-to-pay can be applied more broadly to any contactless payment method in which you tap a card or device to make a payment.
- **Digital Wallets** store payment information securely on a device, such as a smartphone or smartwatch, and use NFC technology to communicate with payment terminals. Payment information, such as a credit card number, is tokenized, meaning the number is embedded in a way that allows you to tap to pay from the phone itself, without ever touching a payment terminal. It is primarily used for remote online transactions.
- **Quick Response (QR) Codes** are machine-readable codes that can store large amounts of data. Once scanned, they open a website that allows transactions to be completed. The use of QR codes increased on a mass scale during the pandemic. For example, restaurants used them for menus, reducing the risk of spreading the disease through handling physical menus. The key value of QR codes is that they add an extra layer of security when used for payments.

The use of QR codes is growing rapidly worldwide. The growth is exponential, with more than $11 trillion in value in 2023 alone, and is set to reach more than $18.5 trillion by the end of 2025. China is the leading market for QR code use, with 85% adoption driven by AliPay's 1.3 billion users and WeChat Pay's 900 million users. One of the fastest-growing markets is Brazil, which has implemented a standard for all QR codes, adding interoperability and consistency across its payments ecosystem, including banks, merchants, and payments networks, and reaching more than 170 million users through its Pix system. This is an exciting new way to pay, and I believe North America will be the next to embrace standards to drive additional growth.

To understand the global landscape of mobile payments, we must look at the rapid rise of QR codes as a primary transaction rail. Figure 3.2 illustrates the regional adoption of QR payments and the specific market leaders driving this change across the globe. The Asia-Pacific region leads the world in total transaction volume with more than 80% adoption in China and India, while Brazil has achieved the highest percentage of adult participation at 93% through its Pix system. North America is shifting toward mainstream use, with the United States

Figure 3.2 Regional QR payment adoption and leaders

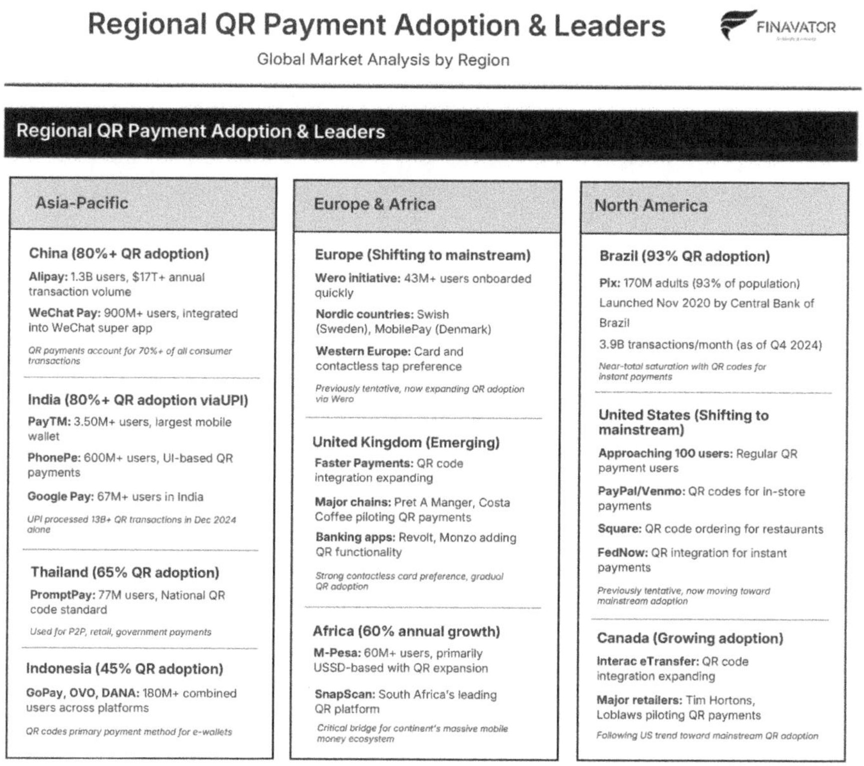

approaching 100 million regular QR users via FedNow and Canada starting to move toward QR payments with some major retailers such as McDonalds and Tim Hortons. In the United Kingdom and Europe, adoption is emerging as a "scan-to-pay" alternative to cards, supported by the Wero initiative and major banking apps like Revolut. Meanwhile, Africa continues to see 60% annual growth, using QR codes as a critical bridge for the continent's massive mobile money ecosystem.

Before diving into new ways to pay, I wanted to share insights from other experts in the world and the power of payments for merchants and the payments-acquiring world.

I reached out to a good friend and fellow Money 20/20 Rise Up alumna, Genevieve Dozier, for her insights on the evolution of merchant payments, drawing on her career, expertise, and perspective across fintech and financial services.

I first met Genevieve in Las Vegas in 2019, and since then, we have shared many stages. Genevieve is a highly respected payments executive with 20 years of experience spanning fintech start-ups, financial institutions, and large corporations, including Truist, Fiserv, and Finova Capital. She has served on the boards of PayTech Women and VizyPay and has received numerous accolades, including being on the Women in Fintech Powerlist, ETA Top Forty Under 40, and the NYC Inspiring Fintech Female award. Recognized as one of the Top 100 Most Influential Voices in Fintech, Genevieve is deeply committed to advancing people-first innovation in payments and financial technology.

When discussing how fintech is shaping a new financial era, Genevieve emphasizes the transformative impact of embedded payments. By integrating card acceptance directly into business software, companies have eliminated the need for separate hardware, creating more seamless merchant experiences, and enabling more efficient operations. She also highlights the shift from traditional card swiping to EMV chip and tap-to-pay technology. "It took the pandemic to accelerate tap-to-pay adoption at the point of sale and for consumers to trust paying with their phones," she notes. "Many people still don't realize this is one of the safest ways to pay as the 16-digit card number is replaced with a token. The business and processor never see the real card number, which means it cannot be stolen or hacked." Since the adoption of chip cards and the liability shift over a decade ago, counterfeit card fraud has nearly been eliminated in the United States.

Genevieve also points to Square, now Block Inc., as a defining disruptor in the past 15 years. By providing sleek, mobile, and tablet-based devices that enable small businesses and entrepreneurs to accept payments easily, Square has fundamentally changed how merchants operate. As of 2024, more than 4 million sellers worldwide use Square's services, underscoring the company's profound influence on business growth and modernization.

She further highlights the broader fintech ecosystem, including platforms such as Stripe, which processed more than $1 trillion in payments in 2023, and global players such as Adyen. These companies demonstrate how fintech continues to reshape commerce and financial services, offering new opportunities for businesses and consumers alike.

I deeply appreciate Genevieve's perspective on merchant services and payments acquisition. Her insights underscore how innovation, security, and user-first thinking are driving the evolution of payments and financial technology and how fintech will continue to redefine the future of commerce for years to come.

Key New Ways to Pay

Now that we have run through embedded payments, real-time rails, and QR payments, I wanted to share two newer ways to pay: "biometric" and "AI agentic" payments. They are both changing how we make everyday payments. Let's start with biometric payments, as I could write a whole chapter on AI agent payments alone but will try to summarize both emerging technologies.

Biometric Payments

Biometric payments are transactions verified using a person's unique biological features. This allows payments without cards, cash, or passwords. By using unique physical characteristics like your fingerprint, face, voice, or even your palm, these systems can verify your identity in a way that feels natural and seamless. Unlike a PIN or card number, these traits are unique to you and much harder to replicate, giving transactions an added layer of security.

When thinking about biometric payment, I think of watching *The Jetsons* cartoon in the 1980s, as so much of that futuristic imaginary world has come to fruition. There was a scene in which George Jetson made a payment with his fingerprint at the checkout. This is a great example of the new ways to pay, and we are just getting started with it.

The top use cases for biometric payments have come from Asia, with China leading the way with retail facial recognition and palm-pay at checkout. In March 2025, Future Market Insights reported that "80% of mobile payment users in China are using biometric authentication."

Amazon Go is one of the first US retailers to have multiple stores where you can just shop and walk out, with payment processed by your face or palm.

Handling such personal data requires care. Privacy, consent, and strong protections need to be built into every system. The potential is real, but success depends on balancing convenience with responsibility so that biometric payments truly support people and their trust in every transaction.

Agentic Payments

In 2007, I managed online shopping malls for airlines when e-commerce was just 1–3% of retail, and trusting your screen to make a purchase felt like stepping into the unknown. Today, we're at a strikingly similar crossroads, shifting from "Search and Click" to "Intent and Execute." The leap in trust required for agentic commerce feels exactly like that early digital frontier. Agentic payments are a transformative force in finance and technology. AI-driven tools are evolving from passive search assistants to autonomous agents.

According to a June 2025 Bank of America Global Research analysis, spending on agentic AI could reach $155 billion by 2030.[4] With numbers like these, it's no surprise that agentic payments are a key topic in fintech and AI circles. If a robot could shop on our behalf, this could help save hours of searching and planning, which could be great in many use cases for consumers. We all want the benefits enabled by new ways to pay, especially when they save time.

I had the privilege of moderating a panel focused on trust at Money2020 Europe in Amsterdam with three impressive CEOs. We connected for a prep call in May 2025, and that's when I first learned about agentic payments. I was excited for the endless use cases and opportunities. I was also a little concerned as the liability models have yet to be defined, leaving many open-ended questions on what happens when there is fraud, the wrong item is purchased, and the list goes on.

Agentic payments represent an exciting step forward and deserve a thoughtful approach. At their heart, agentic AI payment agents are meant to help with everyday purchases, renewals, and bill payments in a way that feels almost effortless. When they work well, they remove friction and create a seamless purchasing experience.

Beyond purchasing goods, consumers have been using autopay since the early 2000s to pay monthly bills on time. This service has become important for many consumers as it helps to save time and to stress less about remembering to pay each bill on the right date. Businesses have been using autopay since the early 2000s and are happy to process scheduled payments, reducing the time and effort spent on receivables. The move toward agentic AI payments seems like a clear next step to help consumers and businesses alike with continuing innovation on autopay that can help save time and money.

This shift toward automation requires vigilance. I am all for innovation and added convenience, yet I am a little concerned that the Internet is now more than 51% bots versus humans.[5] Standards for security, clear consent, and transparency remain essential. Visa has formally updated its Global Core Rules to define "Agentic Payment Providers"; Mastercard is pushing Verifiable Intent standards for audit trails; and American Express is standing out as the first to offer Agent Purchase Protection™, a formal liability model covering financial losses from AI agent errors. We already rely on AI to unlock our phones and open apps with Face ID, personalize what we see in our news or social media feeds, send emails or text messages ("Hey, Siri. . ."), get directions to a new restaurant, and detect fraud in our bank accounts. Agentic payments bring the power and customization of AI to finance. With agentic payments, we can authorize AI to act as our personal assistant.

As a fun example, we might use it to find and purchase tickets to world cup tickets or to help find and purchase vinyl records from your favorite band, rather than spending time searching online or going from store to store ourselves. Agentic payments are transactions initiated and completed autonomously by an AI agent acting on a user's behalf, with minimal or no human intervention at the point of purchase. All transactions are based solely on user-defined goals and constraints.

Agentic AI needs clear direction and consent to help with purchases but can remember context to learn and improve. With its memory, your AI agent can help you book the best flights based on your request for specific dates and times, and complete payment with the best credit card to earn extra airline miles, get discounts, or cashback bonuses.

I am sure it will soon be able to select your favorite window seat over the wing, if that's your preference. Your agent could even order clothing for you and remember your preferred sizes, styles, and colors of items you've favored in the past. In an ideal offering, you will have your own agent that is not shared and shouldn't share any of your data that's not necessary to the transaction, just as you would if you were making purchases yourself. AI can also be trained to make helpful decisions such as suggesting the top credit card offers that could be more beneficial than the one you already have.

Many are starting to call Agentic AI agents "digital teammates" that can help simplify checkout experiences for both consumers and businesses. Figure 3.3 provides a visual roadmap of how agentic payments work and the role of the AI agent in executing autonomous value transfer. Note that it all begins with the user expressing the specifications of their intended purchase very clearly. AI agents will search within the offered parameters, then identify the result back to the consumer before making the purchase. Once approved, the agent moves forward with the purchase through acceptable payment processing procedures, and the consumer receives a transaction of conformation.

The scale of what's coming is hard to ignore. The Worldpay 2026 Global Ecommerce Report forecasts agentic commerce reaching $3.5 trillion by 2031.[6] To capture that growth, Worldpay launched Worldpay MCP, built on the Model Context Protocol, serving as the connective tissue that lets AI agents understand a merchant's payment rules and inventory in real time, enabling tasks like subscription renewals without any manual intervention.

Figure 3.3 How AI payments work

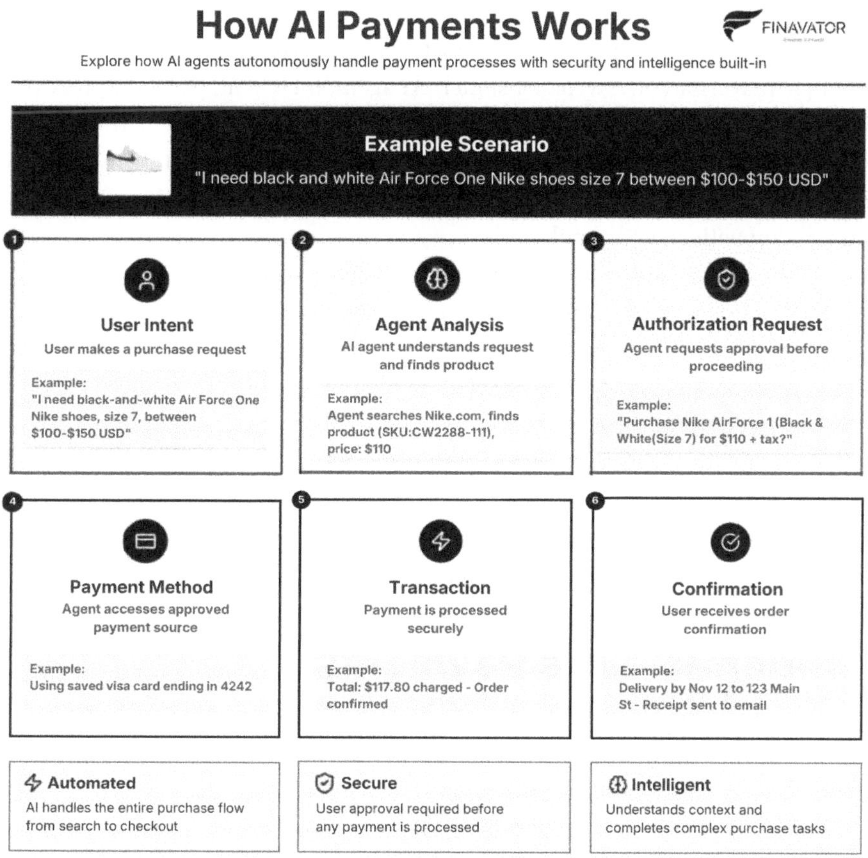

Data Protection and Agentic Payments

One of my biggest concerns around agentic payments is protection. How is my information protected from fraud with each innovation being developed? Thinking about all the places our data is stored with no control over it, which is concerning to say the least. Now more than ever, we need to have access to human data rights to ensure our agentic AI agents allow us to see and control which of our data points our agents can see and share with various sources.

With trust being extremely critical in the digital era, the financial ecosystem needs to be especially careful when it comes to responsibility. As agentic comes to market, it is important to consider all scenarios, including fraud, account takeovers, and who is responsible when something goes wrong during a purchase, as multiple players are involved: consumer, AI agent, merchant, payment processor, network, and bank. It is also critical to ensure that the user is verified with KYC and that the AI agent is verified for know your agent (KYA), and then these two connections are combined with a clear, consented purchase order to start the transaction with an audit trail.

We should also investigate having what many are calling AI agent trust scores for each of our agentic agents to allow merchants and banks to sort the good AI agents from fraudulent ones and set rules as we move forward. Until guardrails are put in place and regulations are established, the financial ecosystem needs to exercise caution around the mass rollout of agentic payments. It is important to test and retest all use cases and to ensure that strong consumer authentication, privacy, and unique tokenization are at the core of every transaction. I would like to see a phased go-to-market approach that has a maximum of $200–$300 purchases for the first six months, similar to when tap-to-pay launched.

Credential-Less Payments

As part of the future of finance, there is also an exciting trend I want to share as it will ideally help move fraud in a meaningful way. This is a shift that is starting to move toward credential-less tokenization, which is a security and access model that allows users to interact with financial services and digital assets without traditional credentials such as usernames, passwords, or stored identity data. Instead, access is granted through cryptographic proofs, tokens, or programmable permissions that verify rights without exposing personal information. This model significantly reduces fraud by eliminating the most common attack surface, stolen credentials, leaving nothing to phish, reuse, or leak in a breach. Transactions rely on time-bound or single-use cryptographic authorizations, making misuse or replay attacks extremely difficult. By minimizing stored sensitive data, credential-less tokenization also reduces insider risk and large-scale data breaches, shifting fraud prevention from reactive controls to security by design.

To summarize, the benefits of the many new ways to pay from QR codes and Real-Time Rails to agentic AI agents as well as embedded finance are endless for customers, businesses, fintechs, and even banks. This evolution is unlocking faster, more efficient payments, helping to drive increased consumer growth as well as potentially generating additional revenue streams.

Expert Interview with Panagiotis Kriaris

I have had the privilege of sharing the stage, both virtually and in person, on multiple occasions with Panagiotis Kriaris, a leading voice in fintech, payments, and banking. Recognized as a FinTech Top Voice on LinkedIn and among the top 200 most influential individuals across 14 European countries, he brings deep expertise across financial services, banking, payments, retail, and e-commerce. His work is rooted in innovation, strategy, business development, strategic partnerships, and building products and businesses from the ground up.

Panagiotis has spent his career at the intersection of business and technology, shaping how payment innovation drives the broader financial ecosystem. When asked why he is so passionate about payments, he explained that payments have evolved from a low-margin operational function into the center of digital finance. "Payments are where innovation is most visible and where finance meets everyday life. They have moved from being transactional to experiential. The more payments fade into the background, the more strategically important they become."

He highlighted the growth of embedded finance as a major catalyst for change. "Financial products no longer require customers to go to the bank. Instead, they appear within the apps and platforms where people already live and work. When payments are integrated into retail, mobility, or business marketplaces, they become effortless and contextual, strengthening loyalty and creating new revenue opportunities."

Panagiotis also discussed the increasing role of biometrics in building trust and security. "Biometrics shift authentication from something you know to something you are. As payments become faster and more invisible, this trust layer is essential. It ensures safety without adding friction and allows institutions to balance security with convenience."

Looking ahead, he expressed excitement about agentic payments, which allow intelligent systems to manage payments on behalf of users. "This is where AI transforms payments from isolated events into adaptive processes that learn and anticipate needs. We are moving toward autonomous finance, where money management becomes proactive and intelligent."

Panagiotis summarized the future of payments innovation through three key takeaways:

- Embedded intelligence
- Frictionless trust
- Autonomous finance

He shared that the most exciting development is the convergence of data, identity, and connectivity, enabled by AI. "Payments are no longer just about moving money. They are about moving information and trust. AI allows payments to become smarter, more connected, and ultimately more useful."

Speaking with Panagiotis reinforced how quickly the payments landscape is shifting toward intelligent, interconnected ecosystems. His perspective highlights how AI, biometrics, and embedded finance are redefining trust, security, and experience in the digital economy, positioning payments as a powerful catalyst for innovation and inclusion.

New Ways to Pay's Alignment to the Future of Finance

Payments are extremely powerful services that are shaping the future of finance, from real-time rails to speed up all transactions to QR codes enabling seamless payments and AI agents that discover products and handle payments autonomously on our behalf, which is predicted to exceed 440 billion transactions by 2030.[7]

I know the topic of payments can be confusing, and they include too many acronyms and new phrases to remember, including RTR, Digital Wallets, BNPL, ISO20022, QR codes, agentic, credential-less payments, and biometric payments. That's why I've included a full, free downloadable glossary available on my website (finavator.com).

As a business owner, I see so many ways for companies to innovate, delight their customers, and create partnerships. Before partnering with or launching any new technology, though, do your due diligence, ensure your onboarding system has the strongest authentication possible to help reduce fraud, and adopt a mindset of leaning into the future. Remember what Amelia Earhart said: "The most difficult thing is the decision to act; the rest is mere tenacity."

Chapter 3 Key Takeaways

1. Embedded finance is adding seamless financial options to our everyday lives that are simple, convenient, and helping to unlock financial inclusion for millions.
2. The world of payments is changing and now includes tap-to-pay, QR codes, instant payments and biometrics, and agentic payments. It can feel overwhelming at times, so take small steps to try new ways to pay, go at your own pace, and ask questions.
3. **Personal lesson:** We all experience high levels of stress at some point in our lives, and the only way I found to win is with a balance between meditation, pushing myself through grit, and building confidence one day or project at a time.

Part II

Trust Is the New Currency

Chapter 4

Trusted Identity: The Key to Thriving in Our Digital World

"The future of digital life will be built on trust. When we secure identity in a way that protects people and preserves privacy, we create a safer, more inclusive digital world."

—David Birch, Global Identity and Payments Expert

As we begin this chapter on the next element of the future of finance, it's important to understand that as both our human needs and technology continue to evolve, this evolution brings new possibilities for how we relate to the benefits inherent in it. We have already seen our use of money shift from physical to digital, as covered in the previous chapters on new ways to pay, unlocking access to the digital economy. That shift has benefited us by providing both convenience and security, while contributing greatly to global economic growth. As we move forward, the element of identity is also shifting from physical forms to digital, enabling new ways to prove who we say we are.

I believe in innovation through technology, including AI, yet I also desire privacy-by-design, as well as what I call "human data rights" and the legal principle of the "right to be forgotten." I would like to see more fintechs work toward building a future with consumer data rights and the right to privacy-by-design at its core.

In this chapter, we will explore how our verified digital identity is becoming a cornerstone of modern life, especially within the realm of finance. It plays a crucial role in driving inclusion, enhancing security, improving and simplifying customer experiences, and enabling new services that expand the level of convenience for us all. The biggest challenge we move further into the age of AI is how to trust the management of all our digital data. Who controls and owns the data? How do we protect it? Who needs access? What access do they get? There are numerous questions arising from this topic, and just as many suggested solutions. It's evolving faster than ever, and the core principles of trust, consent, and security are more crucial than ever.

I started this chapter with a quote from David Birch, as his statement is powerful. David is a respected global voice in identity, payments, and the evolution of trust in the digital world. We all must get on board finding ways to secure our identities from unauthorized access while allowing global recognition of who we are. You will learn more from him later in our in-depth interview.

The management of digital identity is not to be feared but to be understood. Through understanding, we will gain clarity on the best solutions for both protecting and benefiting our digital identities. I understand that many are concerned about digital identity, so I will address current considerations and share insights on how privacy-by-design and triple-blind systems could help protect our data.

I think it all comes down to the question of what systems get built. Is it market-led or regulatory, and will it be centralized or decentralized? How do we ensure it's safe and secure and that everybody's at the table when building an ecosystem of digital trust? Where and when do governments add regulations, and how do we put protection around all of them? Let's walk through this topic together.

Protecting What Makes You, You

Every person on the planet has their own identity. We all have our own names, dates of birth, nationalities, and unique biometrics, those physical and behavioral characteristics that make us who we are. These include, but are not limited to, our fingerprints, facial features, voices, and irises. To interact with our communities, fellow humans, and establishments, whether employers, governments, financial institutions, or even retailers, our identities must be provable. We prove who we are every time we use our driver's license or passport to board an airplane or our insurance health card to see a doctor. We use our identity to order an Uber, open a bank account, rent a place to live, buy a car, or even purchase a home.

Due to the reliance on technology for faster, more efficient business operations, many businesses have stored their information in their own operating systems. That information is part of our digital identity. As we've learned over the years, not all those businesses have enough security measures within those operating systems to fully protect our personal identifiable information (PII). In 2024 alone, more than 3,000 data compromises were reported, affecting more than 1.3 billion individuals.[1]

We are all currently exposed, as our data is extensively shared across various platforms and companies, held by hundreds of companies, and we need an option to move into a future where all aspects of our identities are well-protected through consent and the right to be deleted. This involves us, the consumers of the world, having control over all of our information and who has access to it. The goal is for our digital information to be used when, where, and how we choose through technological tools.

My First Identity Conference

I remember sitting at an IdentityNorth conference in 2018, a couple of weeks into my new role as the chief client officer of a blockchain start-up that was focused on digital identity. It was my first-ever identity conference, and I remember being nervous as I knew nothing about identity beyond what I had learned in the three-day course I took on blockchain, digital ID, and fintech at IVEY in the fall of 2017.

I knew no one in the room, and I remained focused on absorbing all of the many insights throughout the day. One of the most memorable moments was when they had us sit at a round table, with these different-colored sticky notes and markers in the middle. They asked us to write down every word we could think of when we thought of digital identity. Then they gave us a whiteboard, and we put all of the sticky notes on it. We tried to map out which ones were similar and ended up dividing our notes into four categories:

- **Who we are:** Name, email, phone number, passport
- **How we prove it:** Password, PIN, Face ID, two-factor multifactor authentication (MFA)
- **Digital footprint:** Social posts, online cookies, browsing history
- **Where we use ID:** Government, banks, healthcare, travel

It was my first foray into digital identity, but it helped me make new friends and start to understand the terms and ideas behind it early on. Given my background in payments, where identity is key to managing the smooth flow of money and avoiding fraud, I quickly understood the importance of how it's used. Within this chapter, I'll break down the many concepts and insights to help you grasp how it can empower you to protect your identity. I hope these insights intrigue you to advocate for your data rights and potentially find ways to enable them.

What Is Digital Identity?

Just like every person on the planet has their own identity, we also have a digital identity. A digital identity is an electronic representation of an individual's identity that can be used online or in person to verify who someone is. It enables secure authentication, proving who you are, and clear authorization giving the right permissions to whom your data is shared with, which gives access to services in the digital and physical world, replacing traditional physical documents, such as a plastic driver's license, with cryptographically secure digital credentials. The infrastructure behind *secured* digital identity is an encrypted, tokenized architecture developed by industry-leading tech firms, including Apple, Trulioo, ProveID, and Anonybit, to name a few, that can provide the best experience for the end customer. In the US, the American Association for Retired Persons (AARP) is an interesting source for simplifying the complex, especially when it comes to the digital world. One area in which they are involved is the testing of digital identity standards that protect older adults from the rising threat of identity theft and fraud.

Around the world, digital IDs are replacing traditional username and password authentication with a broader set of security-enhanced elements, such as personal information, biometric data, behavioral data, and device identifiers. In simple terms, it's a faster, more efficient, and secure way for us to sign onto a new system, use a new app, check into a hotel, and make purchases, basically, to operate in our everyday world.

When we think of methods to prove our identity, we think of things we touch, like a driver's license or passport, which are government-issued documents and are accepted worldwide by other governments and institutions. There are six main types of identity outlined in Figure 4.1 in the following sections, including those issued by our government, bank-issued, company-issued, mobile-based, education-based, and self-sovereign.

Figure 4.1 Digital ID: Foundation of secure identity verification

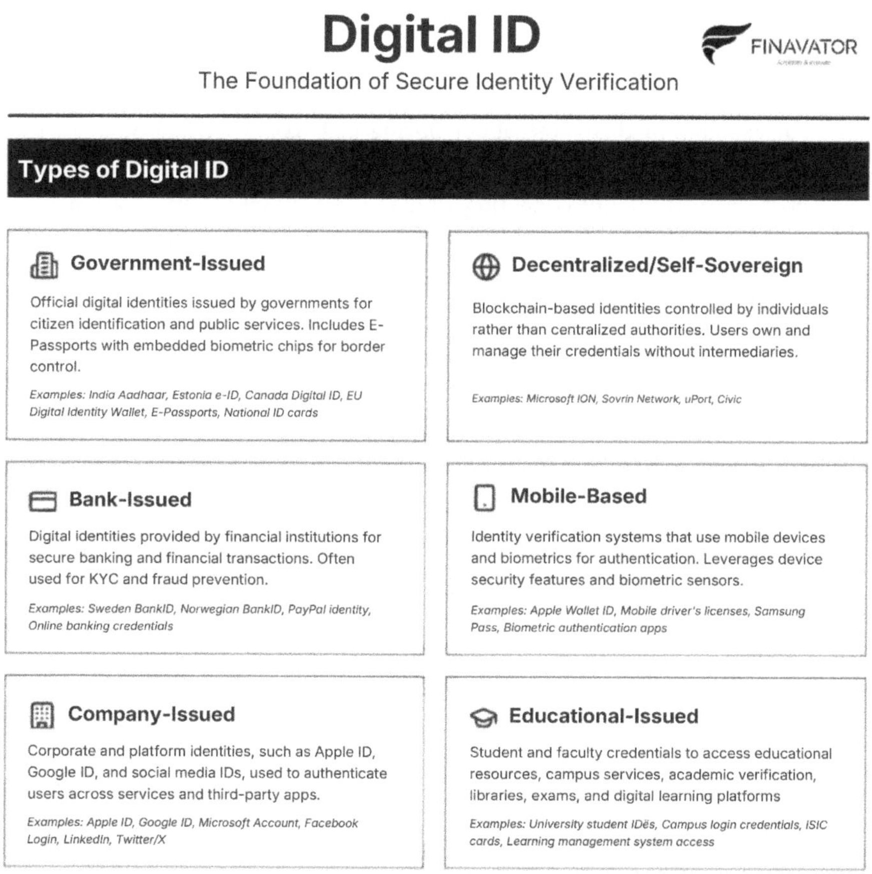

When we think of methods to prove our identity, we think of things we touch, like a driver's license or passport, which are government-issued documents and are accepted worldwide by other governments and institutions. We all have many forms of identity issued by our schools, companies, banks, and mobile providers (see Figure 4.1). As countries work to find the best way to create more trusted identities, they are starting to explore new ways to prove we are who we say we are, including the one I am super excited about, called "self-sovereign ID," which I'll explain here.

- **Educational-issued IDs:** Student and faculty credentials for accessing educational resources, campus services, and academic verification. Used for library access, exams, and digital learning platforms. Examples: University student IDs, campus login credentials, learning management system access convenience.
- **Government-issued IDs:** Official digital identities issued by national or regional governments for citizen identification and public services. Includes e-passports with embedded biometric chips for border control. An example of this came about during COVID, when many countries issued vaccination credentials with QR codes. When a restaurant or airport scanned the QR code, they only saw proof that we were vaccinated, not our name, birthday, health number, or address. Other global examples include India's Aadhaar, Estonia's e-ID, Brazil's (CIN) national ID cards, and other countries' e-passports.
- **Company-issued IDs:** Corporate and tech platform identities and social media IDs for authentication across services and third-party applications. Examples: Apple ID, Google ID, and login credentials for Microsoft, Facebook, and LinkedIn.
- **Bank-issued IDs:** Digital identities provided by financial institutions for secure banking and financial transactions, often used for know your customer (KYC) and fraud prevention. These were first used in Sweden in 2003 and are expanding broadly. They can be equated with a passport or other ID specifically for the completion of financial transactions, including signing contracts or taking out loans. Your identity is secured through an original identifying means, such as a birth certificate or government-issued ID, when you open an account with banks offering this type of identification. These IDs can be used to identify yourself in digital environments rather than creating separate accounts with different organizations. Examples: Sweden BankID, Norwegian BankID, PayPal.

- **Mobile-based IDs:** You use your phone to store a digital version of your physical ID in a digital wallet. They leverage device security features and biometric sensors. Your mobile device ID can use your face recognition for authentication that you are the owner or user of the phone. Examples: Apple Wallet ID, Mobile driver's licenses, Samsung Pass, and Biometric authentication apps. Being able to store that ID on my phone to verify my age when necessary in a restaurant or bar is great. I could potentially even, once approved by the state or province, leave my driver's license at home and just carry my phone. With my credit card already embedded in my wallet, all I need is my phone, and who leaves home without that?
- **Decentralized IDs (DIDs):** The W3C DID specification for creating identifiers that the individual user controls, allowing them to manage their data through blockchain-based identity rather than centralized authorities. Users own and manage their credentials without intermediaries. Each decentralized identity is globally unique, is cryptographically verifiable, and can prove identity across multiple systems.
- **Self-sovereign identity (SSI)** is a model that uses a decentralized identity standard for individuals to fully control their identity data. With SSI, users decide what information to share, with whom, and for how long. An SSI wallet is an application that stores and manages DIDs, identity credentials, and cryptographic keys. It lets users receive, store, and present verifiable credentials securely. Some global examples include the EU Digital Identity Wallet, Microsoft ION, Sovrin Network, uPort, and Civic. Personally, I believe this type of ID has the greatest potential for us, as individuals, to guard our digital identities.

It is important to note that both decentralized ID and SSI use what are called *keys* (public and private keys). The private key stays with the user and is used to sign or approve actions, while the public key is shared so others can verify identity and trust the information. With a traditional identity, you are likely providing more information than necessary to prove who you are, and, historically, that information ends up being stored in someone's system. Now, let's say more than 25 companies (hotels, banks, employers, apps) have copies of your passport. Today, your passport is likely to be saved multiple times, which is concerning given the sensitive data points. In the future, using a mobile ID for your passport, as you see with Apple Wallet, would be a game changer for protecting your data.

If we had access to a decentralized identity passport that revealed only the specific information requested, such as to prove you're over 21, it would show only that. Or if you needed to prove you are who you say you are to check into a hotel, it shows only that. The most important part is that no one can make a copy as you're sharing only cryptographic proof, not the actual data.

With a digital identity, our current physical identities are transformed into digital forms that are authenticated by a recognized source, such as a government entity or, in the case of Sweden, the bank, and are readily accessible to us. We no longer require physical forms of identification to operate in the world. The apps and companies only need access to authenticated proof that we are who we say we are.

The big question about digital identity is: how is it controlled? Since it's all about me, I should have control, right? I believe every aspect of our digital identities should be controlled by us and shared only with our consent, for access to services such as a passport for travel, age to enter a bar, and name and address to book a hotel. The development and use of digital IDs can be controversial. When created and managed properly, using core principles, digital IDs can enhance privacy by simply verifying that I am who I say I am, without sharing my core data. Digital IDs can facilitate additional privacy by simply verifying that I am who I say I am, without sharing my core data. And just as important, digital identity needs to be created in such a way that it also serves the estimated one billion people on the planet who do not have any form of identification, physical or otherwise. Who's to say that those who do not need to travel globally, which currently requires a passport, or those who might never need a driver's license, should not have a form of ID that allows for their inclusion in other aspects of life, such as having bank accounts, buying something online, or attaining the benefits of being able to prove they are who they say they are.

What Is Digital DNA?

Now that you understand the different types of digital identities, I want to share insights into what digital DNA is, as they complement each other and show that we are who we say we are. Digital DNA is your online personality and behavioral data, which creates a digital footprint. It encompasses everything from our biometric data, device signatures, behavioral analytics, and transactional patterns that create a comprehensive identity profile. I simplified the four types of data layers that make up our digital DNA in Figure 4.2: biometric (fingerprint), behavioral (typing patterns), device-based (IP address), and social (content you like online).

When I mention digital DNA, I'm talking about a collection of data that proves "you are you" online: behavioral data, including how you type, your device data, such as where you are located, and biometric data, such as your face, fingerprint, or voice. It's your online footprint, consisting of any data that can be uniquely tied to you. It's what is already out there in the world about you. Your digital DNA is an extension of physical identification documents, such as driver's licenses, passports, and bank cards.

Digital DNA is dynamic and constantly changing based on behavior and usage patterns. Our digital DNA includes our habits and patterns that make us uniquely identifiable through our actions. As an example, your bank could help stop a fraud attempt as they could see that there is a "behavioral layer mismatch" as a fraudster is typing at 45 WPM, while you normally type at 72 WPM. Also, from a navigation perspective, the fraudster goes straight to making a wire transfer, and you always check balances first. Erratic mouse movement or clicking patterns that are not common to you when you log in can trigger potential fraud. This

Figure 4.2 Digital DNA: Blueprint of modern identity verification

Digital DNA

FINAVATOR

The Foundation of Modern Identity Verification

What is Digital DNA?

Digital DNA refers to the unique digital footprint and behavioral patterns that identify individuals in the digital ecosystem. It encompasses biometric data, device signatures, behavioral analytics, and transaction patterns that create a comprehensive identity profile.

Biometric Layer	Behavioral Layer	Device Layer	Contextual/Social Layer
• Fingerprints	• Typing patterns	• Device fingerprints	• Content you like
• Facial recognition	• Mouse movements	• IP address	• Social network
• Voice patterns	• Navigation habits	• Location data	• Social interactions
• Iris scan	• Usage timings	• Network signatures	• What you own online

is where advancements in AI are serving us well. Modern AI-driven biometric systems, such as facial recognition, now achieve accuracy levels exceeding 99.5% under optimal conditions, thanks to deep learning and advanced pattern analysis.[2] AI can detect anomalies better and faster than humans, which enhances fraud detection, including forgery.

The digitization of identities and digital DNA must be based on a foundation of trust with an eye to both simplification and convenience for the user. The world is moving in many different ways when it comes to identity, and my top favorite option is mobile, decentralized, and self-sovereign identities. We can maintain privacy and security by sharing less data about ourselves while still accessing all the services we need.

Trust Is the New Currency

We now live in a world where trust is the new currency; therefore, companies must protect their brands by safeguarding their consumers' data. I still remember when a major hotel chain had a mass data breach that impacted 7.1 million guests. Not long after this came to light, I was checking into my hotel in Las Vegas, where I was attending a digital identity conference. When I got to the hotel, I went to the front desk and was advised to use the self-check-in kiosk, considering I was required to scan my passport to complete my registration. I refused to scan it. As trust had been broken, I didn't want them to store that information.

I ended up speaking with a manager and saying, "Considering the news of the data breach, I am not comfortable scanning my passport as I don't believe it would store my data safely. Hotels shouldn't have my credit card and my passport in your system unless it is encrypted as it can be hacked." I offered to allow the manager to look at both my ID's passport and driver's license to prove I was who I say I was. The manager eventually agreed to complete my check-in without taking a photocopy of my passport, which was great, as it was late and I was tired. I wanted to stand by my principles, especially as I was scheduled to speak the next day about the importance of trust and digital identity.

Another industry statement is that data has become the new oil as it is fueling our digital lives. Therefore, we need to protect it. Had there been a QR code identity verification process similar to the airport in place, the hotel's check-in could have confirmed I am Michelle Beyo without the need for my passport data being shared or stored, and it could have taken less time than it took to call the manager. There would have been no concern on my part about whether to trust the hotel to hold a copy of my ID as they would have any of my sensitive data just that I was authenticated to be able to check in my hotel room.

Identity verification with AI is a simple process. The greatest benefit is that it can complete the process in seconds without having to store any of the information used for assessments.

Benefits of Digital Identity

When you think about digital identity and its benefits, if you have an authenticated or verified digital identity, you shouldn't have to transfer any information fully to anyone. It would give authentication that you are who you say you are. There needs to be some regulation around digital identity, but the potential convenience for end users is phenomenal. Some people feel it's going to change privacy. I believe that when properly protected and supported by robust authentication methods, digital identities can enhance privacy. Moving to digital identities can eliminate threats associated with physical IDs, such as theft and counterfeiting.

There are numerous entities that have to come together for the proper authentication and security of digital identities. However, similar protections are already in place in other areas that could prove useful. For example, when you tap to pay with a credit card, the retailer does not get your actual credit card information. They receive a tokenized identity that's a long, ever-changing number associated with your card. The number confirms the transaction without sharing your personal information.

The same can be done with digital identity. With a digital ID, you wouldn't be giving out your actual identity; rather, you would be providing a verification of it through digital abstraction, which then tokenizes, so your identity isn't shared. It simply verifies that you were there and that someone used your identity. Your information is protected.

Similarly, when you go to the airport and you're checking into your flight, you have to provide your passport with your date of birth, your address, and information about where you're going, and it creates a QR code that you then scan to get through customs and eventually get through to the flight itself. It's not sharing the data with the person who's scanning the QR code; it's validating that you are a passenger at the airport and that you're allowed to go through to this flight.

I had the pleasure of sitting down with Frances Zelazny, one of the early pioneers in the privacy preserving biometric space. I met her in New York in 2021. Since then, we've had the opportunity to collaborate on multiple stages, including co-hosting a full cybersecurity program focused on digital identity in the spring of 2025. Frances is widely recognized as a highly influential voice in biometrics, identity, privacy, and fraud prevention. As the Co-Founder of Anonybit and GM of New Markets at Prove, she has spent her career shaping how digital trust is built and how consumer data can be protected at scale in an increasingly complex, AI-driven world.

When asked about her journey into biometrics and identity, Frances reflected on how her path has always centered on trust. She often states, "Fintech's that don't protect customers will not have customers, and part of the protection is their identity as well as their assets." If you cannot establish who someone is and protect that information, you cannot build a safe digital economy. Her work began long before identity became a mainstream topic, giving her a unique vantage point as digital life expanded, and fraud evolved far beyond passwords and devices.

Frances understood early how innovations in biometrics revealed a structural flaw at the core of digital identity: sensitive data was being centralized, copied, and left vulnerable. As fraudsters became more sophisticated, she recognized the limitations of traditional authentication and the urgent need for architectures that protect biometric data without ever exposing it. Identity has become a weak link. The industry needed a way to anchor identity biometrically while preserving privacy, security, and usability.

This thinking led to the founding philosophy behind Anonybit, a decentralized, privacy-preserving infrastructure that allows organizations to authenticate users without storing biometrics in any single place. Frances explained that this approach is not only technical but strategic, reshaping how companies think about risk. These days, fraudsters collaborate globally, but enterprises have historically protected data in silos. That imbalance is no longer sustainable.

Throughout our discussion, Frances emphasized the increasing overlap between identity, payments, and AI. As financial services move into an era of agentic payments where systems make decisions on our behalf, identity becomes not just an entry point but the safeguard for every transaction. For that world to function safely, identity must be strong, unbreakable, and permanent. The key is securing it in a way that does not create new vulnerabilities.

She also highlighted the expanding role of fintech partnerships in strengthening the ecosystem. No single company can solve identity on its own. Collaboration is essential. Fintech partnerships bring together specialized capabilities that reduce fraud, protect users, and create seamless experiences.

Frances spoke about the rising expectations consumers have for privacy and convenience. They want frictionless access, real-time security, and assurance that their data will never be misused. Identity is not just a technical challenge; it is an emotional contract with the user.

Frances concluded by reflecting on the broader purpose of innovation. The future of finance will be built on trust. When we secure identity the right way, we empower people, protect their data, and build systems that serve them. When trust is strong, innovation can flourish. That is the future she is working toward.

Sitting down with Frances is always inspiring. Her insights show how thoughtful technology can create secure, inclusive, and user-focused experiences, highlighting that the most meaningful solutions are those that enhance security, foster trust, and simplify everyday experiences.

How Digital Identity Protects Our Data

It's vital to move to a data abstraction model when sharing any identity data that filters information down to a "need-to-know" basis, effectively hiding your private details behind an encrypted token. By replacing your real identifiers with these randomized codes, we eliminate the "honey pot" of data and ensure that even if a hack occurs, there is nothing of value for them to steal.

I'm passionate about digital identity as I see the many benefits it can bring to consumers around the world. When I worked at a start-up in 2018, I learned how empowering it was and about the art of triple-blind and zero-knowledge proofs that allowed us to benefit without sharing the data.

- **A zero-knowledge proof (ZKP)** is a cryptographic method that allows one party to prove they know or possess certain information without revealing it. An example of this is age verification when you need to prove you are 21+ to enter a bar. Using a ZKP, your digital ID generates proof that confirms you are at least 21 without revealing your birthdate or any other personal details. The bar is convinced, but your privacy remains intact. This allows you to prove you are at least 21 safely without exposing your home address, name, or birth date.

  Examples of where ZKPs are used include Zcash, Polygon ID, and zkSync.[3]
- **Triple-blind data** is a method for preserving privacy where the data provider, the researcher, and the data processor are blinded to sensitive information, ensuring confidentiality at all stages. This is especially beneficial to banks wanting to improve fraud detection. Three parts are involved: data providers (typically customers), analysts, and a data processing system. Customers provide information anonymously, without names or account numbers. The analysts study spending behavior only, and the system organizes the data to create insights about potential areas of fraud.
- **Privacy-by-design (PbD)** architecture is implemented at the beginning of ecosystem development to ensure the embedding of data protection. It protects individual privacy and data intentionally. It employs data minimization principles, regular audits, and compliance with GDPR.
- **Federated identity systems** allow authorized users to access multiple applications with a single set of credentials. They allow authentication without exposing credentials to service providers using OAuth 2.0, OpenID Connect, and SAML. OAuth lets you grant permission without sharing passwords. Security Assertion Markup Language (SAML) is a standard for single sign-on between organizations, such as allowing employees to use a single login to access several internal systems.

So, we are coming to the point where digital identity consists of data attributes protected by an encrypted method, such as a QR code, to verify that I am who I say I am. That's a tangible digital identity that we're already utilizing and one I believe should become a standard part of our lives.

Key Digital Identity Challenges

The key challenges with some forms of digital identity, such as government-issued digital identity that has not added triple-blind and privacy-by-design principles and has data protection issues, are that their systems are centralized databases, and therefore, they create single points of failure or what is called a *honey pot* of data. This becomes a very attractive target for hackers. Mass surveillance enables tracking citizens' activities without consent. The risk of unauthorized data sharing between government agencies and private companies raises concerns about profiling. For example, the India Aadhaar data breaches exposed 1.1 billion records (2018).

These data breaches are concerning, to say the least. We should all learn from other countries' challenges and build systems that combine self-sovereign (SSI) principles with legal backing (eIDAS 2.0 regulation), ensuring user control and interoperability, and from GDPR compliance standards, with no centralized data honeypot, which dramatically reduces breach risk.

It is important to look at systems that are best in class, and one example I am interested in is the EU Digital Identity Wallet. It is the gold standard for privacy-preserving digital identity and is planned to be mandatory for all member states by 2026. Another reason I see the EU Digital Identity Wallet as a top global solution is its rigorous, legally mandated privacy framework. Under the EU's digital identity regulation, wallets are designed. Hence, all sensitive data stays under the user's control and cannot be reported back to issuers or authorities without consent. Issuers cannot collect or obtain information about how the wallet is used except with the user's explicit consent, effectively banning "call home" tracking or profiling functions that could otherwise be misused to monitor citizens' behavior.

Privacy-first digital identity systems, as outlined in Figure 4.3, show how it limits data sharing to what is strictly necessary and include built-in privacy dashboards that give users transparency and control, showing how and with whom their information is shared.[4]

Figure 4.3 Privacy-first digital ID systems

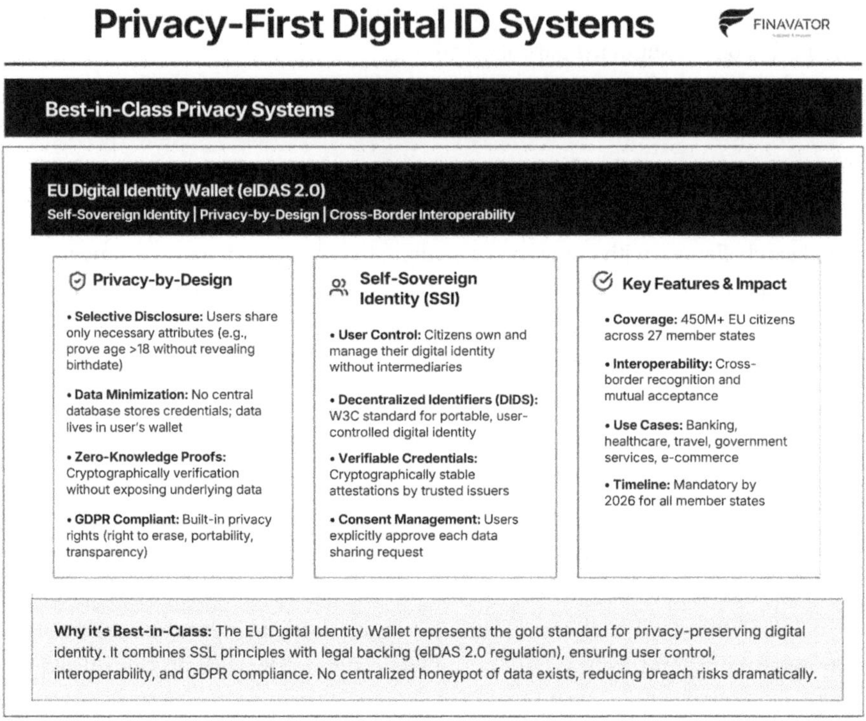

We are seeing some countries avoid creating a digital identity system due to the challenges, which is understandable, but with new, improved, privacy-first systems, this could change over time if the right intentions and safeguards are in place to protect citizens.

The transition from traditional, paper-based identity verification to a trusted digital identity ecosystem is currently in a bridge phase. The market is therefore leveraging specialized platforms to automate the verification of physical documents. These technologies ensure high-integrity registration by using artificial intelligence to instantly validate IDs while maintaining a seamless user experience. Some such providers include Prove (US), Onfido (UK), Trulioo (Canada), and Mitek (US/UK).

Digital Identity Use Cases

Digital IDs can offer considerable opportunities upon implementation. They can be used on a range of devices anytime, anywhere. Users would have greater control over their information. There would be a consistent experience for all users.

A few examples of this are:

- **Financial services:** Consumers and businesses could streamline registration and authentication, secure digital payments, transaction verification, e-KYC, and account opening. By utilizing digital identities, fintech companies can streamline authentication and verification processes and drastically reduce the time and friction involved in onboarding new employees and customers or executing transactions.
- **Interacting with governments:** Citizens could benefit from the ease of using online voting, e-government services, tax filing, benefit receipt, and school enrollment.
- **Talent matching:** HR teams could complete automated background verification and receive efficient payroll services.
- **Online payments:** Businesses could verify consumers, which could help prevent fraud.
- **Healthcare:** Patients can access their records and prescriptions and get help with insurance claims.

As an example, having a digital identity would make getting a driver's license faster and easier. By the time you finish the test, your photo and information will already be integrated into both a physical permit and a digital permit. Once the driving test is passed, the newly issued driver's license can be downloaded into a government app. Once activated, the license could be stored in a digital wallet.

At renewal time, the government app would alert the driver and provide renewal instructions. Through secure authentication, the driver could update their photo or address. Renewal fees would be paid through a mobile wallet. Thus, making the license renewal process a fluid, digital-first touchpoint that eliminates traditional in-person dependencies and redundant data entry.

One of the key advantages of a robust digital identity system is increased security. Technologies like biometrics, AI, and blockchain are used to safeguard identities, making it much harder for fraudsters to impersonate others or carry out unauthorized activities. This is particularly important in a world where digital transactions are becoming the norm. Personalization of financial services is enabled through digital identity. Companies can use the data linked to a digital identity to tailor their offerings to meet the specific needs and preferences of each user. This can range from personalized loan rates to customized insurance packages, enhancing customer satisfaction and loyalty.

Finally, digital identity is a driver for financial inclusion. It allows underbanked or unbanked individuals who may not have traditional forms of ID to access financial services using alternative data. This can empower a larger segment of the population to participate in the economy, potentially reducing economic disparities. The impact of digital identity is vast and multifaceted, influencing everything from regulatory compliance to how companies design user experiences.

While not mandated for all, there's a push toward eliminating paper health records in the United States. When considering a change in providers or even when traveling, having controlled access to your health records can be vital. A digital health record, perhaps with a QR code to access your records across all providers, would greatly enhance your ability to receive optimal healthcare promptly.

With digital IDs, the potential for innovation is massive. Wherever physical IDs must be presented and verified, a digital identification solution can be a game changer. It would make both large and small transactions easier by offering added security and convenience. For example, when applying for a bank account online or renting an Airbnb, it's common to be asked to take a photo of your driver's license and upload it as proof. Also, when signing your kids up for activities such as camp, having to consent to share their personal information, such as their date of birth and health details, is necessary. Security concerns around this can be a barrier to commerce. Having a trusted digital identity that protects our data, such as a decentralized identity in these instances, would greatly enhance the experience for both the consumer and the provider.

When widely adopted, a digital identity system would allow consumers to move beyond the scattered, patchwork quilt of paper and online personal verification to create a more holistic, ubiquitous system that reflects the modern world.

Digital Identity Global Insights

There are many countries that have move toward digital identity, Figure 4.4 illustrates the diverse approaches to digital identity across the globe, comparing government-led initiatives in Estonia and India with regional frameworks in the EU and private-sector models like Sweden's BankID and the US-based Apple ID.

Sweden BankID is a privacy-based electronic identification solution that allows Swedish citizens to prove their identity and sign documents online. First created in 2003, it links a person's personal identity number to their BankID credentials, which are then stored on a computer, smartphone app, or a physical card. A consortium of seven Swedish banks operates them, and BankID data, validated through KYC using a passport or driver's license, shows they were used 7.9 billion times in 2025 alone.[5] As of 2024, more than 8.6 million Swedes between the ages of 18 and 67, or 99.9% of adults, used BankID to access 7,500 services across private- and public-sector platforms.[6]

This ID offers Swedish adults access to more than 7,500 services. The system is built on public-private collaboration, strong security protocols, and high user trust. BankIDs are linked to users' devices and their ID numbers, which cannot be shared or duplicated. Biometric authentication, such as fingerprint or facial recognition, adds another layer of security. The impact has helped transform digital services, enabling seamless interaction with government, banks, and companies, and reducing fraud. BankID has become a key driver in the digital transformation of Sweden's banking sector by simplifying compliance, reducing operational costs, and enhancing the customer experience.[7]

India's Aadhaar program has had some challenges over the years, but it is also one of the world's largest biometric national identification systems. The

Figure 4.4 Digital ID global use cases

Digital ID

Global Use Cases of Digital ID

FINAVATOR

Global Use Cases

Sweden: BankID

① **Overview**

Electronic identification that allows citizens to prove their identity and sign documents online.

② **Key Metrics**

- 95% population adoption
- All major banks
- 600+ auth/year

③ **Impact**

Transformed digital services, enabling seamless interaction with government, banks, and companies. Reduced fraud.

Estonia: e-Residency & Digital ID

① **Overview**

World's first digital residency program offering government-issued digital IDs worldwide, with chip-based national eID cards for citizens.

② **Key Metrics**

- Launched 2002 (eID), 2014 (e-Residency)
- 1.3M citizens +100K+ e-residents
- 99% gov services online

③ **Impact**

Global benchmark for digital government, enabling remote business registration, digital signatures, banking, and tax filing while pioneering borderless identity.

EU: Digital Identity Wallet (SSI)

① **Overview**

Self-Sovereign Identity (SSI) framework under eIDAS 2.0, enabling EU citizens to control their digital identity across all member states.

② **Key Features**

- 27 EU Member States
- User-controlled data
- Cross-border Recognition

③ **Impact**

Enables 450M+ EU citizens to have portable digital identity, interoperable across borders, enabling secure access to public and private services.

USA: Apple Wallet ID

① **Overview**

Store driver's licenses and state IDs in Apple Wallet. Tap to present ID securely using NFC and biometric authentication.

② **Key Features**

- Tap-to-present NFC
- Face ID / Touch ID
- Selective disclosure

③ **Impact**

Privacy-first approach: users share only required info. Accepted at TSA checkpoints and select venues across participating states.

India: Aadhaar

① **Overview**

World's largest biometric identification system providing 12-digit unique identity numbers to Indian residents.

② **Key Metrics**

- 1.38+ enrolled
- 50+ authentication
- 99.9% success rate

③ **Challenges**

- ⚠ Privacy Concerns & data breached
- ⚠ Exclusion due to biomedical failures
- ⚠ Mandatory linkage controversies

④ **Impact**

Enabled financial inclusion for millions, reduced welfare leakage, and raised concerns about surveillance, exclusion, and privacy.

system provides residents with unique 12-digit identity numbers. Large digital identity systems demonstrate the scale and reliability of modern authentication. The Aadhaar program has recorded more than 154 billion cumulative authentication transactions since its launch, with more than 2.29 billion authentications completed in June 2025 alone, reflecting heavy use across finance, telecom, welfare, and other services.[8] This illustrates how digital authentication technologies powered by biometrics and secure protocols are being adopted at a massive scale. These digital IDs have enabled financial inclusion for hundreds of millions, streamlined welfare, reduced leakages, and become the foundation of their digital economy.

Aadhaar has helped enable Unified Payments Interface (UPI) for opening bank accounts. According to a post on Stripe, "UPI moves money instantly between bank accounts via a mobile device. UPI connects hundreds of Indian banks through one interface. With a UPI app such as PhonePe, Google Pay, Paytm, or Amazon Pay, you can send money from your bank account to another account as long as the owner of the second account has a UPI ID."[9] Therefore, anyone with a phone, even if they're homeless, can have access to a bank account as they are identified. The digital ID enables greater inclusion for all.

The Indian system has helped millions by enabling a trusted ID that can be shared and verified, as well as linked to their bank account to make instant payments. While fully government-run national digital identity systems can be powerful enablers of access to services and financial inclusion, they also raise important privacy and security concerns.[10] Critics point out that systems, like India's Aadhaar and its 12-digit unique identity number linked to individuals' biometric and demographic data, have vulnerabilities in how personal data is handled and protected. Centralized storage of identity information creates attractive targets for misuse if exposed through third-party systems or weak integrations, and sensitive biometric identifiers cannot be changed once compromised, unlike passwords or PINs. These risks, along with exclusionary outcomes when authentication fails, highlight that there is still significant room for improvement in how national digital IDs safeguard user privacy and security. Also, as governments change hands every four to eightyears, the system would need to be protected from misuse.

USA Apple Wallet ID, Apple included the ability for users to add a driver's license or state ID to the Apple Wallet in 2022. In late 2025, Apple announced the beta testing of Digital ID, a new way to create and present an ID in Apple Wallet using information from their US passport and present it on an iPhone or Apple Watch.[11] Though it is acceptable only for domestic flights within the United States, with international regulation, there is hope it may become acceptable for international travel.

Expert Interview with David Birch, Global Identity and Payments Expert

It was such a pleasure to interview David Birch. We first met in Las Vegas in 2019 at an identity conference, and since then, we've shared many panels across the fintech landscape. David is one of the most respected global voices in identity and payments. As an author and strategist, he has shaped how governments and financial institutions think about the evolution of trust.

When we discussed his path to fintech, David explained how his background in secure military communications influenced his view on payments. He recognized early on that many financial frictions were actually identity problems. "I started to think that a lot of the things that were problems, costs, and frictions on the payment side weren't really anything to do with payments," he explains. We both agree that our current systems focus on the wrong data. David noted, "In a great many things, who you are is not really the important question. The important question is, what are you?"

We discussed the shift toward agentic commerce, where AI bots handle financial decisions. David believes this is a necessary evolution because humans are too easy to scam. "We can't defend people against AI scamming at scale, so we have to get bots in the way instead," he says. However, this requires a new infrastructure he calls the ABCs of identity. We both agree that the industry is moving toward a model where bots, rather than people, handle the bulk of transactions. David noted, "It's intellectually fascinating to work out how you identify a bot and what it's allowed to do."

David emphasizes that the tools to fix these issues, such as zero-knowledge proofs, are already battle-tested. We both agree that the hurdle is no longer the technology, but the implementation of secure frameworks. David concluded by reflecting on the inseparable nature of protection and privacy. "My bumper sticker is that you can have security without privacy, but you can't have privacy without security," he says.

David's insights on the evolution of digital trust can be summarized in three key takeaways:

- Security enables essential digital privacy.
- Verify attributes not personal identity.
- Trust frameworks for digital agents.

Sitting down with David Birch reinforces that the future of finance is contingent on sorting out identity. By moving away from who we are and focusing on what we are authorized to do, we can finally create a digital economy that is both secure by design and private by default.

Trusted Identity's Alignment to the Future of Finance

To close this important chapter, I wanted to share all the ways digital access to our identity can potentially accelerate the future of finance, from streamlining open banking authentications to enhancing security for transactions while allowing for instant verification and financial inclusion. We need to remember that security is the foundation of privacy and that lasting digital trust requires systems that protect identity and minimize data exposure. The future lies in verifying only what is necessary: authorization, age, and eligibility, without revealing personal details.

As AI systems begin transacting on our behalf, identity must extend to "know your agents" (KYA), creating verifiable, permission-based digital ecosystems. I am excited about the future of finance and what a secure, identity-designed digital access identity can do to help drive the world forward. There are many ways to enable digital access and verify our identities, and the two that seem to offer the most privacy protections are bank ID and Self-Sovereign Identity (SSI).

Understanding digital identity is no easy task, but it is a powerful skill to have, as it can help the ecosystem move beyond the product to onboarding and to new ways of protecting your brand, trust, and data. As per Marie Curie, "Nothing in life is to be feared; it is only to be understood. Now is the time to understand more, so that we may fear less."

Chapter 4 Key Takeaways

1. Security is the foundation of privacy and trust in the digital world.
2. We need systems that mandate triple-blind of all PPI data and employ zero-knowledge proofs to help remove honeypots and protect consumer data.
3. As AI begins to transact on our behalf, identity verification must expand from KYC to "know your agent" (KYA) as well as a clear consent connecting the consumer with the agent. This must also have an audit trail on consumer purchasing requests to safeguard the autonomous future.
4. **Personal lesson:** When sitting in a room taking in all the new terminology, take a deep breath, take notes, and find a way to relate technology to your daily life. This way, you will find ways to simplify the complex to master the subject.

Chapter 5

The Importance of Data Rights: Unlocking Ecosystem Growth with Move Toward Open Data

"For too long, companies profited from people's data. Open data returns control to consumers and replaces extraction with shared value."

—Jane Barratt, Chief Advocacy Officer, MX

Open finance is one of my favorite topics, as it is a crucial element of the future of finance. It empowers consumers to control their financial data. Data portability is an important pillar of open finance, as it enables consumers to share their data with trusted financial services providers by explicitly granting consent to specific data.

An example of this would be asking my bank to share my name, address, date of birth, and bank account details so I can sign up easily with a fintech company that helps me budget. Fintechs, in many countries, would need to be accredited, meaning they've met requirements such as certain levels of security standards and other markers that allow them to join the open banking open finance ecosystem as a trusted third party (TTP).

Starting the discussion on open data with a quote from Jane Barratt, chief advocacy officer at MX, is just perfect, as she is a well-known global expert. Her statement that begins this chapter is something I agree with wholeheartedly. I first met Jane in Marbella, Spain, as we were both on stage at a pivotal Open Future World conference in 2022. Hearing her speak on a panel about data rights, I knew instantly that our perspectives were aligned as we both care passionately about this concern. Her central message is clear: the future of finance should prioritize better outcomes for people, with open data realigning incentives between businesses and consumers. It is a privilege to have her voice open this chapter on open data.

The move to open data reminds me of a transformation that I witnessed in 1999 when I worked for a telco for six years. I sold three-year cell phone plans in which the cell phone number was fully owned by the telco, not the customer. So, if customers were no longer happy with the telco as of service or cost, they had to leave their number behind. Those seven digits had become part of the customer's identity, as their friends and family might have even memorized them. I spent hours helping customers choose the perfect number from the available options, and I even picked both my parents' numbers, which I still have memorized today. It was appalling to me that if you left that telco, you weren't allowed to take "your" number with you.

It wasn't until 2003 in the US (FCC) and 2007 in Canada (CRTC) that number portability was mandated. That mandate required the telco to build an API pipeline between all providers that would allow customers to switch telcos, including the option to move their number, within minutes. That meant freedom of choice, freedom of competition, and data ownership over our cell phone numbers. I feel passionately that this type of mandate should exist across all platforms, and I recently started calling it "human data rights." I believe the future of finance requires us to move from open banking to open finance to open data, with individuals having full rights over where and how their data is stored and accessed.

The Origin of Open Banking

The concept of open banking came about as a response to unsafe data-sharing practices. There was no clear consumer consent, a lack of competition, and the need for greater transparency after the 2008 financial crisis exposed harmful banking behavior. Also, during the financial crisis, banks in the EU and the UK realized that many of their customers had few choices when it came to banking. It wasn't easy to leave their bank if they weren't happy, as they couldn't port their data from one bank to another or to a fintech company.

This led the EU to the creation of PSD2, which was adopted in 2015 and enforced as of January 2018. It required EU banks to provide secure, API-based access to customer data and payments. One of the first standards groups that supported PSD2 was the Berlin Group in 2016, giving Europe a unified technical foundation. The United Kingdom followed and came up with the term *Open Banking* and issued a regulatory mandate from the Competition and Markets Authority (CMA) in 2016, which was implemented from January 2018. The UK helped make open banking a global movement by establishing the first regulated directory and trust framework. It also issued the first clear consumer-protection guidelines and created the Open Banking Implementation Entity (OBIE), which set strict, high-quality API standards and governance, becoming a model for other countries.

Early digital-first banks, called *Neobank's*, were just beginning to appear. However, the process for setting up and logging in was hindered by limitations on how to share financial information. Although they did find a workaround called *screen scraping*. It was not the most secure way of sharing data.

In 2017, the UK had a million consumers screen-scraping to access data, and that is when the government decided to force the CMA9, the nine largest banks and building societies, to not only build secure APIs with national standards for data sharing based on consent but also to pay for the implementation of open banking. The national standards were key as they ensured that data flowed in a way that each bank, fintech, and third-party provider could read, ingest, and share. This was extremely important as it empowered the consumer.

Let's be honest, few people switch banks often, but there is a trend toward consumers banking with a core bank and maintaining multiple other banks or fintech relationships for different aspects of their lives. For example, they might use Revolut when traveling. They might use the Wise app to send money to families abroad and the Greenlight app to send their kids' allowance. With access to open banking, we have more freedom to choose the services that best suit our needs, often reducing costs.

I see open banking as a foundational infrastructure that helps future-proof banks, fintechs, and businesses by ensuring they have consent-driven data. It can help create an audit trail of where our data is and who has access to it. Ideally, we will all have a dashboard of where we've given consent to our data and, therefore, have the right to have it revoked and deleted. This has me excited for a future that places consumers back in control of their data.

I remember when I first learned about open banking in 2018, just after the UK went live with this new ecosystem. When I started to understand how open banking empowered consumers, it ignited something inside of me. I realized this was the key to ensuring consumers not only had control over their data but could also use it to unlock more personalized services.

Open banking unlocks insights into my spending habits to help me choose the best credit card for my needs, the ideal savings account for the best high-interest rates, and, with my financial goals set within the ecosystem, a mortgage that lets me pay less interest while potentially paying it off early. Open banking opens new doors for consumers and will only expand with open finance and open data.

The Evolution of Open Data

To drive the evolution of open data, we have to start with the first step: open banking, which gives consumers the power to move their data from one trusted financial service provider to another. This is followed by the expansion into open finance, which enables consumers to secure faster, cheaper loans or mortgages by sharing their data, helping to derisk the loan. The end goal of open data is consumer empowerment across the entire economy, ensuring that all data is moved with the consumer's consent, enabling a whole new world.

This transformation is far more than a technical upgrade; it represents a deliberate, structured climb from foundational account access toward a comprehensive data-driven economy, as mapped in Figure 5.1.

This layered progression enables use cases that once seemed futuristic, such as instant account-to-account payments and invisible onboarding, placing true individual empowerment at the absolute center of every value exchange.

Figure 5.1 Evolution of open data

The Evolution of Open Data

FINAVATOR

From Banking to Finance to Complete Data Ecosystem

Each layer expands upon the previous, creating a comprehensive data ecosystem

TYPES OF DATA	USE CASES	
OPEN BANKING 1. Account information (balances, account details) 2. Transaction history and payment data 3. KYC and customer identification data 4. Direct debit and standing order information	Account aggregation Account switching Digital onboarding	Payment initiation Personal finance management Creditworthiness assessment
OPEN FINANCE 1. Investment and securities data 2. Insurance policies and claims data 3. Pension and retirement account data 4. Mortgage and loan information 5. Payroll and employment data	Holistic financial planning Cashflow-based lending Insurance switching Employee benefits optimization Enhanced credit scoring	Automated tax filing Buy Now, Pay Later (BNPL) Pension consolidation Round-up investments Micro-insurance products
OPEN DATA 1. Utilities consumption (energy, water, telecom) 2. Healthcare and medical records 3. Government services and social benefits data 4. Travel and mobility data 5. IoT and smart device data 6. Social and lifestyle preferences	Carbon footprint tracking Healthcare financing Subscription management Behavior-driven rewards Smart home energy optimization	Utility service switching Personalized lifestyle recommendations Public benefit eligibility Customized travel solutions Integrated lifestyle dashboards

Open Banking

Open banking is a framework to enable banks, fintechs, and third-party providers (TPPs) to share consent-driven data through APIs upon account holders' request.

One exciting use case that could be unlocked is called *pay by bank*. This is a payment method that allows customers to make purchases directly from their bank accounts, bypassing card networks, or other intermediaries. This is typically enabled by open banking or account-to-account (A2A) payments and is growing in popularity due to its cost-effectiveness, speed, and security.

To enable pay by bank, the system would not only need "read access" to my data but also "write access," meaning it could see my data, which would help inform the products offered to me, as well as "write data" that could allow for a payment to be made from my account. An easy example is me paying my tax bill online by clicking on a pay-by-bank link that verifies who I am and securely processes the payment. This has the potential to revolutionize the way financial institutions operate and interact with their customers.

Another use case for open banking involves digital onboarding. With real-time data sharing, financial institutions can instantly verify customer information. Forms can be autopopulated with customer data, increasing efficiency and enabling banks to make better product offers more quickly, thereby increasing engagement.

Open Finance

Open finance extends data sharing beyond banking to include your wealth, investments, pensions, insurance, mortgages, and other financial products. It gives users even more control and a more holistic view of their financial situation.

One great example is consumers and businesses having enhanced credit scores that could help secure new loans at potentially lower interest rates, as the added insights could help banks and credit unions with de-risk loans. Having a real-time view of a consumer's credit-related information allows for faster approval.

Another benefit is an enhancement in the financial planning sector. Typically, individuals must gather information from several sources before receiving advice on their current financial situation, future needs, and available services. Open finance means both consumers and their financial advisors make better-informed decisions as the data creates a full picture of the consumer's needs and gaps.

Open finance unlocks more than just data; it drives a shift toward true financial health through insights that empower the daily lives of consumers. In the gaming sector, this technology enables real-time player insights that elevate basic compliance toward responsible gambling. Yaspa is driving the adoption of "financial signals" through consent-based journeys which achieves 70% participation, proving that players value secure, proactive protection over traditional, friction-heavy manual checks.

Open Data

Open data refers to the idea that our data can be shared, with our consent, beyond finance, to empower us to have data portability for our health records, social platforms, and utilities. Open data can foster innovation and competition by allowing new players to enter the market and create new products and services.

The example that most excites me is that my healthcare records could be shared through a secure API versus being faxed, yes, *faxed* to my doctor. This is a long-overdue update to the portability of our health records. I know some modern data sharing is occurring in healthcare, though faxing, printing, and mailing are still common practices. We deserve the right to port our health data as it is part of our identity.

It's sad, but true, that there are underinformed individuals who are eligible for government financial and other benefits yet do not take advantage of them. Open data creates opportunities for individuals to both be better citizens and gain greater benefits from being citizens. With open data, citizens can better understand how their communities are run and optimize their use of public services.

As the world moves toward consent-driven data, we are gaining control over parts of our data, with the end goal of an open economy.

How Does Open Banking Work?

To understand open banking, we need to recognize that, as with telcos in the early 2000s, financial institutions have controlled our data. We have limited access to our own data, which limits our ability to empower ourselves. This is starting to change with open banking. We still work with our banks, and they still have our data, but we now have the right to move it. This allows us to quickly secure a mortgage or open an account with another institution. With open banking, people now have a secure channel to easily and consensually share their banking information (account data and transactions) with other banks, fintechs, and third-party providers (TPPs) through APIs.

I find it important to share how the data flows within the open banking ecosystem. For example, with open banking, we can provide a new fintech company with our data from the previous one. The new institution can provide a greater number of tailored products, personalized to our specific situations and needs, backed by that data. This creates a high level of consumer-first relationships. It's all about consumer ease. Figure 5.2 captures the mechanics behind this exchange, illustrating how consent-driven protocols effectively dismantle traditional silos and return agency to the consumer.

Understanding the flow of data in open banking is key to recognizing the power consumers gain when they use their data to inform their choices. This layered progression enables use cases that once seemed futuristic, such as instant account-to-account payments and invisible onboarding, placing true individual empowerment at the absolute center of every value exchange.

This realization, ideally, inspires excitement about possibilities.

Figure 5.2 Open banking, finance and data

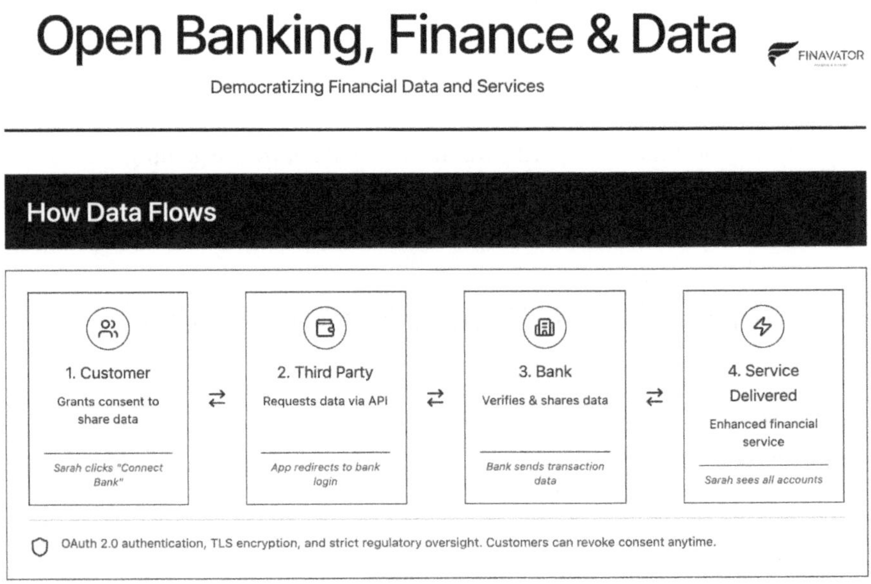

The Five Core Pillars of Open Banking

As with any ecosystem, it is critical for those working on its development to determine and agree on the common denominators at its core. The thought process behind any development needs to include the end goal for the new system, such as who it serves, how it operates, and how it is protected. When thinking about how open banking works, I often describe it by outlining its five core pillars, as defined by the Financial Data Exchange (FDX): control, access, transparency, traceability, and security.

1. **Control:** With open banking, control over financial data shifts from banks to consumers. Consumers gain the right to decide who can access their financial information, when, and for what purpose. This shift gives people true agency over their financial information.
2. **Access:** Open banking enables consumers and businesses to securely share their financial data with authorized third parties through standardized APIs. This access breaks down data silos and creates opportunities for innovation, better products, and more convenient, cost-effective personalized services.
3. **Transparency:** All parties involved, consumers, financial institutions, and third-party providers, are required to operate with clear disclosure about how data is collected, used, and shared. Transparency not only builds trust and ensures informed consent at every step but also enables greater fraud protection.
4. **Traceability:** Every data transaction becomes trackable and auditable. Consumers are able to see who accessed their data, when it was accessed, and for what purpose. This creates accountability on both sides of transactions and allows individuals to revoke access as needed. As the use of agentic AI expands, traceability becomes even more critical for verifying that our agents are acting as intended.
5. **Security:** Robust security measures, including encryption, authentication, and regulatory compliance, protect consumer data throughout the entire ecosystem. Security isn't an afterthought; it's the foundation that makes open banking possible and trustworthy.

Together, these five pillars create an open banking ecosystem where financial data can flow securely, empowering consumers while upholding the highest standards of protection and accountability.

Use Cases

There are many use cases that open banking and open finance unlock that improve consumer experiences when sending payments, planning personal finance, accessing loans or credit, and insurance.

- **Payments and transfers:** Open banking, with write access, allows consumers and corporations to initiate payments directly from their online banking accounts without entering routing data, simplifying the payment experience. Multiple payment options are available within the same payment interface, and payments are often processed in minutes or hours. These might include using payment initiation services through vehicle loan holders. Consumers authorize funds to be withdrawn directly from their bank accounts rather than the old method of writing and mailing checks. Some such providers of this service include Wise (UK), GoCardless (UK), KOHO (Canada), and Venmo (US).
- **Peer-to-peer payments (P2P)** enable customers to initiate secure, frictionless account-to-account payments across all integrated banks and financial institutions. The API-driven, embedded nature of open banking can enable payments with write access, allowing them to be integrated into existing payment flows without manually entering bank details or completing a lengthy authorization form. Some such providers of this service include PayPal, Zelle, Venmo, Apple Cash, and Google Pay.
- **Personal financial management (PFM):** Open banking, followed by open finance, is transforming how customers and businesses manage their finances. Financial data from all their accounts, including current bank accounts, mortgages, investments, insurance, pensions, and loyalty programs, is automatically aggregated in one place, enabling actionable budgeting advice and personalized savings recommendations. For example, if you have three bank accounts, two insurance policies, and wealth accounts, there could easily be seven separate accounts to monitor. Personal financial

management and business financial management (PFM/BFM) provides a way not only to monitor those accounts more easily but to have AI give you some insights as to what's truly best for you. Some such providers of this service include Emma (UK) Rocket Money (US), Cleo (UK and US) and Wealthsimple (Canada).

- **Lending and credit:** Open finance can enable faster, easier access to loans by allowing applications to be submitted and approved through the platform. It might also help you take advantage of the best credit cards or new or additional options to get the most from your mortgage, based on your changing needs or situation. This can help enable a consumer-focused, intelligent offering ecosystem based on the details of who you are, rather than leaving the research of a wide range of offers on the consumer's never-ending to-do list, which for many becomes a "someday" or "never getting around to it" list. Some such providers of this service include Petal (US), ClearScore (UK), Borrowell (Canada), and Zopa (UK).
- **Financial validation:** Open banking automates financial and validation, such as in the use case of responsible gaming, by linking directly to bank accounts for real-time affordability checks. This replaces manual paperwork with high-integrity data categorization to detect "markers of harm" and ensure players only wager what they can afford. Some such providers include Yaspa (UK), Trustly (UK/US/Canada), TrueLayer (UK), and Plaid (UK/US/Canada).

There are now companies that take consumers' rent payments and apply them to their credit scores. This helps a segment of the population that might not have strong credit scores access better lending opportunities, and it can create opportunities for ownership through mortgages or other financial inclusion programs available to those with better credit scores. The bottom line is that more data should lead to better offerings for those who have historically been underserved.

Travel and insurance: Open finance can unlock an interesting aspect: consumers can receive valuable, demographic-specific insights delivered directly to them, eliminating the need to spend hours researching information about their current life and lifestyle. This is a particularly valuable tool for both providers and consumers when it comes to insurance. Also, if you travel often and the data about your travel expenses is available, you might receive a recommendation for travel insurance or a reward offer personalized to you. If you travel infrequently, the data won't generate such a suggestion. In essence, more data allows for the creation and offering of better products.

Open Banking Is Not a Zero-Sum Game

It is important to understand that open banking is not a zero-sum game; it helps enable benefits for the entire ecosystem of consumers, SMBs banks, fintechs, and even governments. I see one of the greatest benefits of open banking for consumers: it expands financial literacy by simplifying how finance works and providing a wide range of choices. Not only do consumers gain control over their financial data, but expanded services are also offered at lower costs and greater convenience. Consumers win through control, and banks win as consumers use more and more banking services.

Who Benefits and How

- **Consumers** benefit through greater control over personal financial data, access to more personalized and innovative financial services, and increased competition that leads to better prices, easier switching, and faster, safer payments.
- **SMBs** benefit from open finance by gaining access to tools to assist with the management and growth of their businesses. These include everything from getting faster, reduced-interest loans to processing transactions to managing payables and receivables. They can participate in the benefits of the digital age with ease.
- **Traditional banks** benefit from open banking through partnerships that can expand their customer base with more customized offerings, leading to customer retention. The traceability aspect of open banking increases the opportunities for banking institutions to remain compliant with AML and fraud protection regulations.
- **Fintechs** benefit from open banking by anticipating and fulfilling the next-level demands of all parties involved. They can scale their own business operations faster and more efficiently through customized services.

- **Governments** benefit when their participation protects their financially vulnerable citizens and fosters innovation. They also benefit greatly when their participation in open banking entices top talent within the fintech industry to locate within their borders.

The Move from Open Banking to Open Finance to Open Data

With open banking, consumers control their banking data and can securely share it with third-party applications or services. The consumer is in control! Banks remain a crucial part of the consumer's life as of their infrastructure. They are good partners and want to expand or deepen their relationships with customers. With consumers having more flexibility to switch accounts, view their payment histories, and retain the security of onboarding through authentication, it's a win for everyone. It allows account aggregation, payment initiation, and personal finance management to become more experiential for consumers.

With open finance, consumers gain a higher-level view than they may have had in the past. They can see the bigger picture themselves rather than relying on multiple sources that may have previously focused on only one aspect of their finances, such as insurance or retirement plans. Open finance extends beyond banking to include insurance, mortgage, investments, payroll data, and more. With this 10,000-foot view of their data, open finance brings new opportunities for consumers in BNPL, cash-flow-based lending, enhanced credit scoring, micro-insurance, and automated tax filing, among others.

Next up are all the opportunities available in an open economy. With all our travel, IoT, social, government, lifestyle, and health data accessible to us, even the data from our personal devices, we get a 50,000-foot view of our needs, thus more effectively managing even more aspects of our lives. This allows us to take advantage of even greater opportunities to enjoy experiences such as customized travel, personalized accounts with benefits we truly enjoy, services that enhance our lifestyle goals, manage our subscriptions, track our carbon footprints, and assist with healthcare management and financing.

With ease of access, enhanced opportunities. With our globally transient society, let's consider what might happen if we want to switch healthcare providers, whether across town or to a completely different country. When an open economy grants us ownership and consent rights to our health data, and it's available in digital form, such moves become not only fast and simple but also could even accelerate life-saving measures.

Open banking does not make consumers responsible for storing their data, but rather for having the right to consent to a trusted party in their ecosystem to share their data through an API with another trusted party to provide a service they want. This creates a safe way of sharing data for the benefit of the consumer.

Let's say I'm with one bank for 20 years and then choose to move to another. Instead of starting at this new bank as a new customer with no experience and receiving only their basic products, I can consent to the new bank accessing my data from my previous bank, which allows them to customize a product offering that suits me. This ensures we have a consumer-first relationship right from the start. Open banking is all about making things easier for consumers.

Faster Access to Credit

Open banking allows faster access to credit largely as now I can share data that can help a lender decide to finance me, where before I was limited to checking my credit rating, and that would be it. Now, there are ways that I can layer in very valuable information about my financial situation without printing or emailing details from multiple sources.

Faster Access to Funds

From a wage-on-demand perspective, open banking provides more insights quickly, so there could be pay-on-demand and pay-same-day offerings. Safety, security, and data use with consent are at the core of this infrastructure. There are payment services that can now be offered once there's a request to pay, which is a second "write" layer of open banking.

So there's "read," meaning they can read the data, and that's the first space many need open bank infrastructure, and then as that infrastructure evolves, it becomes a write access, meaning that you could write against the data and take advantage of an automatic payment infrastructure. Being able to view my financial infrastructure on a dashboard, if I choose, allows me to make more informed decisions, with AI insights added as well.

Ease of Switching Accounts

When we talk about the movement from open banking to open finance to open data, what you're looking at is solving a small use case, but it's a crucial one, as banks are crucial to this use-case infrastructure. After all, they have your data, are good partners, want to help, and want to expand their relationship with their customers by giving them options.

So, you're starting with the ability to switch accounts. You're able to see your payment history; you're able to onboard use authentication that "I am, who I say, I am. Here's my consent. I have a record; I exist somewhere else." There's some inferred security in that, right? So, you're getting to the core of building a system.

What Open Banking Is NOT

I want to be clear. Open banking isn't about you holding your data on your phone or your laptop. It's about you giving consent to a trusted party within the system to share your information *only* as you direct. It's not about putting you in the position of having to store your data. This is about creating an ecosystem for a safe way of sharing your data.

While I think open banking, open finance, and open data are trends, they are trends for transparency and security. There are countries that are phenomenal at open banking already. For example, Ukraine launched open banking in 2025, during war. So, you see, even in a war-torn country, there are benefits from a secure consent-driven data system.

Insights into Global Open Banking

I find the global picture of open banking fascinating, as so many countries are moving toward it in so many ways. Keeping informed of the how and why of each approach is essential. When I think of open banking, my thoughts turn first to the United Kingdom. I feel it spurred the whole global movement. To understand why certain philosophies are successfully driving mass adoption while others stall, Figure 5.3 provides a side-by-side benchmark of leading global frameworks.

When looking at the global open banking landscape, it is imperative to start with the country that created open banking back in 2018, the United Kingdom; followed by the first country to launch a consumer data right (CDR) in 2020, Australia; then, the fastest market to enable both open banking and open finance, which is Brazil, starting in 2021 with full launch completed in 2022. These contrasts highlight a clear strategic lesson: clear central bank mandates, as seen in Brazil, the United Kingdom, Australia, and the United States, provide the regulatory velocity needed for true ecosystem maturity and financial inclusion. It is also important to share insights on the largest market-led countries, the United States and my home country of Canada, which is moving forward with plans to launch by the end of 2026.

The United Kingdom

The United Kingdom launched its open banking framework in 2018, requiring the CMA9 banks to provide secure APIs and create the Open Banking Implementation Entity to deliver the program. By 2024, the CMA confirmed that the final Open Banking Roadmap had been completed and that adoption had grown to more than 10 million consumers and SMBs, with 2025 showing steady growth. UK consumers now benefit from both read and write access to their data, enabling widespread use cases such as tax payments, personal finance management, and lending. Through the Smart Data Initiative, these principles are now expanding beyond banking into pensions, investments, and insurance, forming the foundation of open finance.

The Open Banking Limited (OBL) Annual Impact Report 2025 indicates 18B+ annual API calls, averaging 1.5–2 billion monthly.

Figure 5.3 Global open banking insights

Global Open Banking Insights

Comparing Leading Open Banking Frameworks Worldwide (2025)

FINAVATOR

UNITED KINGDOM

Launch Date:
January 2018

Framework & Standards:
Open Banking Standard (OBL), PSD2/PSR compliance, OAuth 2.0, RESTful APIs

Active Users:
11.5M+ (2025)

API Calls:
18B+ total annual, 1.6B+ monthly (2025)

Access Type:
Read & Write (AISP & PISP)

Top 3 Use Cases:
Tax payments (HMRC), Personal Finance Management (PFM), Lending

Key Features:
600+ regulated TPPs. Transitioning to JROC (Joint Regulatory Oversight Committee) to move beyond banking into "Smart Data."

BRAZIL

Launch Date:
February 2021

Framework & Standards:
Open Finance Brasil (Central Bank mandated), FAPI (Financial-grade API), OAuth 2.0, mTLS

Active Users:
52M+ (2025)

API Calls:
15B+ monthly (2025)

Access Type:
Read & Write

Top 3 Use Cases:
Pix payment initiation, Credit limit increases, Insurance

Key Features:
The world's most successful integration of Instant Payments (Pix) and Open Finance. Fastest adoption rate globally. 900+ institutions.

AUSTRALIA

Launch Date:
July 2020

Framework & Standards:
Consumer Data Right (CDR), CDR Technical Standards, FAPI, OIDC

Active Users:
2.5M+ active users (2025)

API Calls:
350M+ monthly (2025)

Access Type:
Read & Write (Action initiation legislation passed 2024/2025)

Top 3 Use Cases:
Mortgage switching, Energy price comparison, Wealth management

Key Features:
"Economy-wide" mandate including banking, energy, and telecommunications. Comprehensive consumer protection. Covers 99% of bank accounts.

UNITED STATES

Launch Date:
Market-driven (2015); Regulatory-led (2024+)

Framework & Standards:
CFPB Section 1033 (Final Rule), FDX Standards, OAuth 2.0, Screen scraping transition

Active Users:
130M+ via aggregators (2025)

API Calls:
20B+ monthly across aggregators (2025)

Access Type:
Transitioning to Read & Write

Top 3 Use Cases:
Digital wallet funding, Neobanking, Credit underwriting

Key Features:
Largest user base globally. CFPB 1033 Final Rule (Oct 2024) mandates 100% tokenized API access, ending screen scraping by 2026-2030.

Australia

Launched in 2020, open banking is part of a bigger national reform to drive competition, spark innovation, and empower consumers. They were the first country to create a consumer data right (CDR), enabling consumers to regain ownership of their data from companies and banks. The launch started with open banking and then moved to open finance, open energy, open telco, and finally open data. This powerful right is enforced by the Australian Competition and Consumer Commission (ACCC), an independent Commonwealth statutory authority.

Initially, Australians had read-only access, enabling use cases such as product comparison, financial management, and service switching. They added write access to enable new payment use cases for consumers. An example of this is pay-by-bank.

Reports show tremendous adoption with 2.5M+ active users with 350M+ API calls monthly.

Brazil

Brazil's open banking journey is one of my favorites, as it built a full open finance ecosystem within 24 months, supported by clear regulation and a mandate from the Central Bank of Brazil. Their ecosystem enables three key aspects of the future of finance: real-time rails, open banking, and digital identity. Their approach completed a four-phased open banking ecosystem, launched in 2021, with each phase addressing a key initiative.

Brazil's open finance ecosystem has grown rapidly, with 52 million active users, which is the fastest adoption rate globally. API calls are massive at more than 15 billion monthly.[1]

Brazilian consumers have read-write access, with the top use cases being Pix payment initiation, credit limit increases, and insurance. At the same time, the Gov.br digital identity platform has been accessed by more than 130 million unique users in 2025, enabling secure access to thousands of governments and private sector- services online.[2] These digital IDs are based on blockchain technology to make them safer, reduce fraud, and make it easier for public agencies to share information.

United States

The United States launched market-driven open banking in 2015, driven by proprietary data-sharing agreements. Market growth has happened through partnership, and one of the key elements has been the role of aggregators such as Plaid, MX, Finicity, Yodlee, Akoya, and many others. They have helped expand adoption by more than 130 million active users, reporting more than 20 billion API calls monthly across the entire aggregator ecosystem. Open banking helps enable everyday use cases from digital wallet funding, neobanking, automated budgeting, lending, payroll deposits, credit underwriting, and so many more.

As of August 2025, the implementation of Dodd-Frank Section 1033 has created a period of significant regulatory "recalibration." While the Consumer Financial Protection Bureau (CFPB) previously finalized its "open banking rule," the framework has been moved back into an added review phase and is currently on hold for reform. Another important ecosystem partner is the Financial Data Exchange (FDX), which is the official standard-setting body recognized by the CFPB to define the technical rules for secure, password-free data sharing in North America. As of January 2025, FDX established a unified API language already serving more than 94 million consumer accounts, helping aggregators and financial institutions scale secure data sharing while reducing reliance on screen-scraping.[3] This practical foundation maintains industry momentum even while the specific implementation timelines and fees of Section 1033 face ongoing regulatory shifts. Top use cases with read-only access include digital wallet funding, neobanking, and credit underwriting.

Canada

Canada is behind in its open banking journey, yet I still have hope as it is my home, and we are finally starting to see progress. The Consumer-Driven Banking Act was put into law by royal assent on March 26, 2026. While an early 2027 launch is expected, the ecosystem still needs a hard date mandate for effective industry planning. Framework success depends on not having a one-size-fits-all accreditation model, rather a tiered model, similar to those in the UK and Australia, to ensure competition is not limited to the largest players and that fintechs are not sidelined by high barriers to entry. There is also mention of write access for payment initiation to be added to consumer-driven banking after Canada's RTR is finally live (expected by the end of 2026 as it enters its final testing).

The global open banking landscape is ever-changing and empowering consumers and SMB through many key use cases. As you can see, some countries such as the European Union, United Kingdom, Australia, and Brazil have advanced quickly as they had regulatory mandates with clear dates that forced the entire market to come together at the same time. North America has taken a more market-led approach, which means some providers have moved further ahead due to focus and effort, while others are further behind as they haven't focused on open banking enablement. I believe we all win when we work together with a mission to empower consumers, and regardless of regulatory mandates or market forces, I can see the market come together, and it is inspiring. The momentum of this movement is now visible on a global scale, with Figure 5.4 tracking the maturation of these initiatives across dozens of jurisdictions as of early 2026.

Figure 5.4 Global open banking

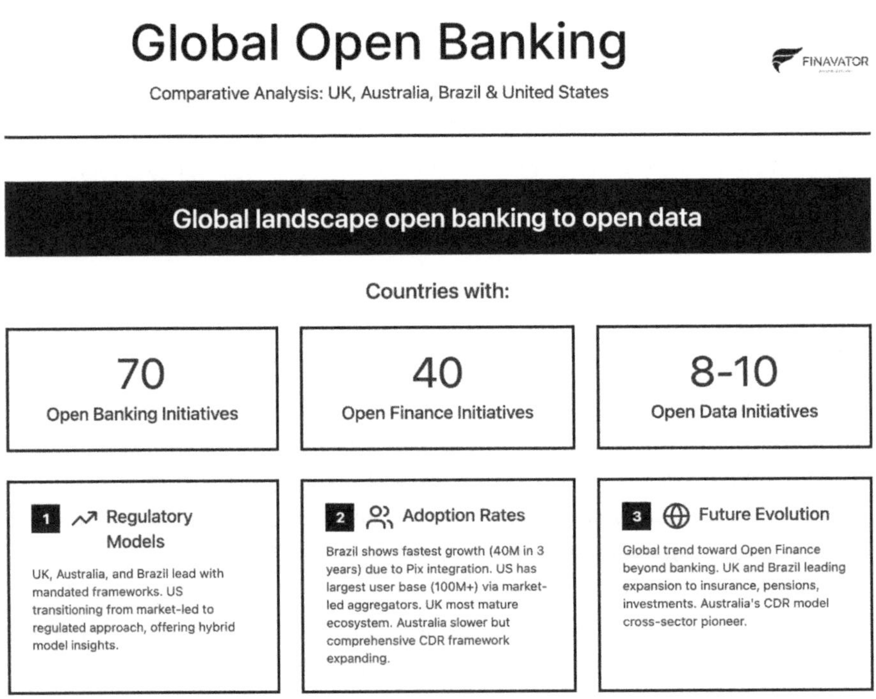

As of early 2026, the global transition toward a data-driven economy is unfolding in three distinct waves. Currently, approximately 70 jurisdictions having implemented open banking frameworks. This movement is rapidly maturing into open finance, with roughly 40 countries now expanding data-sharing principles to include insurance, pensions, and investments. At the frontier, a pioneering group of 8–10 nations, led by Australia's Consumer Data Right (CDR), is moving toward a full open data economy, where data portability extends across all sectors of the globe.

The scale of this shift is reflected in the user base: the global open banking population surpassed 470 million in 2025, with projections targeting 600 million users by 2027.[4] This growth is fueled by a fundamental shift in value creation. According to a 2024 analysis by Boston Consulting Group (BCG), the widespread adoption of data-sharing ecosystems could unlock $2.6 trillion in annual economic value, representing 2.5% of global gross domestic product (GDP). While financial services are the catalyst, the high value put on data will drive innovation across healthcare, transportation, agriculture, and education, effectively re-architecting the global economy.[5]

I am an advocate for open finance as it has the potential to empower consumers and business owners first in banking followed by finance and even across their whole lives in healthcare and beyond. When I speak on local and global panels, I like to push the discussion beyond open banking to the potential GDP growth that can be created with consent driven data across open data as it can help drive new opportunities. It's not just about open banking or open finance or open telco, for that matter; it's about open data.

Open Data Leads to Human Data Rights

In my opinion, open data equates to "human data rights." I'm passionate about this topic. A 2021 McKinsey report outlines the importance of open data. It shared that 1–5% of GDP could be unlocked when a country moves toward an open data infrastructure, which allows consumers the right to port their data from one institution or organization to another in banking, finance, insurance, telcos, energy, health, social media, AI, and beyond.[6] This concept of open data was championed by Australia's move to legislate a consumer data right (CDR) across five sectors, with consent at its core and the intent for consumers to own their data with a safe and secure way through APIs to share it.

Open data is the next evolution from open banking, which is a consumer banking infrastructure, to open finance, which allows consumers to move their wealth and insurance data, followed by open data to allow control over telco, energy, and social media, and therefore gives the consumer control with consent-driven consumer data.

Expert Interview with Eyal Sivan, "Mr. Open Banking"

The first person I thought of interviewing about the importance of data rights was Eyal Sivan, widely known as Mr. Open Banking. I first met Eyal in 2019; what was meant to be a quick coffee chat turned into a three-hour discussion on open banking, which was then just a whisper in North America. Today, Eyal is the host of the *Mr. Open Banking* podcast and a globally recognized advocate for financial data rights.

Eyal's journey began during a 15-year career at a major Canadian bank, leading API strategy. In 2017, a conversation with Gunnar Berger of Nordea Bank changed his trajectory. "When I heard that regulation was going to drive banking innovation. . .it was a little like being struck by a bolt of lightning," Eyal recalls. He realized that standardized APIs would force banks to compete on service rather than creating artificial moats based on hoarding customer data.

We both agree that open banking is really the thin end of a much larger wedge. Eyal explains, "It introduces the notion of standards-based data sharing with consent of the person who owns that data." We discussed how, once this notion of standardized, mandated, and regulated data sharing spreads, we are really talking about an entirely new Internet. This shift will fundamentally change how we relate to our data and to each other.

When discussing the economic impact, we both agree that open banking is a catalyst for massive growth. Eyal compares its potential to the early days of the Internet, noting, "In the early 90s, nobody could have accurately predicted the impact the Internet would have. The Internet is the global economy." We discussed how this infrastructure will grease the wheels for small businesses by automating accounting and credit applications. By allowing these businesses to run more efficiently, we see a significant wealth transfer that creates a new volume of economic activity.

The conversation shifted to the hottest topic in finance: AI. We both agree that for agentic finance, where AI assistants make decisions for you, to work, open banking is mandatory. Eyal notes, "Agentic AI is essentially the last nail in that question's coffin. If you want agentic AI to power your banking, you need open banking to do it." To really help with your financial life, an agent needs to know your full financial picture.

Eyal also provided a candid update on the North American landscape. He described the U.S. regulatory path as a roller coaster, citing the legal battles over Section 1033 and the controversial move by major banks to charge for data access. In Canada, we are both optimistic about the commitment to digital public infrastructure and the advancements made in the new 2025 budget. We agree that Canada is moving toward a generalized data portability right, which is fundamental to the future of open data.

Eyal's insights on the intersection of data rights and open finance can be summarized in three key takeaways:

- Gateway to universal open data.
- Unlocking efficiency and economic growth.
- AI requires consent-based plumbing.

Eyal concluded with a powerful reminder about the value of our digital lives. We both agree that while society has become laissez-faire with data, we must regain control. "Think about building a whole new kind of Internet," he urges. "Protect your data like you protect your children, like you protect your homes." Sitting down with Eyal reinforces that open banking is the foundational infrastructure for a future where individuals, not institutions, own their digital destiny.

Data Rights' Alignment to the Future of Finance

When I think about the future of finance, open data is one of the first initiatives that comes to mind, as I believe data ownership and portability are the fuel that drives a safe and secure economy. As consumers and business owners, we should be able to have personalization while also protecting our privacy and to live our lives with some degree of autonomy. Standardized open banking with consent-based data sharing in financial services is just the beginning. As these principles expand into other sectors, individuals will gain control over a wider range of personal data, reshaping how we interact with the digital economy. Small businesses will benefit from easier access to financial services, lower interest rates, and new solutions that reduce operating costs. This creates a ripple effect across the economy, driving growth and enabling innovative business models.

In the world of finance and with the ever-evolving power of AI, we should defend our data just as we defend our homes and kids. Agentic AI can act effectively only if it has secure, standardized access to data that user's controls. Open banking provides the regulatory and technical infrastructure to make consent-driven AI feasible and trustworthy.

Chapter 5 Key Takeaways

1. Open banking is an important pillar of the future of finance, as it enables consumer control through consent-driven data sharing, which can lead to open data.
2. Enabling consent-driven data sharing helps to realign incentives between businesses and consumers, replacing data extraction with a model of shared economic value. This is why I believe in a global human data right, as it will help empower consumers around the world to have control over their own data from banking, finance, health, and beyond.
3. **Personal lesson:** It may be unpopular to believe we can protect our data, but it is a core value I hold and will continue to advocate for on behalf of everyone.

Chapter 6

Defense-by-Design: Cybersecurity, Compliance, and AML

"True cybersecurity begins at the earliest stages of development when products are being architected, controls are being defined, and responsibilities are being established."

—Amber Scott, Co-founder, Chairperson, and Strategic Advisor at Outlier Compliance Group

The next element in the future of finance is cybersecurity. Most people are familiar with the term. It often brings to mind feelings of fear and the mindset of "I need to defend against multiple threats all at once." Although

I am not a cybersecurity expert, I feel compelled to raise potential cyber challenges when working on new, innovative products for fintechs or banks. It's not that they are unaware of the challenges, as they have large security departments. My concern is due to the large number of ongoing threats in the market. I firmly believe that we must all think of cybersecurity as a defense-by-design tool added in the product design stage. Financial firms have significantly increased their cybersecurity spending in recent years.

I know how important data protection is and realize the brand harm that could occur, especially if attention isn't paid to every detail of a new payment launch. This approach is one of trying to achieve and maintain "cybertrust." When customers trust that their personal preferences and information are safe within an ecosystem, they are less likely to take their business elsewhere.

In our ever-changing world, with the rise of AI, it is critical to understand how cybersecurity affects customers' trust in our businesses. If an organization is holding login and customers' personal information, it is crucial to think about ways to maintain and improve its cybersecurity. Our data is fueling our digital lives and empowering us to access personalized products and services. It can also work against us if it is hacked or leaked; therefore, it is critical that the companies, banks, and fintechs we work with protect our data by ensuring it is stored securely. Now more than ever, it is not only a compliance mandate but also critical for brand protection. This is especially true if the service is helping with holding or moving money.

Of all the topics in this book, cybersecurity is the one I have the least personal experience with. Yet after building many products in the financial services industry that touch payments, e-commerce, loyalty, and identity, I have learned to rely on compliance and legal experts to ensure that we build with cybersecurity in mind from day one. That's why I chose the quote from Amber Scott that begins this chapter. Amber is the co-founder, chairperson, and strategic advisor at Outlier Compliance Group, and someone whose wisdom and experience I trust implicitly when it comes to this topic. We will hear more from Amber's expertise at the close of this chapter.

While building new products, whether they be for payments, loyalty, or identity, cybersecurity is one of the top considerations in this digital era, especially as we face new challenges from rising instances of fraud, account takeovers, and now the potential of AI being used in nefarious ways. I have found that cybersecurity and compliance experts are always thinking three steps ahead to ensure that organizations are not only offering the most innovative products and services to their consumers but also protecting data and ensuring compliance at the federal, state, or provincial level.

Cybersecurity is crucial to the future of finance, especially when building next-level product offerings; it is vital to use a defense-by-design approach. Defense-by-design is a security approach in which potential threats are anticipated during the design phase and protective measures, such as encryption, access controls, and fail-safes, are integrated into the architecture. This ensures security is inherent, reducing the risk and impact of attacks. Working with a cybersecurity expert to create a preventive system to protect against cyberattacks is critical to the continued success of any business, not just those in the finance world.

My Journey into Understanding the Scale of Cybercrime

In 2021, I had the pleasure of being the emcee for a two-day conference in New York focused on cybersecurity in finance for chief compliance security officers (CISOs). This conference featured an incredible keynote speaker, the former professional impostor Frank Abagnale, who went from being one of the world's most notorious con men to a highly respected authority on forgery and secure documents. He has been a world-renowned consultant and lecturer for more than 25 years. He is also the co-author of the book *Catch Me If You Can*, which was made into an amazing movie.

Mr. Abagnale's words stuck with me: "Funds stolen through fraud are almost never recovered, so fraud prevention is the best form of protection."[1] The other expert speakers at that same event discussed deep insights into major cybercrimes, fraud rings, increasing cyber threats, and everything that was happening on a global scale. I remember the weight of knowing what was keeping a lot of CISOs up at night, and it was concerning, to say the least. I had not been aware of the amount of money criminals spend to target and attack individuals and companies through ransomware, phishing, account takeovers, malware, and more. I promise to share more details throughout this chapter.

My passion for privacy-by-design comes from having the honor of hosting Dr. Ann Cavoukian for a keynote at an OFNC 2024 event. I was deeply inspired by her mission to embed trust into the very fabric of our digital systems. While leading jurisdictions such as the European Union (Digital ID Wallet), Australia (CDR), Brazil, and the United Kingdom (PSD3) have already embedded privacy-by-design ISO 31700 principles into their regulatory frameworks, North America has yet to move toward this important shift. By championing the universal adoption of these principles, we can move beyond reactive compliance, transforming privacy into a proactive driver of innovation and consumer empowerment. It is time for every nation, especially Canada, to honor this legacy by ensuring that "defense-by-design" becomes the foundational bedrock of a secure and inclusive global financial ecosystem.

The inner workings of fraud and cyber threats are concerning. I clearly remember leaving that conference incredibly concerned about how to protect my family's data and how to be aware enough to help my clients connect with the right experts to put up a stronger defense. It was quite an eye-opening event for me that caused some sleepless nights.

Personal Safeguards

One of the things I do to protect my family from cyberthreats is to follow a series of small tips I have learned over the years. I am not sure if they are perfect, and I am always open to other suggestions. Unfortunately, there is no course on how to protect your family from cybercrime, but there should be one in schools or offered by the government, given the level of threats today. Please note that these are not proven tips but simply ideas to consider.

First, I sat my kids down and shared some potential threats they needed to be aware of, as knowledge is power. Then I told them we needed a safe word to prove to them that a request via text, email, or even a call was really from me. If they felt the request was odd, they were to ask for the safe word and, if it was not given, report the message and call me.

I also sat down with my Finavator team to share a safe word for our work requests. I explained that I would never email to ask them to send me digital gift cards, as a popular scam at the time involved fraudsters pretending to be employees' bosses and urgently asking them to send gift cards. Upon review, the sender's email address was, obviously, not the boss's email. I wanted to be sure my employees were aware of that scam and to make them aware that scams are ever-changing, so everyone is a little more hyperaware at work and at home.

I then spoke with my parents and shared the same information about threats, that I would never email them with a new phone number and to be suspicious if that were to happen. If they received an odd message, I showed them how to check whether it was really from my cell phone number or email address, to call me to double-check before clicking links in questionable emails, and to report them as spam when appropriate. When verifying suspicious requests sent via email, text, or phone call, it's wise to contact the actual provider at a known number or email address. Never forward a questionable email to anyone, as it could cause them to click a fraudulent link.

I have also shared with my family and employees that it's important not to share their true birthdate online unless required to verify their identity for government, banking, or medical purposes. No one needs to know your birth date or your Social Security number, unless it's a mandate. Those personal identifiers are not something you should volunteer without a specific purpose. We need to be more selective about who we share our data with and what data we share.

Given the volume of cyber threats today, it's important to be extremely cautious. Do not click on links that look suspicious. Always check the email address that messages come from. When they're real, the email address will appear to be from that person or company's domain. A fraudster's email is likely to use a deceptive sender name or domain or include subtle misspellings. Fraudsters are known for masking email addresses or creating addresses that look similar to the company we know (e.g., @Blockbuuster or @Blockbster versus @blockbuster).

I received an email recently, supposedly from my bank or from someone pretending to be my bank, asking me to verify my cell phone number immediately by clicking a link in the message. If I had clicked on that link, I believe there would've been malware. When I checked to verify who it was from, the emailer's address had nothing to do with my bank's name.

Being proactive about cyber protection is the only way to go. Be aware of potential threats and either report them as spam or take a photo and send it to the real company, but don't forward them, as doing so could spread the scam. If we are proactive and report, we might help prevent scammers from compromising our identities and protect our clients and loved ones as much as possible.

Cybersecurity Is Not Just an IT Issue

As our lives become increasingly digital, from online banking to social media, the risk of cyberattacks grows. These breaches can lead to identity theft, financial loss, and compromised privacy. Proper cybersecurity measures safeguard individuals, businesses, and governments by securing networks, devices, and data from unauthorized access and cyber threats.

- For individuals, this means protecting sensitive information such as Social Security numbers and bank details.
- For businesses, it extends to safeguarding proprietary information and maintaining the trust of customers and partners.

Sophisticated cybersecurity measures are crucial for maintaining the integrity of critical infrastructure sectors, such as healthcare, energy, and transportation, which rely heavily on digital systems. A breach in any of these can have widespread consequences, affecting everything from the availability of essential services to national security. In essence, cybersecurity is not just an IT issue but a foundational aspect of a secure and functioning society in the digital age. Understanding its importance and applying robust security measures can help mitigate risks and protect against the evolving cyber threat landscape.

Cybersecurity Defined

Cybersecurity is the practice of protecting systems, networks, and programs from digital attacks. These cyberattacks are usually aimed at three things:

- Implementing effective cybersecurity accessing, changing, or destroying sensitive information
- Extorting money from users via ransomware
- Interrupting normal business processes

Implementing cybersecurity measures is particularly challenging as there are more devices than people, and attackers are becoming more innovative. Cyber Awareness Month (Cyber Month) is an international initiative that takes place every October, aimed at educating the public on how to strengthen their cyber health against cyber threats. It shows how big the problem is when we officially have an "awareness month."

In my experience building digital programs, I've always reached out to a cybersecurity and compliance expert or firm to ensure we elevated our security process for new launches. Each of these experiences has deepened my understanding. There are many aspects of cybersecurity, including, but not limited to, application security, data security, network security, disaster recovery plans, operational security, cloud security, critical infrastructure security, physical security, and user education. When new products and services, or infrastructure upgrades, are planned, it is critical to review and, if necessary, implement additional cybersecurity measures to avoid becoming one of the many organizations that fall victim to cybercrime.

According to IBM Security's Cost of a Data Breach Report 2024, the average global cost of a data breach has risen to $4.88 million USD, up from $4.45 million USD in 2023, marking the largest increase since the pandemic. Organizations in the financial services sector face even higher costs, averaging $6.08 million USD per breach, which is 22% above the global average. These costs include breach detection and response, operational downtime, lost revenue, and long-term reputational damage.[2]

Protect Your Data

To understand cyber threats, it's important to know what cyber criminals are looking for. Basically, they are looking to steal our identities and then take advantage of the benefits we have or have worked for. What they want is a concise record of our identities and assets. They want our first name, last name, birth date, address, and, preferably, passport and driver's license information, and Social Security number. They're looking for our personally identifiable information (PII). Their goal is to compile all the information they can get about each of us and then to use it to gain financial benefit.

Once they have enough information, they might sign up for a credit card using the stolen identity and, if not stopped, could max it out with purchases. They sometimes do this by having a card shipped to a different address, if not stopped by a compliance check, such as know your customer (KYC), or by accessing an existing card virtually. Millions of Americans alone have had their identities stolen, costing them money and making it more difficult for them to prove they are.

In many data breaches, criminals try to steal your information to sell it on the dark web. Regularly changing your passwords is a good habit. Making them more challenging for hackers is important. You may have seen posts on social media asking people to show photos of their pets. Those who do it will often mention the pet's name and guess which part of their favorite password it is. You got it. It's their puppy's name, Charlie, Copper, Howie, or Luna, plus the number from their house address, and the hacker cracks their password. If they use the same password for all accounts, the hacker will be able to access all of them. To protect your information, changing your passwords every three months is a good habit. Also, make sure your passwords are complex, with 12–20 characters that include both uppercase and lowercase letters, numbers, and symbols. Then, ensure that no one but you knows what they are.

I use a password manager that has passed an independent third-party security audit and is a zero-knowledge proof design, meaning the vault password data is encrypted before it leaves your device. It also monitors my emails for data breaches. We need to be hyper-vigilant when it comes to protecting our devices and our data. Sadly, it's come to this: we have to be very aware of threats and suspicious of texts, emails, social media, and phone calls to maintain protection.

A good way to enhance protection is to use multifactor authentication (MFA), especially for important financial accounts and those connected to sensitive PII. Many of us already use this in our banking apps. When we log in, we're asked for a six-digit code that's sent to the cell phone number listed on the account, and we have to enter it for the app to open. These are good ways to help verify that the user is the correct account holder, but an even better way is to have an authenticator app on your phone, like Google Authenticator, that prevents redirection of the text code to a scam phone, which, unfortunately, has happened, as text is not as secure as an authenticator app. The important thing to remember is to add at least one way to verify that you are who you say you are, to make it harder for scammers and safer for you.

Cyber Threats Targeting Finance

It is concerning to consider the many ways financial services companies need to protect us from cyber threats, and it can be challenging to learn about them. However, it is important to understand as many as we can to help avoid the threats out there on any given day. Some of the top threats include:

Ransomware attacks encrypt systems, locking out the owners and demanding payment to restore access. Ransomware attacks are one of the most damaging cyber threats facing organizations. According to the 2024

Sophos State of Ransomware Report, the average cost of recovering from a ransomware attack has risen to $2.73 million USD, a sharp increase from previous years. Organizations affected by ransomware also face significant operational disruption, often requiring extended periods of time to fully restore systems, recover data, and return to normal operations.[3]

I remember an attack in 2023 that impacted many hotel chains in Las Vegas. It affected room keys, slot machines, ATMs, reservations, and their brands. I was heading to Las Vegas for a conference in October of that year, and three days into the attack, I canceled my booking as I was not sure if they could recover in time. I booked a hotel that was not part of the attack instead, and now that I think about it, I haven't stayed in one of that chain's hotels since. I am not even sure it was a fully conscious decision; the brand just has a stain on it in my mind.

Account takeovers (ATOs) occur when attackers gain unauthorized access to a person's online account, often exploiting reused passwords or stolen credentials. According to the 2024 Sift Digital Trust Index, 24% of US consumers reported being victims of ATO in the previous year, highlighting the widespread nature of this threat. Once an account is compromised, attackers can steal payment information, make unauthorized purchases, or access other linked accounts, creating a cascade of fraud. Large organizations, including banks, subscription services, and online retailers, are particularly vulnerable, making ATO a major concern for both consumers and security teams.

Phishing and social engineering threats arise when users are tricked into revealing credentials or sending money through scare tactics and high pressure. These tactics are aimed primarily at individuals and remain the most common causes of data breaches. A recent Guardz report indicates that 94% of organizations have experienced phishing attacks and that phishing was blamed for 36% of all US data breaches in 2023. The average cost of a phishing-driven breach is estimated at US $4.91 million.

It is becoming more challenging to tell if an email, text, or call is really from your bank or service provider. Some ways you can try to protect yourself include taking security awareness training and, if you have employees, making it mandatory for them every quarter. Make sure to add MFA to all accounts, as well as anti-phishing tools and email filtering.

I set up a virtual private network (VPN) on my family's mobile devices and computers many years ago. It helps protect our IP address, which is connected to our home Wi-Fi. We need to be more aware of the threats to our families and ourselves.

Deepfakes are AI-generated videos, images, or audio that can convincingly mimic real people, often making fabricated content appear authentic. Globally, the technology is advancing rapidly, with potential applications ranging from entertainment to education, but it also poses significant risks to security, privacy, and trust. One notable misuse occurred in the United Kingdom, where scammers used a deep-fake, cloned voice of a company CEO to trick employees into transferring approximately $243,000 to fraudulent accounts.[4] Beyond financial fraud, deepfakes have been used to spread disinformation, manipulate elections, and damage personal reputations. To address these risks, organizations are adopting AI detection tools that flag manipulated media and implementing multistep verification processes for sensitive transactions. Governments and regulators worldwide are beginning to introduce guidelines for responsible AI use, while companies are investing in employee education and cybersecurity training to raise awareness of these threats. In Denmark, policymakers are leveraging intellectual property (IP) and data rights to give individuals and companies legal tools to challenge and remove deepfake content, strengthening accountability and protection against misuse. While deepfakes offer innovation opportunities, a combination of technology, policy, and human vigilance is essential to prevent global misuse.

Protecting Our Identities

There is more than one type of identity. There is what is called "hard" data, such as your physical attributes, including your fingerprints, date and location of birth, and biological family. These prove who we are. This information is typically used by governments and other entities to identify us as we apply for driver's licenses, passports, or even bank accounts.

The other is "soft" identity and involves digital attributes about you. It is flexible and dependent on context. For example, we can use a soft identity of our choice to create fun email and social media accounts, such as summer-sun@____.com.

This aspect of our identity doesn't directly affect our physical identity. It involves only what we choose to share when setting up accounts. Some attributes connect with us, but they're what we call *soft*. They are not authenticated or verified by recognized authorities for legal purposes, so they can't be used to prove who we are.

If our email is hacked, it could be a huge problem, as we typically use it to communicate with our financial institutions, healthcare providers, and possibly our employers. If our social media account gets hacked, that's a different type of challenge. The hacker can gain access to our friends and our network. And depending on how much information is on there, from our birthday to where we live or the last names of cousins, this could lead to our mother's maiden name, which is typically used to identify us when applying for credit. Having that information in the wrong hands can create major challenges. You can see how hackers might gain benefit from something we might consider a minor detail. It is all part of our identity and should be protected. I have taught my teenage kids to use different names and make up a birthdate for online use to protect their identities, and I do the same.

Cybersecurity Challenges

The two biggest threats to cybersecurity are the speed at which evolving threats manifest and the volume of information being stored.

Evolving threats: One of the highly challenging elements of cybersecurity is the evolving nature of security risks. As new technologies emerge and as technology is used in new or different ways, new attack avenues are created.

Data deluge: Organizations can gather a lot of data on individuals who use one or more of their services. The more data collected, the greater the likelihood of becoming a target for cybercriminals who want to steal PII.

Cybersecurity Awareness

Just as we recognize the need for insurance, everyone in our society should be made aware of the importance of cybersecurity from a young age. Education on how to stay safe in any cyber environment should not be limited to a young age; it should be a continuing education for everyone. There are two resources

I have found helpful: the first is part of National Cybersecurity Month from the US government, focused on families, from CISA.[5] The other is from the Canadian government and is called Get Cyber Safe.[6]

Those involved in cybercrime have large budgets to develop innovations to gain access to data and trick people into falling for their schemes. Businesses also need sufficient budgets to protect data, whether it's their own or their customers'. Continued employee awareness training is critical, as employees may unknowingly introduce threats and vulnerabilities into the workplace via their laptops or mobile devices.

Why Is Cybersecurity Important?

At an individual level, a cybersecurity attack can result in everything from identity theft and extortion attempts to the loss of important data, such as legal documents. Everyone relies on critical infrastructure such as power plants, hospitals, and financial services companies. Securing these and other organizations is essential to keeping our society functioning.

We also benefit from the work of cyberthreat researchers, such as the team of 250 at Cisco's Talos, a threat intelligence research organization that investigates new and emerging threats and cyberattack strategies. They reveal new vulnerabilities, educate the public about the importance of cybersecurity, and strengthen open-source tools. Their work makes the Internet safer for everyone.

The Elements of Cybersecurity

The cybersecurity field can be broken down into several different sections; the coordination of which within the organization is crucial to the success of every cybersecurity program. These sections include the following:

- All forms of security (application, network, operational, cloud, physical, data, and critical infrastructure)
- Disaster recovery/business continuity planning
- End-user education

- Cybersecurity threats
    - **Personally identifiable information (PII):** Names, addresses, national identification numbers, such as passports and driver's license numbers, Social Security numbers, and credit card information

Compromised PII often leads to a loss of customer trust, the imposition of regulatory fines, and even legal action when there is a real risk of significant harm from the compromised PII. The reputational damage alone could be fatal to an organization. The diversion of funds to rectify a loss, as well as the amount of time it takes to do so, could delay the development of new product launches that might otherwise grow a brand.

Core Concepts of Protection

The core concepts of protection include defense-by-design, privacy-by-design, and a cybersecurity framework, as shown in Figure 6.1.

Figure 6.1 Defense-by-design and compliance

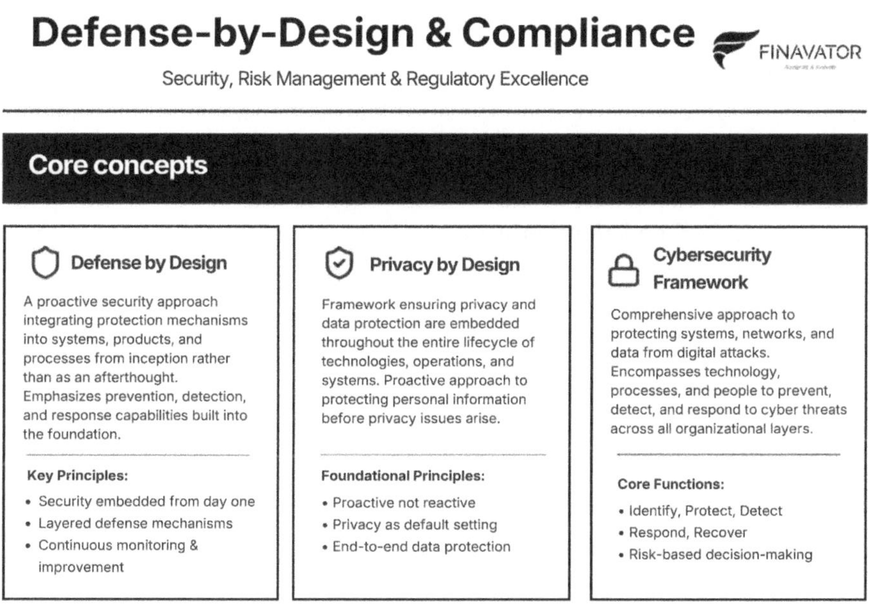

Aligning these principles ensures that protection is not a reactive "patch" but an inherent part of the architecture, maintaining the digital trust required to move value in a modern economy.

Defense-by-design: A proactive security approach integrating protection mechanisms into systems, products, and processes from inception rather than as an afterthought. Emphasizes prevention, detection, and response capabilities built into the foundation. Most technology now uses an opt-in model by default in their terms and conditions (T&Cs), which requires users to manually opt out of data sharing. While this often meets legal requirements, it does not align with what I would call privacy-by-design, which favors data minimization, explicit choice, and protective defaults, meaning sensitive data collection should be "off" by default. Consumers can protect themselves by changing settings, but real privacy improvements need to be considered that embrace building with Privacy-By-Design ISO Standard when building.

The following are the key principles:

- Security embedded from day one
- Layered defense mechanisms
- Continuous monitoring and improvement

Privacy-by-design: Frameworks that ensure that privacy and data protection are embedded throughout the entire lifecycle of technologies, operations, and systems. This is a proactive approach to protecting personal information before privacy issues arise.

These are the foundational principles:

- Proactive, not reactive
- Privacy as a default setting
- End-to-end data protection

Cybersecurity framework: A comprehensive approach to protecting systems, networks, and data from digital attacks. It encompasses technology, processes, and people to prevent, detect, and respond to cyber threats across all organizational layers.

These are the core functions:

- Identify, protect, detect
- Respond, recover

- Risk-based decision-making that helps to integrate security as a foundational building block requires a unified strategy that spans the three core pillars outlined in Figure 6.1

The Benefits of Cybersecurity

The benefits of implementing and monitoring cybersecurity practices include:

- Increased business protection against cyberattacks and data breaches
- Prevention of unauthorized user access
- Improvement of recovery time after a breach

This could add protection for end users and endpoint devices while following regulatory compliance and enabling business continuity. Focusing on cybersecurity can improve a company's reputation and increase trust for developers, partners, customers, stakeholders, and employees.

What Does Cybersecurity Mean for Your Business?

Cybersecurity is a business problem that has been presented as such in boardrooms for years. Yet accountability still lies primarily with IT leaders. In the 2022 Gartner Board of Directors Survey, 88% of board members classified cybersecurity as a business risk.

Organizations have become far more vulnerable to cyber threats as digital information and technology are now so heavily integrated into day-to-day work. But the attacks themselves are becoming far more sophisticated by targeting both information and critical infrastructure.

Cyber-risk incidents can have operational, financial, reputational, and strategic consequences for an organization, all of which come at high costs. This has made existing measures less effective, and organizations need to step up their cybersecurity game.

The simplest explanation of the importance of cybersecurity is as follows: information drives business, and businesses rely on technology to store it.

Cybersecurity practices aim to protect them. The benefits, however, go much further. A good cybersecurity posture protects:

- **Financials:** Downtime reduces revenue, reputational damage discourages new customers, and fines for noncompliance can be costly.
- **Reputation:** Bad press from challenges, such as data breaches that create downtime, negatively impact goodwill.
- **Customers:** Loss of data can have far-reaching effects on the lives and businesses of those with whom you do business.
- **Employees:** Cybercriminals aren't just trying to get customer information. They're after employee data, too.
- **Compliance:** Businesses have a responsibility to protect customers', patients', and clients' personal and business data, depending on their industry and regulatory compliance requirements.

How to Guard Your Business Against Cybersecurity Threats

Every person and organization must implement cybersecurity practices to meet their unique needs. Let's review some of the best practices for achieving this.

Best Practices for Businesses

Strong cybersecurity postures typically involve a five-step process:

1. Establish **perimeter security** to make it harder for hackers to penetrate your data systems. This involves using firewalls, VPNs, antivirus software, and network segmentation.
2. Implement **access control** devices. Determine who, in your organization, should have access to which data. Then, establish authorization controls that require authentication, including MFA. Provide continued information and training to employees as protective measures. Include the requirement of complex passwords that are updated every 90 days.

3. Apply **data protection**. Encode data both while it is stored (at rest) and while it is being transmitted.
4. Employ continuous **monitoring**. Take advantage of security information and event management (SIEM) solutions that collect, analyze, and manage data across the organization. It can provide both threat detection and compliance monitoring.
5. Create an **incident response plan** with a budget that can be upgraded as new technologies evolve. Implement redundant backups as part of a recovery plan, assuming a breach will occur at some point. Be prepared to spend time and money on forensics in the case of a breach.

Cybersecurity for Individuals

According to the Motley Fool, in the first half of 2025, the Federal Trade Commission (FTC) received 748,555 reports of identity theft, a 196,357-case increase over the first half of 2024.[7] This suggests 2025 could be a record-setting year for identity theft. While the Identity Theft Resource Center (ITRC) saw a decrease in reported identity crimes overall, it also reported an increase in the number of individuals experiencing multiple identity-related concerns.

While working from home and other remote locations is increasingly common, the same technology that makes remote work possible also creates opportunities for hackers and cybercriminals to steal data. Working remotely can leave you more vulnerable to digital attacks than you might be in a business office where protections are enhanced. A lack of strong personal cybersecurity habits can put not only your PII at risk but also the information you share with employers, co-workers, and clients.

Personal Cybersecurity Risks

Your smartphone, whether iOS or Android, can be tracked. Even when location services are turned off, it's important to understand how exposed we all are when using mobile devices. They can be tracked through the mobile towers used, the Wi-Fi and Bluetooth services used, and even through apps and web browsing. Ad tracking services provided by shopping sites to locate stores or restaurants near you can be used as inexpensive spy tools to provide your location.

Some of your apps, once opened on your smartphone or tablet, collect a lot of information about you. It's important to understand each app's terms of service before permitting it. Check where an app was created before deciding whether to download it. Different countries have different data regulations. Some apps access personal data, such as your contact lists, photos, calendars, health data, microphone access, information about the devices you use, and your location. Consider changing settings for location, microphone, and camera access to "only when using" your apps.

The Future of Cybersecurity

Cybersecurity has become a critical issue for both individuals and businesses, as the threat of cyberattacks continues to grow every day. We all have more sensitive information being stored and transmitted online, making it even more important to protect against cybercrime. Between 68% and 89% of financial institutions planned to increase their investment in security in these areas in 2025: cloud security, identity and access management, fraud detection and prevention, data encryption, security operations centers, API security, and credential-less tokenization.[8] Key growth drivers for these investments include a 300% increase in cyber threats from 2020 to 2024. This is also increasing due to the high adoption rate of digital banking. Another factor was cloud migration and the addition of AI-powered fraud.

As you see in Figure 6.2, the global cybersecurity market was valued at approximately $172 billion in 2024 and is projected to grow significantly, with estimates suggesting it could reach around $373 billion by the early 2030s as organizations invest more in defense against escalating cyber threats and digital transformation expands.[9] The financial services vertical market size alone in 2025 was 25% of the global cyber market. The projected finance sector size in 2030 is upwards of $85 billion. With consumers adopting new technologies, businesses have a responsibility to provide them with a high degree of protection. The key use cases for these investments revolve around fraud detection and prevention as well as payment card security. Financial organizations are investing in biometric authentication, identity, and access management, and data encryption, within core banking systems and mobile banking app security.

Beyond simple market valuations, Figure 6.2 reveals the critical growth drivers and investment priorities currently dictating the global defense landscape. This shift toward "cyber resilience" forces organizations to move beyond traditional backups, favoring air-gapped recovery strategies that can withstand the escalating sophistication of AI-driven threats.

Despite significant improvements in cybersecurity measures in recent years, so too have cybercriminal techniques. The future of cybersecurity looks to be a constant battle between those who would protect information and those who would steal it. Future cybersecurity will also be shaped by regulation and legal frameworks. Governments are increasingly passing laws and regulations to protect sensitive information and hold organizations accountable for data breaches.

Figure 6.2 Global cybersecurity in finance

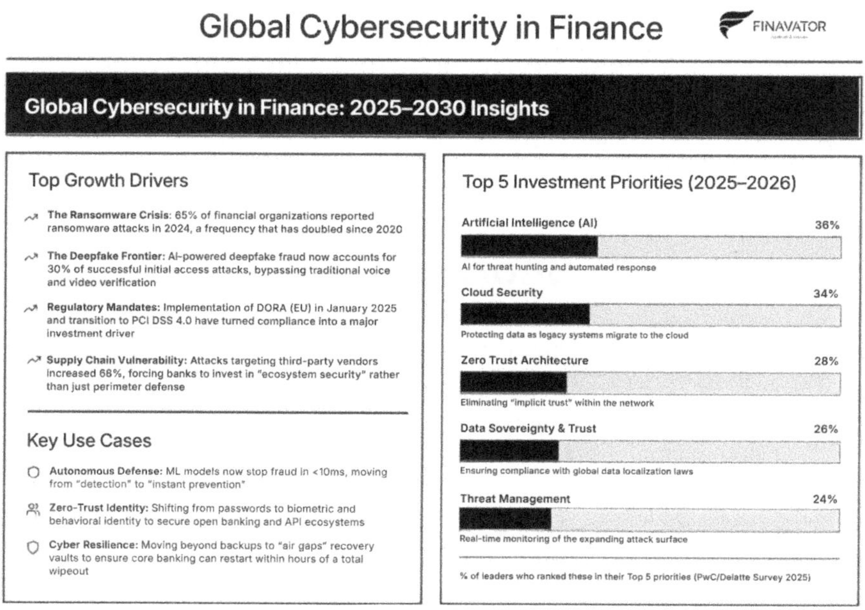

This includes laws that require organizations to implement security measures, such as encryption and multifactor authentication, and that impose penalties for data breaches. Organizations will need to stay informed about and compliant with the latest laws and regulations.

Cybersecurity and AI

According to the World Economic Forum, AI is bringing profound advantages to cybersecurity. In fact, as of this writing, it is one of AI's top applications. AI is transforming the cybersecurity landscape by automatically detecting inconsistencies, finding patterns, focusing on areas of threat, and recommending solutions. Some benefits of using AI in cybersecurity monitoring include improved threat detection, faster detection, automation, accelerated troubleshooting, bot blocking, and a better overall user experience.

It is also important to note that some experts have expressed concern that AI gives attackers a greater advantage than defenders by making phishing attacks more realistic. AI lacks human judgment, can generate false alerts, and struggles to keep up with new threats. We need to find ways to use AI to defend faster than attackers are attacking. I hope we see consumers have more protection against risks, but the future is unknown; therefore, I continue to bring the need back to awareness and diligence.

Workforce Shortage and Skills Gap

A major cybersecurity challenge is a shortage of qualified cybersecurity personnel. The 2024 ISC2 Cybersecurity Workforce Study reports a global workforce of 5.5 million, leaving a 4.8 million talent gap worldwide. Demand for skills like AI/ML security is surging, and by 2030, more than 10 million cybersecurity jobs are expected to need filling.[10] It is truly a growing field (see Figure 6.3).

As the amount of data businesses collect and use grows, the need for cybersecurity staff to analyze, manage, and respond to incidents also increases. Unfortunately, there is a significant and widening gap between the demand for

Figure 6.3 Global cybersecurity in workforce

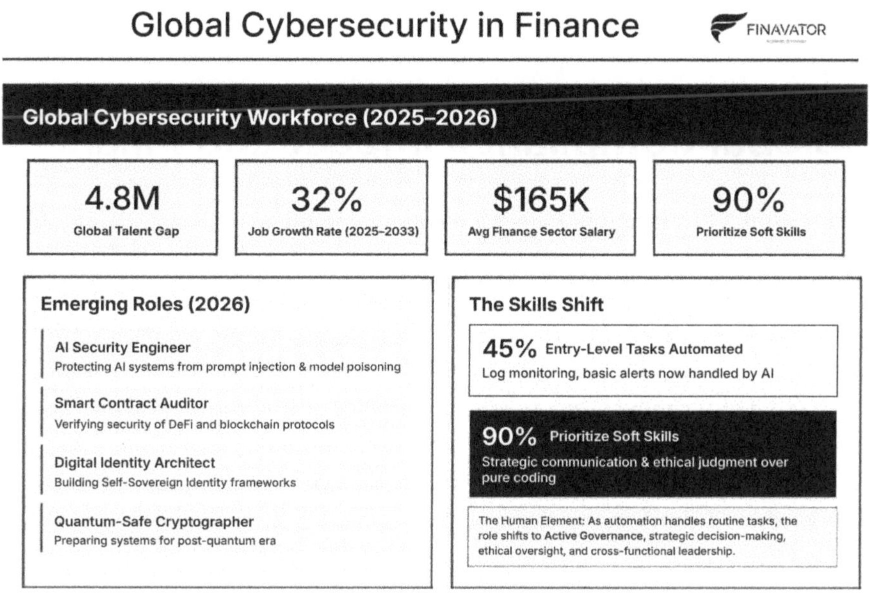

cybersecurity professionals and the available workforce. This gap leaves all businesses at greater risk of cybercrime. Government agencies and public-sector organizations struggle to compete with the salaries and benefits offered by the private sector. The shortage of cybersecurity professionals is being felt across many sectors, including education, healthcare, and especially within small businesses.

We are currently facing a structural bottleneck in digital safety. Figure 6.3 visualizes the widening talent gap and the specialized roles required to defend a complex financial future.

Addressing this 4.8 million–person gap through roles like AI security engineers has become more than an HR task; it is a strategic imperative for long-term organizational governance.[11]

If you're on a board or even working within an organization, it's becoming more and more vital to become aware of the cybersecurity profile of that organization. If it's lacking, finding an expert partner in the cybersecurity industry will need to become a key line item in future budgets. Every time you level up in any other business practice or in providing innovations in product offerings, it's critical to level up cybersecurity as well.

Global Compliance Impact and Pillars

When I think of innovation, I also think about compliance. I know I'm not the average person, but when I worked at a global prepaid company, helping launch a reloadable retail-sold prepaid card coast to coast, I quickly realized how much there was still to learn. I needed to learn about KYC and the compliance that's needed to offer financial services. It's about trying to ensure the customer's safety. Some of it can be heavy weighted, but a lot of it is common sense, and I just felt aligned to its purpose. Data should have consent audit trails. Businesses should be required to simplify complex fees and explain them properly to consumers, which I think many challenger banks and fintechs have done a really good job of.

AML and Cybersecurity

Beyond compliance, I think of anti-money laundering rules and reporting. Since money laundering is a major problem, involving $2.21 billion annually, regulations are strict.[12] Yet, in 2024, reports show that less than 1% of illicit funds laundered were successfully seized.[13]

Anti-money laundering (AML) is a legal framework that requires financial institutions to prevent, detect, deter, and disrupt money laundering. They achieve this by monitoring transactions and reporting suspicious activities, conducting customer due diligence, and maintaining records. According to the LexisNexis True Cost of AML Compliance 2024 report, global spending reached 213.9 billion dollars as nearly all financial firms saw their expenses climb over the last five years. Rather than replacing human expertise, companies are now layering in advanced artificial intelligence to help their teams keep pace with faster and more complex digital threats. By 2026, this combined approach has become the standard for building secure systems that protect both consumer privacy and the future of automated payments.[14]

Means of preventing money laundering include:

- **Know your customer (KYC)** is the process of verifying a customer's identity and assessing risk to prevent fraud, money laundering, and terrorist financing. This includes identity verification, address confirmation, source-of-funds checks, and ongoing monitoring.
- ***New* know your AI agent:** As AI begins to help make purchases on our behalf, there is a need for greater due diligence in monitoring AI agents, algorithms, and automated systems to ensure compliance, transparency, and accountability in financial services. This includes AI model validation and testing, algorithm bias detection, explainability and transparency, AI decision audit trails, and responsible AI governance. This is an emerging area of legislation and practice.

When innovating, it's vital to take into consideration compliance and legal requirements. Innovation is encouraged, but within specific parameters. The goal is always to provide a better customer experience in a simple way. When customers understand the innovations, those innovations fit within regulatory and compliance rails, and all of that enhances business; we have created a true win-win-win situation. It is realistic to assume this can happen. In fact, according to TheSumsuber, "In 2025, major economies introduced or updated regulations to strengthen verification, protect users, and combat fraud."[15]

Key Regulatory Frameworks

When building financial products, it is important to work with a cybersecurity expert or department that understands the many regulatory frameworks, including global and regional regulations. When thinking of regional frameworks, the major ones that come to mind are the EU's GDPR for data protection, the Bank Security Act (BSA) in the United States, and the Personal Information Protection and Electronic Documents Act (PIPEDA) in Canada.

The key global standards include the Financial Action Task Force (FATF), which sets international AML standards; ISO 27001 for information security management systems; and the NIST Cybersecurity Framework, which provides a comprehensive approach to managing cybersecurity risks.

Expert Interview with Amber Scott, Co-Founder, Chairperson, and Strategic Advisor at Outlier Compliance Group

When I think about cybersecurity and defense-by-design, the person who stands out for both her leadership and long-standing commitment is Amber D. Scott, MBA, CBP, CIPP, CAMS, FIS, co-founder, chairperson, and strategic advisor at Outlier Compliance Group and a self-described compliance geek with a deep passion for technology.

I first connected with Amber on LinkedIn in 2019, shortly after founding Finavator. Since then, we have continued an open and thoughtful dialogue about the future of compliance, cybersecurity, and financial crime prevention. Over time, our conversations have moved far beyond regulation alone into broader discussions about organizational resilience, leadership accountability, and how companies can prepare for risk in increasingly interconnected digital environments.

When asked about her approach to cybersecurity, Amber consistently returns to the principle of defense-by-design. She explained that "many organizations still treat security as a final checkpoint rather than as an essential building block." For her, "true cybersecurity begins at the earliest stages of development when products are being architected, controls are being defined, and responsibilities are being established. Waiting until systems are live to address risk is no longer a viable strategy."

Amber spoke at length about how cybersecurity has evolved from a technical discipline into a business imperative. "Today's threats are no longer isolated events. They have financial, legal, reputational, and regulatory consequences that ripple across the entire organization. Leadership teams can no longer afford to view cyber risk as something that sits solely within IT or security departments. It is now a matter of governance and enterprise responsibility."

We also discussed the rapid acceleration of financial crime in the digital age. Amber noted that "fraud has become more organized, automated, and difficult to detect. Cybercriminals do not operate in silos, yet many organizations still approach risk with fragmented systems and disconnected teams. This mismatch leaves institutions vulnerable." In her view, alignment between compliance, security, risk, and operations is not optional. It is fundamental.

Technology, while powerful, is not a silver bullet. Amber emphasized that "tooling alone cannot replace leadership, judgment, and accountability. Strong programs are built through clear ownership, continuous testing, and realistic risk assessments. Technology should enable teams, not obscure responsibility."

Another key theme was the customer experience. As security measures become more sophisticated, organizations must ensure protection does not come at the cost of usability. Trust is not built through friction alone. The goal is to create environments that feel seamless for legitimate users while remaining hostile to fraud.

She also highlighted the role of leadership tone. Culture begins at the top, and the way leaders communicate about risk sets the standard for how teams behave when pressure is high. Organizations that invest in awareness, training, and empowerment are better positioned to withstand disruption and recover quickly when incidents occur.

Amber's perspective can be summarized through three central themes that shape the future of cybersecurity and compliance:

- Cybersecurity frameworks are key.
- It is important to have full enterprise accountability.
- Risk needs to be integrated into the design.

Speaking with Amber reinforced an essential truth. Cybersecurity is not just about stopping attacks. It is about designing systems people can depend on. Every digital interaction depends on earning and maintaining that trust.

It has been a privilege to learn from Amber and to engage in these conversations over the years. Her perspective reflects the direction the industry is moving, where cybersecurity is no longer a technical requirement but a strategic responsibility embedded in how organizations operate and lead.

Defense-by-Design's Alignment to the Future of Finance

When thinking about the future of finance, I first consider how we protect our data, as cyberattacks continue to increase on a daily basis. Sophos and IBM reports show $25 billion in annual losses in finance, including ransom payments, recovery costs, and lost business, with 70% of firms targeted in 2025. Subsum's and Onfido/Entrust's separate identity fraud reports show that 35% of breaches involve AI-generated content, with a 400% YoY increase in voice and video deepfakes. With 92% of firms lacking real-time vendor security monitoring, supply chain attacks are creating a crisis across the entire ecosystem.[16] Insufficiencies in cybersecurity *can* be corrected when we dedicate today's powerful resources to them.

We need to see compliance not only as mandatory but also as a crucial way to protect our clients' data and our brand. In my mind, cybersecurity needs to be embedded from the beginning, not added after systems are built. It is important to see cyber risk as a business risk that, as Amber said, "must be owned at the organizational level." We will find that the real protection comes from aligning technology, people, and processes. As Albert Einstein said, "Intellectuals solve problems; geniuses prevent them." I won't pretend to think we can prevent cybercrimes fully, but we can definitely reduce exposure with the right design and engaging top cybersecurity experts.

Chapter 6 Key Takeaways

1. Defense-by-design needs to be a core principle with security embedded from day one.
2. Privacy-by-design should be the default setting with end-to-end data protection.
3. Modern financial safety requires moving from monitoring past transactions to real-time prevention by building a defense-by-design from the start. Also shifting to cyber resilience systems that are designed to recover instantly and withstand AI-driven threats by default.
4. **Personal lesson:** I have learned that when building new products, it is essential to lean on compliance and legal guidance to mitigate risks while still driving innovation.

Part III

Groundbreaking Technology

Chapter 7

AI's Superpower: Transforming Finance

"AI is a tool, not a magic button. Too many organizations rush to inject AI at the very beginning of their processes when it really belongs at step thirty-seven."

—Russell Moore, CEO of Amotivv

As we step into Part III of mastering the future of finance, I am excited to finally dive into the elements that are the groundbreaking technologies driving its transformation, starting with the superpower of AI. Although I am by no means an expert in AI, I have spent hours learning and days trying different tools and have had the pleasure of sitting down with many experts to summarize the key benefits of AI in finance for you.

Artificial intelligence was created in 1956 when John McCarthy, Marvin Minsky, Claude Shannon, and Nathaniel Rochester, all with IBM, organized a workshop that officially gave birth to AI. Their proposal, made at the Dartmouth Conference, was that "every aspect of learning can be precisely described so a machine can simulate it." Fast-forward to today, and we see AI making waves across our everyday lives, as we rely on technology from Alexa and Siri to ChatGPT, and it is also sparking a powerful impact on the world of finance with chatbots and agentic payments.

Like many of you, I have witnessed the birth of the World Wide Web, the cell phone, and the digital payment, which have all amazed me, but AI is a next-level experience as it is not just changing the way we interact, talk, and pay; it is changing the way we learn, think, build, and trust. There are many quotes on the future of AI, but I felt compelled to choose one from Russell Moore to start the chapter, as he was one of my first guests on my "Step into the Future of Finance" podcast on Spotify and an impressive AI expert I could speak with for days on end. He is the CEO of Amotivv, a company that makes AI auditable with the right to be forgotten. His excitement for how AI is and will continue to benefit all of humanity is contagious. His thinking, encapsulated in the quote, is critical to what I believe will be the best way of using AI-driven innovations into the future of finance.

While historically one of the biggest challenges in finance has been literacy, AI is beginning to level the playing field by unlocking simplified financial recommendations tailored to individual needs, leading to financial inclusion. Using AI, complex financial products can be simplified through vocal explanations and explainer videos. Financial literacy is not an easy problem to address as it's complex, emotional, and personal for every consumer. We all start at different levels and have unique financial needs and goals.

Fintechs have been among the first to use AI to personalize digital experiences and meet consumers' unique needs, such as explaining the best ways to use prepaid and credit cards to build credit scores and offering tips on saving that will drive a high level of interest. AI enables fintechs to address challenges in niche and underserved segments with product depth and at scale, a challenge that has historically been a challenge with traditional digital products.

For example, Greenlight, a fintech company, was built to help teens manage their allowance and savings. The use of AI within Greenlight helps bring to the surface age-appropriate financial lessons and usage patterns to suggest financial tips. If a child spends most of their money on games, the app may suggest ways to save or offer budgeting tips. Kids can also get paid for completing chores, which helps build a connection to work and to earning money early in life.

Greenlight offers these hyper-personalized experiences without sacrificing consumer privacy and security; it must comply with regulations, including the Children's Online Privacy Protection Act (COPPA). Default privacy settings must favor minimal data collection for minors. Stronger rights to data deletion and access controls apply to minors. Parental consent is often required before collecting or sharing children's data (including financial data), and such consent requirements state that the data must not be sold. This shows that greater privacy can be achieved in AI use in finance when mandated, which is encouraging.

A "privacy-first for everyone" model is possible, where adult financial data isn't exploited and is treated as a fundamental right, not a commodity. The EU and countries such as Switzerland, Singapore, and Brazil provide adults with very strong financial data privacy, often close to child-level protections, by requiring consent, limiting data use, and enforcing strict penalties for misuse.

As consumer AI becomes more mainstream, we are seeing the rise of tools that function like "financial coaches" and "AI CFOs" offering personalized guidance, real-time financial monitoring, and sophisticated financial analysis. These are only a couple of the many innovative ways AI can be used to help unlock consumer benefits.

When I First Recognized the Potential Impact of AI

The first time I remember hearing about AI was in 2011 when IBM's Watson beat the all-time champions of the US game show *Jeopardy!* This was a big moment for AI, as it communicated in natural human language, processed more than 200 million pages of unstructured data to find answers in three seconds, and learned from each experience to improve performance over time. That win for IBM's Watson was a win for AI, as it made mainstream news, boosted public awareness, and showed that AI was not science fiction; it had practical applications.

I was struck further by the power of AI in its early stages at an IBM Innovation Studio event in Toronto. IBM demonstrated how its AI platform, Watson Enterprise, could automate HR recruiting through advanced, AI-driven résumé sorting to select top candidates for interviews. I don't remember how I got invited to that particular event, but I distinctly recall being amazed by the power of AI and what it could achieve. I remember getting home that night, thinking if AI could already simplify the hiring process, what would the future world be like for my then two-year-old daughter if AI continued to improve at a mass scale? I never would have imagined what is possible today, and I am still trying to imagine what will be unlocked in the years to come.

Innovators in financial services are expanding the use cases and value of machine learning and AI. We now experience AI throughout our daily lives, whether we realize it or not: it is the core of how fraud detection works and how products and offers are personalized, and we are seeing a transformation in how we spend money, with frictionless payments. Advancements have also been made in how we manage our health. AI continues to impress me in so many ways.

A couple of my favorite ways to use AI in 2025 and 2026 were:

- Having my personal DJ on Spotify create the soundtrack of my day, filled with everything from the Red Hot Chili Peppers to the Beatles to "Diary of a CEO."
- Using Figma to create not only presentations but also impressive infographics with sources that are included in this book.
- Using ChatGPT, Claude, and Copilot to help with researching everything from recipes to bake with my kids and deep dives into the latest payment trends.

While AI can be a force of good in the world and in finance, it can also, unfortunately, fuel criminal activity, corruption, and deepfakes. To understand its impact, I will share its incredible potential and the key aspects that need regulation to lessen potential challenges in future AI finance trends.

Components of AI: From Machine Learning to Agentic AI

I think we all understand that vast amounts of data are created in the world of finance. Before going deeper into how AI is impacting the world of finance, I think it's helpful to understand what it is and how it works. By simple definition,

AI results when computer systems are programmed to perform tasks based on analyzing large amounts of data, which typically requires human intelligence and effort, but it's not just analysis that makes up AI. NVIDIA CEO Jensen Huang describes AI as being like a five-layer cake. The key components are energy, chips, infrastructure, models, and applications.[1] When you think about it, each of those components is an industry within itself, providing a large volume of jobs.

Nuances exist within the models and applications as well. Financial institutions need to connect with experts to understand these distinctions and deploy AI effectively. I believe understanding these six basic nuances in models and applications will prove helpful.

Rather than treating "AI" as a catchall term, I think it's helpful to see modern AI as a layered system in which each level builds on the one before it to enable greater capability and complexity. These layers represent different approaches, model types, and system behaviors rather than single, uniform technology.

The Six Layers of Modern AI

1. Artificial Intelligence (AI)

   The broad umbrella for systems designed to perform tasks that typically require human intelligence.

   Examples: IBM Deep Blue, Apple Siri, SAP enterprise decision systems
2. Symbolic and Statistical Methods

   Rule-based systems and probabilistic models that provide structured, interpretable decision-making.

   Examples: FICO credit decision engines, Oracle rules engines, IBM expert systems
3. Machine Learning (ML)

   Systems that learn from data to make predictions or classifications without explicit programming.

   Examples: Google search ranking, Netflix recommendation systems, PayPal fraud detection
4. Deep Neural Networks

   Multilayer neural models are capable of learning complex patterns, such as those in vision and speech.

Examples: Apple Face ID, Tesla Autopilot vision systems, Meta image recognition

5. Foundation Models

   Large, pre-trained models that serve as adaptable engines for many downstream tasks.

   Examples: OpenAI GPT models, Google Gemini, Meta LLaMA

6. Generative and Agentic Systems

   Application-level systems that generate content and autonomously plan or take actions on behalf of users.

   Examples: ChatGPT, Microsoft Copilot, Meta Smart Glasses

Considering AI through these six layers helps organizations better understand its capability, risk, and governance needs. It also enables more responsible deployment, stronger privacy controls, and clearer decision-making as AI systems scale.

The Development of AI in Finance

The advancements in AI since its inception have arrived in phases, with each generation coming faster and making a bigger impact. There has been greater acceleration and adoption of AI in the last three years than in the previous 70+ years. Just having the term "AI" become mainstream is a big step. The general public now understands that when they interact with a digital product in natural language, such as customer support chatbots or ChatGPT, they are interacting with AI. They trust this AI not only to respond to their task but also to trigger follow-up actions, such as freezing their account, creating a complaint ticket, or sending a notification. Those uses alone have increased trust in AI's value.

To help break down the progression of AI from its beginnings to our everyday use, Figure 7.1 outlines its key milestones across four phases.

This historical trajectory points directly toward a 2030 autonomous finance ecosystem, where intelligent agents operate within a unified ledger that merges identity with programmable value.

Figure 7.1 AI evolution in finance.
Sources: The History of Artificial Intelligence (Harvard University), Artificial Intelligence in Finance (OECD Report), McKinsey Global Banking Annual Review (2023 and 2024).

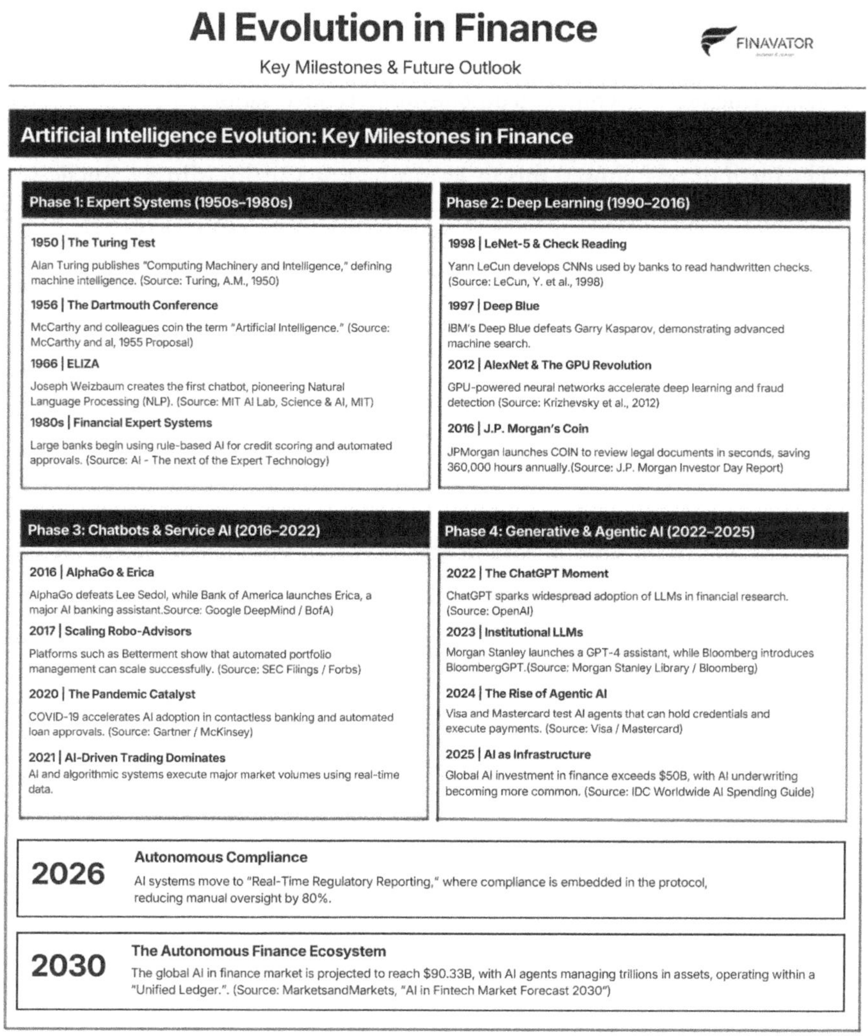

Phase 1: Expert Systems (1950s–1980s)

The first phase was the longest, from AI's development in 1950 to the 1980s. AI's initial developers operated from the understanding mentioned earlier that "every aspect of learning can be precisely described so a machine can simulate it." The first milestone was Alan Turing's 1950 paper, in which he proposed the Turing test to evaluate whether a machine can imitate human conversation. This foundational concept established criteria for machine intelligence.

The birth of AI followed this in 1956 when McCarthy, Minsky, Rochester, and Shannon formally established AI as a field of study at the Dartmouth conference.[2]

Developments in the 1960s and 1970s gave us SHRDLU, an early natural-language understanding program, and ELIZA, the first chatbot to project human traits.

AI systems were used in finance in the 1980s for credit scoring, loan underwriting, auditing, and decision support.[3]

Phase 2: Deep Learning (1990–2016)

The second phase of innovation, between 1990 and 2016, focused on deep learning. Progression from the 1990s and mid-2000s has shown us models for AI decision-making based on learning from datasets, analysis, and fine-tuning. Machines proved capable of learning! Financial institutions began personalizing products based on predictions of customer behavior.

There were breakthroughs in natural language processing (NLP) and a machine's ability to make decisions based on patterns recognized in learning data. This is distinctly different from the first phase, in which machines made decisions based on hard-coded, explicitly programmed rules. It also allowed pattern recognition for fraud detection, risk assessment, and portfolio prediction.

You may remember hearing about IBM's Deep Blue beating chess master Garry Kasparov with algorithmic thinking, which was also being used for trading and financial modeling. Innovation continued as we saw the rise of voice assistants like Siri and Alexa. During this time, banks began experimenting with the use of AI for fraud detection and risk assessment, bringing a whole new level of trust to customer relationships. This was so successful that major banks established AI research labs to further develop credit-scoring, market-prediction, and trading algorithms. Leading technology companies like Google and Meta (Facebook at the time) open-sourced deep learning frameworks, democratizing access to them, and the impact grew even bigger.

Phase 3: Chatbots and Service AI (2016–2022)

During the third phase of AI development, from 2016 to 2022, the most notable innovations were in chatbots and advanced reinforcement learning. In 2016, Bank of America became the first major bank to launch an AI-powered virtual assistant, "Erica," to handle routine customer service inquiries and reduce wait times. These same features are now commonly offered by banks through their own chatbots.

It is important to note that the world stopped in 2020 as we faced the challenges of COVID-19. As terrible as the pandemic was, it massively accelerated the adoption of AI for contactless banking, fraud detection, and automated underwriting. By 2021, algorithmic and AI-driven trading systems executed a majority of equity market volume. Portfolio management became mainstream with automated rebalancing. The data was doing the hard work in finance, and high-frequency firms began leaning on it for microsecond decision-making.

Phase 4: Generative and Agentic AI (2022–2026)

The fourth phase, which has come at us even faster, involved generative AI. The major evolution here, compared to phases 2 and 3, is the ability of machines to learn from massive datasets and perform many general tasks (also known as large language models). This is thanks to the volume of data accumulated on the Internet over the last few decades and the computational power available.

The biggest milestone during this phase was the release of ChatGPT by OpenAI on November 30, 2022. ChatGPT changed the game for AI worldwide by demonstrating the transformative capabilities of generative AI. Those in the world of finance began piloting large language models for research analysis, customer service, contract review, and compliance documentation.

As a payments geek, I am very excited to see developments in agentic AI, as Visa and Mastercard pilot agent-initiated payments. This is not yet live as I am writing this book, though I am sure it will be by the time you are reading this.

Most major financial institutions deploy AI at scale, underscoring the rapid growth in investment in AI-driven automation, analytics, and customer experience solutions across the financial sector. AI is here to stay, as consumers and businesses alike are using AI agents to execute search recommendations and rebalance portfolios. Even payments are being transformed by AI, with agentic systems enabling autonomous transaction processing across financial institutions.

I am happy to see that some regulatory frameworks for AI governance are being established in some major markets, such as the California Transparency in Frontier AI Act (SB53). In 2025, California enacted state-level legislation requiring large AI developers to disclose safety processes, establish transparency protections, and enable reporting of critical safety incidents.

Future Vision: An Autonomous Finance Ecosystem

By 2030, we are expected to see an autonomous finance ecosystem, with industry projections suggesting AI could manage trillions in global assets, enhance regulatory compliance for portfolio optimization, and make financial decisions autonomously. "The global AI in finance market is projected to grow from USD 38.36 billion in 2024 to approximately USD 190.33 billion by 2030, driven by broad adoption across operations, compliance, fraud detection, and analytics."[4]

There is also the potential for quantum machine learning to be deployed for portfolio optimization. As AI agents manage trillions in assets while fully complying with regulations, we will see human-AI collaboration as the standard model. AI did not arrive overnight; Figure 7.1 provides a roadmap of the milestones that took us from early academic theories to today's generative and agentic systems.

AI in Our Daily Lives

I am particularly excited to share information about AI as we are already reaping many benefits from it. I think we're all aware that AI is used in scientific research, but we have already received numerous personal benefits from it as well. Some common uses of AI include navigation apps (e.g., Google Maps, Waze) that save us time on our daily drives and assistants such as Siri and Alexa that can help with reminders or answer simple questions. Netflix, Spotify, and Amazon rely on AI to suggest entertainment options we might enjoy based on past selections. AI is also used in spam detection, and don't we all appreciate that for email, phone, and text communications?

While there is much debate about how many jobs AI will take over in the years to come, this will depend on what, if any, regulations are put in place to protect them. It is fair to say these are some of the same concerns society once had about industrialization, automation, and computerization. While initial transitions in those areas faced some challenges, fine-tuning has made it so that we rely heavily on time-saving and convenience-enhancing devices to improve our lives. Improving the human condition is the foundation of all technological advancement. AI can definitely be a threat to certain jobs, I must admit, but it can also be a force for good. The key is to keep the discussion going as we continue to evolve and find ways to harness the good.

The AI Technology Stack in Finance

In finance, AI encompasses machine learning algorithms, natural language processing, computer vision, and neural networks to process vast datasets, detect patterns, predict outcomes, and make decisions with an accuracy and speed unmatched by humans. Data is aggregated from structured and unstructured transaction records, market feeds, documented customer interactions, regulatory filings, and social media.

The most common use of AI in finance that people are aware of is fraud detection. Patterns are recognized, anomalies are highlighted, and fraudulent activities are discovered. When you receive an email or text message from your credit card company questioning purchases, those communications are generated due to discoveries made by AI.

When predictive models are applied to those same datasets, forecasts are made about everything from market movements to whether you are a good credit risk for a loan. AI systems can make investment recommendations in the best interest of customers. On the business side of things, they can also execute loan issuance decisions autonomously faster than humans. Automated decisions can even trigger compliance alerts before they become issues, thus allowing banks and fintechs to make necessary adjustments.

There are eight foundational layers within the AI technology stack in financial services. Each layer enables the intelligent automation, pattern recognition, and decision-making capabilities that power modern financial operations.

1. **Infrastructure**
   Provides the computing, storage, and networking foundation required to run AI systems at scale, including cloud platforms, accelerators (GPUs/TPUs), and secure networking.
2. **Data Layer**
   Manages data ingestion, processing, normalization, quality controls, and lineage for market data, transaction data, customer data, and third-party sources.
3. **Feature & Data Products Layer**
   Transforms raw data into curated, reusable features and data products that models can reliably consume. Includes features such as stores, metadata management, and versioned datasets.
4. **Models**
   Statistical, machine-learning, deep-learning, and generative models that produce predictions, classifications, recommendations, or generated outputs such as fraud detection, credit risk scoring, forecasting, or natural-language responses.
5. **Training and Deployment**
   Supports model training, validation, testing, approvals, versioning, and controlled deployment into production environments, ensuring repeatability and operational stability.

6. **Inference and Monitoring**
   Handles real-time and batch execution of models through APIs or workflows, including logging, performance monitoring, drift detection, and alerting.
7. **Applications**
   Operational and analytical systems that consume AI outputs, such as fraud alerting platforms, underwriting tools, risk dashboards, trading systems, and decision-support applications.
8. **Consumer Interfaces**
   Front-end touchpoints where customers experience AI directly, including mobile banking apps, chatbots, voice assistants, robo-advisors, and personalized financial dashboards.

Cross-Cutting Layer: Governance, Risk, and Compliance

Governance, risk management, and compliance span **all layers** of the stack, providing explainability, audit trails, privacy controls, security safeguards, and regulatory compliance required for financial institutions.

One of the most valuable aspects of AI in finance is that models continue to learn. They retrain when new data is made available: fraud algorithms adapt to emerging attack strategies, credit models incorporate macroeconomic shifts, and trading systems learn from market regime changes. The results of this analysis are of great benefit to businesses and consumers alike. Accelerated decision-making allows for actions to be taken when the timing is best!

AI's Transformation of Finance

In finance, AI has been proven to increase operational efficiency, enhance risk management, and allow financial institutions to provide personalized services. The use of AI tools is a competitive necessity, especially in banking, investment, and insurance.

Operational Efficiency

AI assessments of operations, overhead, and revenue patterns point decision-makers toward actions that can make the greatest positive impact on the bottom line. AI is shrinking common challenges inherent in data entry, document processing, and account reconciliation, freeing human staff members for more strategic and customer-facing operations. By automating redundant tasks, more time and resources can be applied to strategic initiatives. In this case, AI complements, rather than competing with, workers. While the adoption of AI may lead to job losses in some departments, banks like JPMorgan Chase and Wells Fargo are reporting increased human productivity and are considering increasing their tech head count.[5]

On the personnel front, AI background checks and assessments can help financial institutions identify top candidates to hire while reducing risk and time to fill open roles. AI, if designed with the intent to reduce bias in hiring, has the potential to provide a more inclusive work environment and personalized training and career development resources for individuals. This would allow workers to acquire new skills and remain competitive in an AI-enhanced job market.

Risk Management

Not only does AI analyze massive amounts of transactional data to identify potential fraud and detect financial crimes, but it also draws on a wide range of data to improve credit-risk assessments. The faster financial institutions can assist, the better. Because of its speed of operation, AI reduces the risk of false-positive alerts and can quickly flag potential issues, informing consumers and helping prevent fraud.

Personalized Services

Chatbots and virtual assistants offer 24/7 customer support, enhancing the customer experience and reducing long wait times for assistance. AI can also help analyze customer behavior against financial goals to provide personalized financial advice, which can, in turn, generate increased revenue.

One of the tools I find most useful for my business and my kids is the new AI budgeting and planning offering embedded in bank and fintech apps, which provide personalized services, education, and tips to help achieve financial goals. Also, having the ability to automate monthly bills, saving amounts, and long-term education planning is a win for anyone who takes advantage of these new tools.

Software Integration

As a business owner in this category, I often find it hard to dedicate time to accounting and administrative tasks. AI has been extremely helpful to me, especially its integration with QuickBooks. Accounting software companies have added AI-driven features to analyze monthly revenue flows and identify challenges for business owners. Some features are also helpful for loan assessments and for accessing additional cash flow, as AI can turn historical data into forward-looking insights that help banks and credit unions de-risk loans and speed up approvals by leveraging larger datasets. They are also reducing time spent on matching category expenses, as AI can "read" receipts and invoices, reducing accounting costs, reducing errors, and giving business owners real-time visibility into their finances. Overall, AI for small- to medium-sized businesses can be game-changing across accounting, operations, marketing, and sales, and ultimately serve as a powerful tool for innovation and growth.

While many future use cases for AI in finance are still being dreamed of, there are many we already rely on and benefit from. I tip my hat to the geniuses who created the many user-friendly apps and services that some consumers don't even recognize as being AI-driven, just that they're great tools.

Consumer AI-Interface and Experience

Consumer interfaces are the front-end touchpoints where users interact with artificial intelligence. In everyday financial activities, these interfaces make complex AI capabilities accessible, improving engagement, convenience, personalization, and security. Figure 7.2 shows eight valuable interfaces detailing the specific

Figure 7.2 Consumer AI interface and experience

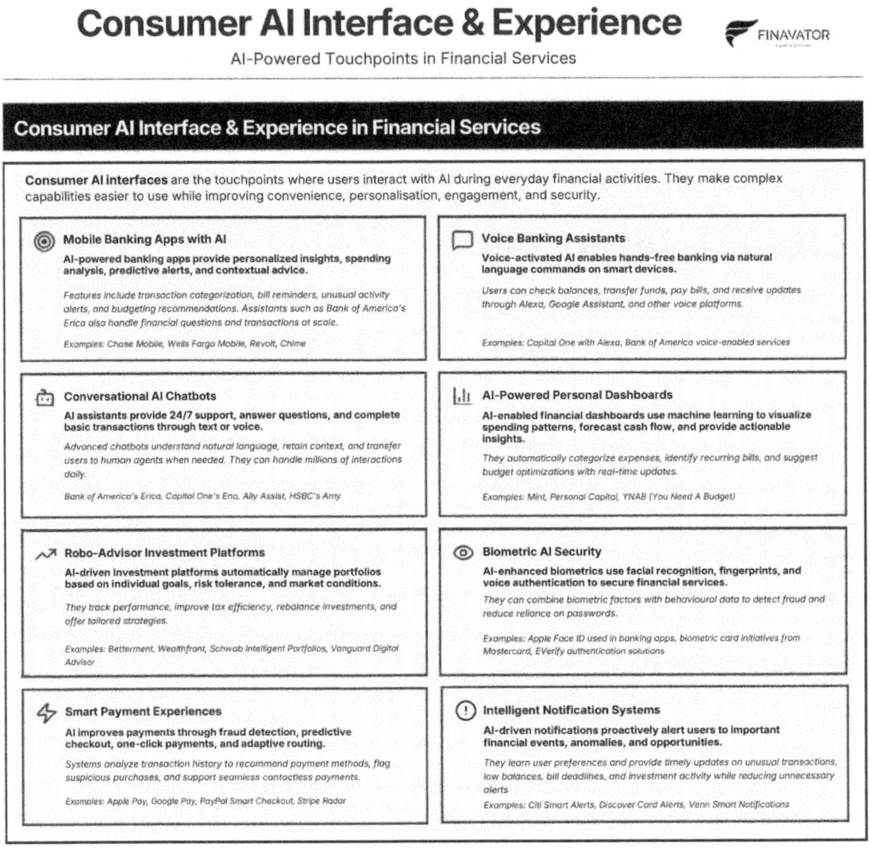

touchpoints where complex background logic is translated into the intuitive, front-end experiences we now use daily. Let's discuss each.[6]

Whether through biometrics or proactive alerts, these interfaces empower users by masking technical complexity and making high-level AI capabilities feel available to all.

1. **Mobile Banking Apps with AI**
   Some of the features provided by AI-powered mobile banking applications include personalized financial insights, spending analyses, and predictive alerts. Some include intelligent transaction categorization, bill

payment reminders, notifications for unusual activity, and personalized savings recommendations based on spending patterns.

Examples: Chase Mobile, Wells Fargo Mobile, Revolut, Chime

2. **Voice Banking Assistants**

   Hands-free banking is available through voice-activated AI systems that use natural language commands through smart speakers on tablets and mobile devices. Users can check balances, transfer funds, pay bills, and receive financial updates via voice commands with Amazon Alexa, Google Assistant, or Siri.

   Examples: Capital One with Alexa, Bank of America with Google Assistant

3. **Conversational AI Chatbots**

   AI-powered virtual assistants provide 24/7 customer support, answer questions, and complete transactions via text or voice. Advanced chatbots understand natural language, remember conversation context, and seamlessly hand off to human agents when needed.

   Examples: Bank of America's Erica (1B+ interactions), Wells Fargo's Fargo, HSBC's Amy

4. **AI-Powered Personal Dashboards**

   Intelligent financial dashboards use machine learning to recognize spending patterns, forecast cash flow, and provide useful insights. Dashboards are designed to categorize expenses, identify subscription services, predict upcoming bills, highlight unusual spending, and suggest ways to optimize budgets. They provide real-time updates with predictive analytics.

   Examples: Mint, Personal Capital, YNAB (You Need A Budget)

5. **Robo-Advisor Investment Platforms**

   AI-driven investment platforms manage portfolios based on user goals, risk tolerance, and market conditions. Interfaces show portfolio performance, automatically rebalance assets, improve tax efficiency, and offer goal-tracking visualizations. Users answer simple questions to receive personalized investment strategies.

   Examples: Betterment, Wealthfront, Schwab Intelligent Portfolios, Vanguard Digital Advisor

6. **Biometric AI Security**

   AI-powered biometric systems use facial recognition, fingerprint scanning, and voice authentication for secure access. Advanced systems combine multiple biometric factors with behavioral analysis (typing patterns, device usage) to detect fraud. Face ID, Touch ID, and voice recognition eliminate passwords while improving security.

Examples: Apple Face ID for banking apps, Mastercard biometric cards, HSBC Voice ID

7. **Smart Payment Experiences**
AI enhances payment interfaces with fraud detection, one-click checkout, and predictive payment suggestions. Systems analyze transaction histories to pre-fill payment details, suggest optimal payment methods, detect suspicious purchases in real-time, and enable seamless contactless payments with instant verification.
Examples: Apple Pay, Google Pay, PayPal Smart Checkout, Stripe Radar
8. **Intelligent Notification Systems**
AI-driven alerts proactively notify users of important financial events, anomalies, and opportunities. Smart notifications learn user preferences to deliver timely alerts for unusual transactions, low balances, bill due dates, investment opportunities, and potential fraud.
Examples: Citi Smart Alerts, Discover Card Alerts, Venmo Smart Notifications

Challenges/Concerns

While speed-to-market is important in the continued development of AI capabilities, I tend to advise erring on the side of caution when developing any new tool to ensure protections and regulations can be put in place. Having been involved in the world of fintech for decades, I have seen incredible products and services come to market, many that offer broad inclusion for those who have previously been underserved. I have also seen new technologies that have posed challenges and required changes to better suit the market.

Newer strategies focus on minimizing data collection, keeping core data in its original repositories, and using attribute-based indexing and privacy-by-design principles to enable AI reasoning without creating large, duplicated data stores that could be exploited by attackers.[7]

I often speak about the need for greater awareness among those with the power to implement safeguards and standards regarding AI's impact on the future. There are several areas that I believe need to be addressed. These include:

Privacy-by-design, as covered in Chapter 6, applies whether it's held by a government, an employer, or an organization that transacts business. The European Union has enacted the General Data Protection Regulation (GDPR), widely regarded as the global gold standard, which gives all EU residents the right to access, correct, and delete personal data.

North America is a bit behind in instituting similar regulations. The California Consumer Privacy Act (CCPA) is similar but narrower compared to GDPR, as it only provides privacy rights for residents of California, mainly to consumers, not to employees, and is an opt-out data right model, versus opt-in. Currently, the rest of the US does not have the same protections in place.

On the global front, the UK (UK GDPR) and Brazil (LGPD) are most similar to Europe's GDPR. Australia's Privacy Act offers weaker but growing protections, while Canada's PIPEDA remains less comprehensive, still lacking key GDPR-level rights and enforcement mechanisms.

Data is as valuable to the current era as oil was to the petroleum age. When allowed, your data can be stored, analyzed, and used as a source of learning. Protecting your data is not easy and takes effort as you turn off training, some personalization, and background collection. Even that is still not going to fully protect you, as data about us is everywhere, but it is a good place to start if this concerns you at all, as many feel that we have already lost the battle of data privacy. As for me, I still have some hope that we can fix aspects of data protection to help the next generation.

AI safety: One of the biggest challenges in the development of AI is that AI-driven systems are only as good as the data upon which they are trained. In finance, AI safety concerns include biased and opaque decisions, cybersecurity threats, systemic instability from autonomous models, data privacy risks, and misuse by attackers, with real examples of fraud, market risk warnings, and biased outcomes appearing across the industry. This is a documented ethical concern for financial AI systems. Autonomous AI trading systems can amplify volatility or trigger market disruptions. For example, the Bank of England warned that advanced AI systems could unintentionally manipulate markets or contribute to financial crises if unchecked.

AI adoption is outpacing accountability, leaving open questions about who is responsible when automated systems cause harm; ongoing legal cases include a $1.5 billion settlement by Anthropic with authors overusing copyrighted books to train AI models and multiple wrongful death lawsuits alleging harmful impacts of AI chatbots on teens' mental health.[8]

In finance, accountability gaps around AI have surfaced in multiple areas: firms have been charged for misleading claims about AI usage, algorithmic tools have produced discriminatory credit decisions, and regulators have warned that AI-generated disinformation could create systemic risks. These cases highlight ongoing unresolved questions about responsibility and oversight in the financial sector.

Many AI systems are hard to explain or audit. For example, regulators warn that opaque AI models in finance make it difficult to justify decisions like credit denials or trading actions, raising accountability concerns. There needs to be some form of accountability built into AI-driven systems that have the potential to breach privacy or negatively impact other human rights.

- **HR:** Without oversight, historical biases can be perpetuated, allowing for inequality in hiring practices, pay scales, and career advancement.
- **Spreading misinformation:** The term for this is "AI hallucinations." This is when generative AI models produce factually incorrect information based on patterns in training rather than on verified facts. This can be caused by insufficient training data or unusual user prompts.

Ethical AI

While AI-driven advancements are accelerating the pace of change in all areas of life, leaders must have the courage to stand up and commit to fostering innovation responsibly and with ethical foresight. Without adequate regulation and oversight, even strict governance, AI could generate opportunities for misuse.

An article in *Time* magazine from October 2023 stated, "AI needs to be regulated like nuclear weapons."[9] The analogies used indicate the powerful potential negative impact on human life should AI be misused, while, when properly harnessed, the tremendous value of good for human life. We are seeing many experts increasingly discussing this analogy as they call for stronger global AI safety frameworks.

I am a glass-half-full person and want to highlight that for AI to be a force for good, we should at least be concerned about the challenges AI could cause without clear safety frameworks, as we did eventually add seat belts to our cars, warning labels to alcohol, and food and drug safety laws.

Job Displacement

According to the McKinsey Global Institute, AI could generate $13 trillion by 2030 and increase global GDP by about 16%. It may also replace millions of jobs and automate 25% of many jobs.[10] While this disruption occurs, AI can also create a demand for new roles similar to other periods of disruption. Many roles still require a human touch to enable trust, as well as a need for emotional intelligence, leadership, and management to remain irreplaceable. Blind trust in AI outputs can lead to costly errors. For example, even outside AI-specific failures, excessive automation has shown how a lack of oversight leads to mistakes in financial systems. Countries might need to enact laws to protect human-centric positions, including planning funding to retrain displaced workers.

Regulatory

Historically, progress is much slower than technological advancements. Globally, governments are beginning to put guardrails around AI, with the European Union leading through its binding AI Act, the United Kingdom adopting a principles-based regulatory approach, and the United States and Canada relying on a mix of executive actions, sector-specific rules, and proposed legislation rather than a single comprehensive AI law.

A major milestone came in September 2024 with the Council of Europe's Framework Convention on Artificial Intelligence, the world's first international AI treaty signed by 56 countries, including the United States, the United Kingdom, Canada, Japan, Australia, and most of Europe. These countries agree that the use of AI systems is to be consistent with human rights, democracy, and the rule of law. It is technology-neutral and promotes AI progress and innovation, while managing the risks it may pose.[11]

While this treaty is an important step forward, AI governance still needs stronger enforcement, clearer responsibility, and deeper global coordination to reach the level of consistency and effectiveness seen in long-standing nuclear treaties.

In the United States and in the AI race to achieve AI super-intelligence first, regulatory restraints on AI have currently been removed. This has created both positive and negative outcomes, as AI development could move so quickly that challenges cannot be fixed in the future. However, if the United States doesn't create it first, that could cause other challenges.

Energy

The pros and cons of data center placement have been featured in the news for quite some time. While the centers create jobs and generate tax revenue, they have very specific needs and demands regarding the amount of energy required to operate them and their reliance on freshwater supplies for cooling. Communities need to be educated on both sides of this equation before making long-term commitments, unless new developments in technology change those demands.

When thinking about AI and the growing energy crisis, Sue Ennis, president of Realbotix, was one of the first people who came to mind. I met Sue in 2018 when we worked together at a blockchain company focused on digital identity and consent, and I've long admired her ambition and attention to detail when it comes to scale.

In our interview, Sue shared a clear, grounded perspective on how AI is reshaping finance not just through software and algorithms but also through the physical infrastructure that powers it. From energy arbitrage and data center expansion to grid constraints, water usage, and sustainability, Sue broke down what many overlook when discussing AI innovation.

She also highlighted how stablecoins and tokenization are helping legitimize digital currencies, reduce friction in global payments, and expand access to financial systems, while emphasizing the importance of regulatory clarity and responsible design.

To close, what stood out in this conversation was how interconnected everything is. AI, finance, energy, water, regulation, and trust are no longer separate conversations. Sue reminded us that the future of finance will be shaped as much by electrons and infrastructure as by code and capital. Leaders who understand that infrastructure matters, that the current power system is a bottleneck, and that sustainability by design is important will be the ones best positioned to build systems that scale responsibly and sustainably.

The Global Impact of AI

While the continued development of AI models in finance has the world buzzing, some regions are experiencing greater impact than others. For example, North America, dominated by US banks and fintech innovation hubs, accounts for 43% of market usage. The Asia-Pacific region accounts for 31% of the market share, led by China's Ant Group and Tencent AI initiatives, while Europe accounts for 19%, driven by a strong regulatory focus on ethical AI and GDPR compliance. The remaining 7% of the market share is "the rest of the world," working to adopt AI for financial inclusion.[12]

When it comes to the future outlook for AI in finance, as you will see in Figure 7.3, the emerging technologies as we head toward the year 2030 are in the following areas:

- **Generative AI:** GPT-powered financial advisors and automated report generation
- **Quantum ML:** Portfolio optimization and risk modeling at unprecedented scale
- **Edge AI:** Real-time fraud detection on mobile devices without cloud latency
- **Federated Learning:** Privacy-preserving AI training across institutions
- **Explainable AI (XAI):** Transparent models meeting regulatory requirements

Figure 7.3 AI in finance market overview

Key industry predictions are that by 2027, 90% of banking interactions will be AI-mediated. By 2028, it's predicted that AI will manage $16 trillion in global investment assets. By 2029, it's predicted that there will be a 70% reduction in financial crime through AI surveillance. By 2030, it is believed that AI will handle 80% of all financial decisions. All of this is projected to result in $1 trillion+ in annual cost savings across the global financial sector.[13]

These predictions only reinforce my stance that regulatory practices must evolve to protect both businesses and consumers from abuse of AI models. Global AI governance frameworks must be standardized and fast!

The economic ripple effect of AI is increasingly defined by regional dominance. Figure 7.3 summarizes the trends and technology outlook currently driving this global impact.

The analysis confirms a definitive shift toward local, on-device processing, or "edge AI," to safeguard privacy. This move is expected to support a projected 20–25% reduction in operational costs, while the total market is projected to scale toward $190 billion by 2030.

Expert Interview with Russell Moore, CEO of Amotivv

When I think about artificial intelligence and its impact on finance, Russell Moore stands out for both his technical depth and his ability to make complex concepts accessible. As the CEO of Amotivv, he has spent years at the intersection of payments and innovation. His company solves a critical problem called AI memory persistence, which allows digital systems to remember context and maintain relationships over time. Instead of starting fresh with each interaction, his platform enables AI to deliver personalized experiences that improve the more you use them.

I first heard Russell speak at an industry panel years ago, and I was struck by how he talked about AI like a tool rather than magic. Since then, our paths have crossed multiple times. I had the pleasure of speaking with him in Atlanta in the summer of 2025, and he was one of the first guests on my podcast. His perspective comes from building and deploying this technology at a mass scale rather than just theorizing about it.

When asked about his approach to AI, the answer is always the same. He believes "it is a tool and not a magic button." He says that "too many organizations rush to use AI at the very beginning of their processes when it really belongs much later as an optimizer. The technology works best when placed strategically to automate specific tasks. If you treat it like a cure-all, your project will likely fail. Success comes from understanding exactly where the technology adds value to the business."

He compares this moment in AI development to the early days of the Internet. "Most people do not know the technical rules that make the Internet work, but they use it every day. Right now, new standards are being set for how AI agents communicate and how they maintain memory. These foundations will unlock everything that comes next, just like Internet protocols did decades ago." We are building the future right now, even if few people have yet to realize it.

Throughout our discussion, the emphasis kept returning to memory as the main differentiator. Without memory, AI cannot maintain context or build real relationships. Russell shared a story about a digital twin he built from thousands of emails and patents. When that data was lost due to a vendor issue, it felt like losing a real person. That loss became the catalyst for his current work in creating secure memory for AI systems.

We also talked about how AI will change our expectations for everyday experiences. He calls this our tolerance for technology. "In the past, people were willing to wait a long time for a web page to load, but today we get annoyed if it takes more than two seconds." That tolerance keeps shrinking, and AI is accelerating that shift. Russell has already developed a single view of all his payment tools, including credit cards and digital currencies connected by AI. Soon, this level of personalization will be expected by everyone.

When I asked about getting started with AI, his advice was very practical. He warns that "you should never put anything into a general AI tool that you would not share with a total stranger." You should keep bank account numbers and Social Security numbers out of these systems. However, he highly recommends using AI for contracts. He strips out his personal identifying information and has the AI explain what the terms actually mean before he signs. He has not signed a document in years without doing this first.

Another key theme was data ownership and avoiding being locked into one vendor. He compares this to how we own our phone numbers today. In the past, if you switched phone companies, you lost your number, but now the law allows you to take it with you. He believes the same must happen with AI data. "Organizations often build sophisticated systems only to find they cannot move their data to a new provider." Users must demand ownership and control over their digital history.

One story stuck with me about a large financial institution. They wanted to use AI to fire most of their call center staff to save money. Russell gave them the opposite advice. He suggested using AI to eliminate the boring tasks that make the job miserable so that experienced employees would want to stay. The institution ignored this advice and cut the workforce, but their costs ended up increasing 10-fold as the technology could not fully replace human judgment. They eventually had to rebuild their entire team from scratch.

When implemented, the results of AI can be staggering. Russell's team needed to move a large database, which usually takes seven people several months and costs one million dollars. "By using AI strategically, they finished the job in just seven hours for only $1,000." This is the kind of transformation that is possible when AI helps humans work faster.

Russell's final point was clear. "AI is no longer optional. If you participate in society, you will be participating in AI. It is becoming as essential as the Internet or cell phones. The only choice is whether you will be someone who develops it or someone who uses it." Either way, people need to be aware of how their data is used and demand ownership of it. You would not let someone take your physical property, so you should not surrender your digital data either.

His insights can be summarized through three central themes:

1. AI as a strategic tool
2. Memory as a foundation
3. Human and AI collaboration

Speaking with Russell Moore reinforced an essential truth. AI is not magic; it's also not a silver bullet. It's a powerful tool that, when used strategically and built on the right foundations, can enhance human capability in ways we're only beginning to understand. Implement AI where it genuinely optimizes and automates, not as a replacement for human judgment and connection. Semantic memory that carries across interactions transforms AI from reactive software into a cognitive partner capable of true personalization. The goal is to empower people, not eliminate them, while fiercely protecting data ownership and avoiding vendor lock-in.

It has been a privilege to learn from him and to engage in these conversations. His perspective reflects where the industry is heading, where AI is no longer just a technical innovation but a strategic imperative embedded in how organizations operate and compete.

AI's Alignment to the Future of Finance

The future of finance will not be shaped by AI alone but by how thoughtfully we integrate it with human expertise and how fiercely we protect an individual's right to own and control their data. In 2026, we are witnessing a definitive shift toward autonomous compliance. In this new era, AI systems enable "real-time regulatory reporting," where compliance is embedded directly into the protocol, reducing manual oversight by up to 80%.[14]

We are already seeing these changes permeate our daily lives, from chatbots providing instant suggestions for the best mortgage rates and bank interest to agentic AI executing autonomous payments. Looking ahead to 2030, the global AI market in finance is projected to reach $90.33 billion. In this vision, AI agents will manage trillions in assets, operating within a "unified ledger" that seamlessly combines identity, money, and programmable logic.[15]

With AI moving at such a breakneck pace, much may have already evolved by the time this book reaches your hands. I cannot predict every turn the future will take, but it is undeniably exciting to witness the profound impact AI is having on our financial ecosystem and the world at large.

Chapter 7 Key Takeaways

1. AI is reshaping the world across all sectors, especially the future of finance, from agentic payments and identity to fraud, complaints, personalization, cybersecurity, credit risk, and more. It is important to stay informed.
2. I hope we focus on building ethical AI, even though it might be one of the hardest tasks we face, to ensure we harness the power of AI with global guidelines, similar to the Nuclear Treaty, to avoid the challenges that can occur without a rulebook.
3. **Personal lesson:** AI is an impressive tool that can help us in so many ways when used with care and with an effort to protect our sensitive data.

Chapter 8

Why Blockchain Matters: From Tokenized Assets to Digital Economies

"Just as the Internet democratized access to information, blockchain has the potential to democratize access to financial systems through programmable trust, enabling digital assets, instant payments, and making identity sovereign."

—Malcolm Clarke, VP Digital Assets Ecosystem at Western Union (Ex-Disney, Ex-Zelle, Ex-TD)

Our next element in the future of finance is blockchain. As I write this chapter, I find myself trying to navigate a divide within the industry. Some practitioners are deeply bullish on blockchain's potential to reshape finance, while others remain skeptical after years of pilots that have not always delivered. Both perspectives are valid, and understanding this tension is essential to evaluating where blockchain truly fits in the future of finance. We will dive into all sides, the key use cases, the wins and losses over the years, and the potential ahead.

I was new to the blockchain world when I agreed to serve as chief client officer for a blockchain start-up focused on digital identity and keeping consent on chain in June 2018. This was one of the most daring moves of my career. I left my safe, secure payments role to leap into the unknown. The idea of being part of a start-up was both exciting and filled with uncertainty. I remember feeling like the new kid in school. Everyone seemed to know the ins and outs of the whole ecosystem. I had basic knowledge of blockchain as the backend for Bitcoin (BTC) and that Bitcoin had taken off in 2017, so there was a lot to learn.

Around this time, I attended my first blockchain conference and was pleasantly surprised at the difference from the traditional industry events I attended. Futurist brought together industry professionals to discuss blockchain from cryptocurrencies to Web3, and it changed the way I thought about the industry in so many ways. I noticed the difference immediately: neon lights instead of fluorescent boardroom lighting, unstructured discussions instead of formal panels, fun food instead of catered sandwiches, live podcasts instead of prepared speeches, drinks, DJs, and, most of all, the relaxed atmosphere with many dressed in sweatpants, running shoes, and baseball caps instead of business suits and heels. It felt like a space built for creativity, curiosity, and experimentation, which was refreshing.

Blockchain promised a world of limitless possibilities, at least according to the whitepapers, pitches, and early experiments. A blockchain use case that left a strong impression on me came from a friend working in blockchain innovation labs. Lucia Gallardo, CEO of Emerge, presented at the first Futurist Conference in 2018 and described her mission to use blockchain to help track agricultural supply chains for social good. Her vision gave consumers unprecedented transparency, allowing them to verify exactly where produce originated, including information on organic certifications and waste reduction. I left the conference energized by the possibilities that the industry would spend the next eight years attempting and often struggling to realize. Today, major logistics companies like FedEx and DHL continue to explore these solutions, while the technology has also expanded to address financial inclusion for smallholder farmers. Platforms like EthicHub provide unbanked farmers with ethical loans at 9.9% interest, an alternative to local predatory rates that can exceed 60%.[1] Apps like ThankMyFarmer allow consumers to send direct tips to producers, creating a secondary revenue stream for farming communities.

After months of coffee chats and conversations with others in this space, I began to see what blockchains could truly enable. Beyond crop tracing and Bitcoin, the technology could validate transactions, execute smart contracts, enable end-to-end traceability, and store data in distributed, tamper-proof records. Its potential to make data trustworthy and immutable was exciting. It's the reason I chose the quote from Malcolm Clarke, VP of Digital Assets Ecosystem at Western Union, to start this chapter. I love how he projects that democratized "access to financial information through programmable trust" will enable digital assets and instant payments and make identity sovereign. His 20-plus-year career includes experience transforming global payment ecosystems through digital innovation, blockchain infrastructure, and large-scale identity solutions.

A fundamental limitation of blockchain is that it is "blind" to the physical world. While nodes can immutably record and secure data, they cannot verify accuracy on their own. The bulk of real-world data, such as crop quality or weather measurements, is stored off-chain and referenced by the blockchain. This creates the well-known Oracle Problem: if a sensor malfunctions or a human enters incorrect data, the blockchain will faithfully record it. Reliable oracles and verification mechanisms are therefore essential for bridging the digital ledger with reality. New tools are helping bridge this gap, but the battle is far from won; these systems must prove they work for more farmers, in every corner of the globe. We will cover this more later in the chapter.

Few know that Ethereum's blockchain was created and launched in Toronto in 2015. Its impact worldwide has been profound, and as Vitalik Buterin, Ethereum's founder, notes, its power lies in enabling decentralized applications that go far beyond simple cryptocurrency transactions.

It is fitting that Ethereum's blockchain is increasingly recognized as "tru/stware," a foundational infrastructure designed to industrialize trust for the digital world economy.[2] As our lives move deeper into the Web3 era, blockchain is transforming global finance by shifting the control of identity from centralized silos to the individual. Through decentralized identifiers (DIDs) and verifiable credentials, Web3 identity is now being stored securely on user-owned devices, while only the cryptographic proofs of these records reside on public ledgers.[3]

This shift is evidenced by Kinexys by J.P. Morgan (formerly Onyx), which reports processing more than $1.5 trillion in transaction volume.[4] Through its Project EPIC, Kinexys is demonstrating how on-chain privacy and "composability" allow institutions to verify a user's creditworthiness or legal status without ever seeing their private data. Furthermore, blockchain serves as the backbone for the rapid expansion of stablecoins and central bank digital currencies (CBDCs).[5] By leveraging zero-knowledge proofs, these ledgers can protect a user's privacy during high-speed transactions while maintaining the transparency and regulatory compliance necessary for a trustworthy global financial system.

It is important to note that blockchain is tamper-evident: it is a resilient system that, even as technologies like quantum computing evolve, any attempt to change your records is instantly visible, providing a secure foundation for our digital future. We will look at use cases and experiments to demystify what blockchain has become: a specific, powerful toolset that is quietly reshaping how the world trades trust. Let's begin with the backend technology of blockchain first.

What Is Blockchain?

Blockchain is like the Internet, operating in a decentralized manner. Few truly understand how the Internet works, yet we all use it. Blockchain is a foundational Trustwave layer that allows us to manage databases in a permanent, trackable, and auditable way, effectively industrializing the production of digital trust. While this technology began as a ledger for currency, it has evolved into the backbone of a new Internet architecture known as Web3, a concept we will explore in greater detail later in this chapter. Think of blockchain as a digital record book, a distributed ledger, shared across a network, where everyone can see the same unchangeable record rather than records being stored in a single, centralized location.

Transactions in that ledger are recorded in blocks linked together, which is why it is called block*chain*.

The three key concepts of decentralization, transparency, and immutability are what make blockchain so efficient and effective:

1. **Decentralized:** No single person or company controls the blockchain. Thousands of computers worldwide maintain identical copies, making it impossible for any single entity to manipulate the data.
2. **Transparent:** Transactions on the blockchain are visible to everyone. Depending on the blockchain used, transactions can be private, public, or verifiable. While you can see the transactions, identities are protected through cryptographic addresses.
3. **Immutable:** Once data is recorded, it cannot be changed or deleted. The cryptographic linking of blocks makes altering historical data computationally infeasible, creating a permanent record.

To understand why blockchain is often described as "trustware," Figure 8.1 breaks down the foundational pillars from decentralized, transparent, and immutable characteristics that ensure data remains an auditable record of truth.

Figure 8.1 Blockchain technology

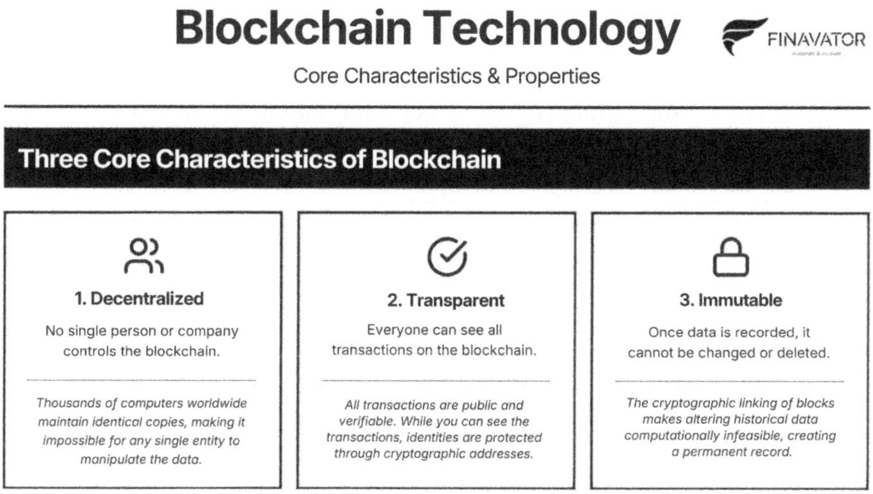

Decentralization and immutability are the anchors of this infrastructure, providing the tamper-evident security needed to build the next-generation Internet.

A blockchain consists of three fundamental components:

1. **Nodes**
   These are the network participants (people and their computers). Thousands of independent nodes maintain copies of each blockchain, eliminating single points of failure. The number of globally reachable nodes has increased significantly over the years, reaching 24,099 as of the end of January 2026, marking the highest level of network decentralization in history.[6] They create decentralization.
   There are two types of nodes:
   A full node downloads and validates entire blockchains, which requires powerful computers with significant energy needs. A full node can also be a mining node, as it is responsible for verifying transactions and adding new blocks to the blockchain. These nodes perform complex calculations to solve mathematical problems, enabling them to create new blocks and receive cryptocurrency rewards.
   A light node (aka simplified payment verification [SPV]) stores summaries of blocks and verifies individual transactions. This verification can happen on devices with lower storage capacity, which require less energy.
2. **Blocks**
   Blocks are the containers of units of information, the data. Transaction data is added to blocks, along with cryptographic proofs, timestamps, and metadata, creating verified records. The transaction or smart contract information is then added to a block, but only after nodes have reviewed it to verify and validate it. Once verified, the records can't be disputed.
3. **Chains**
   Chains are unique cryptographic links between each block, appearing in a specific order. It is therefore very clear to all nodes when any piece of data changes, as the code for the other blocks will no longer match. This ensures the data cannot be altered, creating a tamper-evident record.

Use Case: Strengthening Traditional Wills with Blockchain Records

Imagine you have spent a lifetime building your estate and want to ensure your assets are distributed after your death exactly as you intended. In a traditional system, a will is a physical document that can be lost, hidden by a disgruntled relative, or contested in court for an extended period. By recording a cryptographic fingerprint (hash) of your will on a blockchain, your final wishes become a permanent, verifiable part of the digital record, reducing uncertainty, disputes, and delays for your family.

1. The Final Wishes (The Broadcast)

When you finalize your will, you don't just put it in a safe place. You digitize the document and generate a cryptographic hash of its contents, which is then broadcast to a secure, private network. This hash serves as a unique digital fingerprint: if the document is ever altered, the hash will change, immediately signaling tampering. Details included in this process might include "This is the final version of the will for (Person A), recorded on January 15, 2026." This creates an immediate, timestamped proof of existence that the network recognizes.

2. The Witnesses (The Nodes)

Instead of relying on two people in a room with you, the network nodes, including your law firm, government estate registry, and bank, act as digital witnesses. They verify your identity (via biometrics) to confirm it is you signing. They "vouch" for the will's authenticity before it is officially sealed.

3. The Digital Seal (Hashing)

Once verified, the will is hashed, creating a unique digital fingerprint of every single word. If an unhappy beneficiary tries to change anything, the hash no longer matches the original. The discrepancy is instantly obvious to banks, courts, and other legal parties.

4. The Permanent Legacy (Immutability)

When the time comes to execute the will, there's no need to hunt for a paper original. The document itself is stored in secure off-chain storage, while the blockchain holds only its cryptographic hash. This ensures the document's integrity: any alteration to the document would produce a different hash, immediately revealing tampering. The blockchain record is immutable; it cannot be deleted, replaced, or destroyed. Banks and registries can instantly verify your instructions and release funds to your beneficiaries. The mental and emotional burden on your family is reduced, replaced by the certainty that your legacy is protected exactly as you intended.

With a decentralized network, there is no single point of control. Data is distributed across thousands of nodes around the world, making the blockchain system resilient and transparent. The trust value of blockchain stems from the validation of transactions through consensus protocols, such as proof of work or proof of stake.[7]

In use cases such as digital identity, cryptocurrency ownership, and voting records, a decentralized blockchain is likely the best approach. However, there is also a type of *centralized* blockchain that offers the same efficiency but has a single point of authority. An example of this is a company's database, which may not require validation by multiple participants.

Another aspect of blockchain usage is *privacy*, which depends on the use case. With a *public* blockchain, like Bitcoin or Ethereum, anyone can participate. That means anyone can read, write, or audit the data stored in the system. A *private* blockchain might be used in a controlled environment with a select group of people to facilitate transactions, such as obligations and terms of a strategic partnership. It allows only the parties involved to validate the information that is shared. In finance, blockchain provides a transparent payment system that validates designated aspects of transactions before they can be completed. It provides an audit record of what occurred, often reducing both errors and costs.

Common Uses of Blockchain

Thus far, the most common uses of blockchain include supply chain management, digital currencies, smart contracts, and banking and payments. As in the coffee bean supply chain example, tracking can be applied to any product, from manufacturing through delivery, to ensure authenticity and prevent counterfeits.

Digital currency is far more than just "crypto." It is a multilayered ecosystem where different tools serve different purposes. While decentralized assets like Bitcoin and Ethereum operate independently of the traditional banking system, other forms are designed to work within it. Stablecoins act as digital versions of the dollar for fast, everyday payments; tokenized deposits allow traditional banks to move money 24/7; and CBDCs are digital versions of national cash issued by governments. All of these run on blockchain technology, allowing value to move as instantly and easily as sending a text message.

Smart contracts were first introduced and described as code that could replace lawyers, run companies, and even judge complex disputes on their own. In reality, legal and technical limits made that vision unrealistic. Today, smart contracts are best known as practical automation tools. They are self-executing digital agreements on a blockchain: when a specific condition is met, a predetermined action happens automatically. For example, funds can be released once a transaction is verified, or a stablecoin can be exchanged for a digital asset instantly, removing manual settlement delays. In supply chains, payments for a shipment could be triggered automatically upon delivery verification with no invoicing or follow-ups required. This practical approach has already reached significance with more than $27 trillion in value processed via smart contracts as of 2025.[8] Their main benefit today lies in reducing intermediaries, speeding up settlements, and lowering costs for financial services, digital assets, and other routine operations.

Instant settlement: In the world of banking and payments, stablecoins and blockchain technology enable instant settlement of transactions between financial institutions at lower costs than before. Before blockchain was used, international fund transfers could take several days. This can greatly improve efficiency. Fintechs such as Ethereum and Solana are often used by businesses for these transactions.

Other records, such as those generated by governments or the healthcare industry, can also benefit from blockchain's tamper-proof data encryption. Data breaches and identity theft can be reduced considerably with blockchain applications, thereby increasing trust. In fact, blockchain has the potential to improve social and economic systems on a global scale.

My Blockchain Learning Curve

I had heard about blockchain before 2017, but it was always passing, and it went over my head; I hadn't yet taken the time to fully understand what it was or what it could do. After helping to work on a test pilot for top-up payments via QR codes and seeing the future of finance flourish in other markets, I sought out a course to learn more. I found an impressive, executive course at Ivey Business School at Western University in Toronto, focused on fintech, digital identity, and blockchain, taught by Professor Michael King, a multibook author, in the fall of 2017.

We were required to complete an 80-hour preread of global articles, case studies, and insights on emerging technologies before being allowed to join the three-day course, which alone tells you how intense it was. This was attended by top executives from banks, wealth firms, and insurance companies, as well as me. I felt overwhelmed as everyone introduced themselves; I was a senior director at a fintech company. I soon realized that my work on payment innovation and within fintech meant I was in the right place and had a lot to contribute.

That course changed my life. It helped me understand the power of fintech even back in 2017, the impact fintechs could have on financial inclusion, to what blockchain was, and to how it could revolutionize the future. It helped me grasp what digital identity is and why it is so important for consumers to be empowered when identity is implemented with data protection.

When Professor King began discussing blockchain, what it powered, and its potential, I was intrigued. It was a hot topic, and I had many questions about how it worked, its auditability, what nodes were, and how it would revolutionize the future. I soaked up so much knowledge in those three days! I pushed myself beyond my usual limits in reading and focus, and I made some good friends who were there as well.

One of those new friends, Malcolm Clarke, featured as the opening quote for this chapter. When I met Malcolm, he was focused on digital identity and payments at TD Bank, where he created one of the first bank-backed private digital identity blockchains, Verified.me. His work on this led to patents that are still valid, describing how digital identity and payment move and create private, immutable chains. Malcolm has remained a leading voice over the years, with roles at Disney, Early Warning (Zelle), and SMBC. He is currently the vice president of Assets and Ecosystem at Western Union. Malcolm also shared a comment that struck me as the right next step for the ecosystem: "Our challenge now is not proving the technology works but ensuring it scales responsibly so moving value, or a digital item becomes as simple, secure, and ubiquitous as sending a text message."

My other new friend was Rajan Bansi, the business head of the micro-investing platform InvestEasy at RBC Bank, who is now the head of portfolio at a well-known investment firm and holds many board seats. I learned so much from both as we worked on a project together during that course.

My passion for innovation was solidified through Michael King's teaching, which prepared me for a "hot seat" moment when I had to explain blockchain to a room of older donors instead of the students I had prepared for. I pivoted on the fly, comparing blockchain's evolution to the early days of the Internet to help the audience grasp its role in driving transparency and trust. Seeing the audience finally grasp these complex concepts was incredibly rewarding and solidified my passion for helping others step into the future of finance.

Benefits vs. Challenges

As I mentioned at the start, there are both supporters and skeptics of blockchain's potential. Let me break it down for you. Supporters of blockchain emphasize its ability to enable trust-minimized coordination, programmable money, and global settlement without centralized intermediaries. From this view, decentralized infrastructure unlocks financial inclusion, automated markets, and entirely new economic models such as DeFi, tokenized assets, and autonomous agents. Proponents also point to growing institutional adoption, including JPMorgan's Kinexys platform, Fidelity Digital Assets, and U.S. Spot Bitcoin ETFs, as evidence that blockchain is transitioning from experimental technology to core financial infrastructure.

Key Benefits

24/7 Global Settlement

Transactions settle instantly across borders, without banking-hour limitations or weekend delays.

Programmable Money

Smart contracts enable automated execution of complex financial agreements without intermediaries.

Transparency and Auditability

Immutable ledgers provide real-time verification and complete transaction history for compliance.

Reduced Counterparty Risk

Cryptographic security and decentralized validation minimize reliance on trusted third parties.

Financial Inclusion

Open networks enable access to financial services for unbanked and underbanked populations globally.

Tokenization of Assets

Real-world assets can be fractionalized and traded with improved liquidity and reduced barriers.

Key Wins

- BlackRock's BUIDL Tokenized Treasury Fund, officially known as the BlackRock USD Institutional Digital Liquidity Fund, was available in March 2025, with AUM amounts above $1.7 billion as of early 2025.[9]
- DeFi adoption by mainstream players remains cautious: Total tokenized assets (about $25 billion) and institutional DeFi participation are growing but not yet widespread.

Challenges

Skeptics, however, argue that many blockchain implementations are over-engineered solutions to problems already addressed by existing databases and payment rails. They highlight persistent challenges around scalability, regulatory uncertainty, fragmented user experience, and recurring security failures. From this perspective, blockchain often introduces complexity without delivering proportional benefits, except in narrow domains such as censorship-resistant assets or speculative trading.

Scalability Limitations

Most blockchains still lag far behind centralized payment systems in raw throughput. Visa processes around 8,500 transactions per second (TPS) on average,[10] while major public blockchains handle far fewer: Bitcoin around 7 TPS and Ethereum roughly 15–30 TPS on the base layer.[11]

Regulatory Uncertainty

Fragmented global regulations create compliance complexity and slow institutional adoption.

Poor User Experience

Complex wallet management, irreversible transactions, and technical jargon create barriers to adoption.

Security Vulnerabilities

Smart contract bugs, bridge hacks, and key management failures have led to billions in losses.

Energy Consumption and Transaction Costs

Proof-of-work blockchains consume significant electricity, raising environmental sustainability concerns. Users also pay the blockchain network to process, secure, and record transactions. These transaction costs are called "gas fees," typically paid in cryptocurrency. Fees are based on the complexity of the transaction.

Integration Complexity

Connecting blockchain systems to legacy infrastructure requires substantial technical investment and redesign.

Notable Failures

Terra/Luna Ecosystem Failure (2022): $40+ billion wiped out when algorithmic stablecoin UST depegged, exposing flaws in unsustainable economic models.

Mt. Gox Exchange Hack (2014): 850,000 BTC stolen ($450 M at the time, $60+ billion at 2021 peak), the largest crypto exchange failure, highlighting custody risks.

As you can see, there are many benefits and many challenges, and the future will include both traditional and blockchain-based technology.

The Search for Product-Market Fit Pilots, Prototypes, and Pivots

The current reality of blockchain is best understood through the outcomes of the past eight years of experimentation. After the surge of enthusiasm in 2018, blockchain was widely tested across industries ranging from shipping logistics to estate law, as organizations explored where the technology could add real value.

The use cases highlighted in Figure 8.2 represent the most significant of these experiments. While not all of them displaced the legacy systems they aimed to disrupt, each one offered a critical lesson. They taught us the difference between what can be done technically and what should be done economically. Some paved the way for the financial plumbing we use today, while others proved that sometimes, a standard database is actually the better solution. Let's look at them more closely.

These examples demonstrate that when blockchain is applied to specific frictions, it moves from experimental theory to essential core infrastructure. A perfect example of this is cross-border transaction settlements.

1. Instant Global Payments (P2P/B2B Settlement)

Blockchain and digital currencies such as USDC (a stablecoin) and Bitcoin enable instant, global money transfers. Until recently, the usual way to transfer money internationally was to use intermediary banks, paying fees and incurring

Figure 8.2 Financial blockchain use cases

Financial Blockchain Use Cases

High-Impact Application Chart

Financial Blockchain Use Cases: High-Impact Chart

Use Case & Business Value	Live Example	Key Stats
Instant Global Payments (P2P/B2B Settlement) USDC and Bitcoin enable instant global transfers outside banks and SWIFT, reducing fees from 3–7% to under 1%.	**Stripe** USDC payments settle instantly. Companies moved 20% of volume to stablecoins, cutting costs by half.	**$10B** savings by 2030. **85–90%** of major institutions are piloting adoption.
Securities Settlement (Atomic Settlement) Settlement moved from T+2 to T+1 and is progressing toward 24/7 atomic settlement, reducing risk and volatility.	**J.P. Morgan Kinexys** Uses JPM Coin to settle billions in intraday repo transactions.	**97%** of investors expect tokenization to transform asset management.
DeFi (Decentralized Finance) Smart contracts support direct trading, lending, and borrowing with fewer intermediaries, creating faster and more transparent services.	**PayPal & Aave** PYUSD earns rewards through DeFi protocols for global commerce.	**$250B** locked in DeFi as of early 2026. Institutions use it for assets and treasury operations.
Tokenized Securities (Digital Ownership) Blockchain tokens enable 24/7 trading, faster settlement, and fractional ownership.	**BlackRock BUIDL Fund** $2.3B in assets, offering U.S. Treasury yields with 24/7 liquidity.	**$18.9T** projected by 2033. nables batch verification, thousands of identities in one transaction
Digital Identity & KYC (Private Verification) SSI, DIDs, and ZKPs verify identity or status without exposing personal details.	**Mastercard Crypto Credential** Uses off-chain verification and an on-chain badge to confirm compliance. **Sovrin Network** Provides verifiable credentials for finance and DeFi.	**70–90%** less manual compliance. Thousands of identities can be checked at once.
Blockchain in Supply Chain Finance Blockchain improves SME liquidity, releases financing at milestones, and processes Letters of Credit in hours instead of days.	**Walmart & IBM Food Trust** Shares secure supply-chain data and traces food origins in seconds.	Helps close a **$2.5T** trade gap and cuts settlement times by **50%.** Letters of credit: **days to hours.**
Blockchain-Enabled Insurance & Instant Claims Smart contracts use flight or weather data to trigger automatic payouts and reduce manual claims.	**Etherisc** Flight and weather data trigger automatic insurance payouts.	Payouts in **days vs. months.** 100% automated claims processing.
Institutional Access via Spot Bitcoin ETFs Spot Bitcoin ETFs provide regulated Bitcoin access without direct self-custody, reducing custody barriers.	**U.S. SEC Approval** Approved ETFs from BlackRock, Fidelity, and ARK 21Shares provide Bitcoin exposure through regulated markets.	**$124B+** in AUM within 2 years and **$2T+** cummulativetrading volume.

multiday delays, via a bank and Society for Worldwide Interbank Financial Telecommunication (SWIFT). SWIFT is a network that banks use to communicate securely with each other. Blockchain-based transfers allow peer-to-peer and B2B entities to bypass intermediary banks, reducing average transaction fees from 3 to 7% to less than 1%.[12] This shift is projected to save global businesses more than $10 billion by 2030, according to Juniper Research,[13] with institutional adoption reaching record highs as roughly 85–90% of major financial institutions now pilot or fully integrate these systems.[14]

Live use case: Stripe now allows businesses to accept USDC payments that settle near-instantly, a move that Stripe reports has helped some companies shift 20% of their volume to stablecoins, cutting costs by half.

2. Securities Settlement (Atomic Settlement)

While traditional securities settlements historically required a two-day (T+2) period, major markets like the U.S. and Canada officially transitioned to a one-day (T+1) standard in May 2024. To eliminate remaining time-sensitive risks and price volatility, the industry is now moving toward "atomic settlements," the simultaneous, 24/7 exchange of assets for digital currencies. As noted by J.P. Morgan Kinexys, "This blockchain-powered shift allows for near-instantaneous trades, with 97% of institutional investors agreeing that tokenization will revolutionize asset management."[15]

Live use case: J.P. Morgan (Kinexys) uses its JPM Coin to settle billions in intraday repo transactions, allowing banks to borrow and lend cash for just a few hours with surgical precision.

3. Decentralized Finance (DeFi)

Decentralized finance (DeFi) is a global ecosystem of blockchain-based applications that reduces reliance on traditional intermediaries like banks. Automated smart contracts allow users to trade, lend, and borrow directly, with transactions executed instantly and securely.

In 2018, many thought this technology could mean the end of banks. It is now clear that it represents the future of bank technology, not replacing banks, but making financial services faster, more transparent, and automated. Smart contracts were once hyped as code that could replace lawyers or run companies. Today, they are practical tools that automate payments, stablecoin swaps, and other routine processes, reducing intermediaries, lowering costs, and speeding up settlements. As of early 2026, $250 billion is locked in DeFi applications (TVL) according to DeFiLlama, showing the scale of value in this ecosystem.[16] Institutional players are increasingly using DeFi to manage real-world assets and streamline treasury operations.[17]

Live use case: PayPal now allows customers to use its PYUSD stablecoin in DeFi protocols such as Aave to earn rewards or to use digital dollars for global commerce.[18]

4. Tokenized Securities (Digital Ownership)

Turning tangible or digital assets into blockchain tokens enables 24/7 trading, instant settlement, and "fractional ownership." According to a Ripple Report published in 2025, this is expected to reach $18.9 trillion by 2033.[19]

Live use case: BlackRock's BUIDL Fund has surpassed $2.3 billion in assets, offering institutional investors a way to earn US Treasury yields directly on the blockchain with 24/7 liquidity.[20]

5. Blockchain in Supply Chain Finance

In 2018, the industry focused on putting the entire supply chain, from raw materials to retail, on a shared distributed ledger, with the idea that greater transparency would improve verification and consumer trust. By 2025, financial institutions were using blockchain to help bridge the $2.5 trillion global trade-finance gap, unlocking liquidity for small and medium-sized businesses. Smart contracts can trigger financing automatically when supply chain milestones are met, reducing reliance on paper-based systems and cutting settlement times by up to 50%. Digitized letters of credit can be processed within hours rather than days, and immutable record-keeping strengthens security and accountability in cross-border trade finance.[21]

Live use case: Walmart has teamed up with IBM to use the IBM Food Trust Network, a blockchain-enabled platform that lets food suppliers, processors, and retailers share secure data about products from farm to table. By using blockchain, Walmart can trace the origin of food items in seconds, improving safety and reducing risk compared with traditional tracking methods.

6. Digital Identity and KYC (Private Verification)

In 2018, the fintech industry introduced self-sovereign identity, using blockchain-based decentralized identifiers to give users total control over their digital personas. As covered in Chapter 4, this technology promised a major shift toward a password-less future, replacing traditional logins with secure credentials stored directly in a personal crypto wallet. While early adoption stalled due to complex key management, the industry has pivoted toward a portable and reusable identity model that balances personal control with institutional trust.

For businesses, this blockchain-enabled verification can reduce manual compliance workloads by up to 90% by eliminating redundant document handling. Companies such as Mastercard now use these digital credentials to verify users for blockchain transactions, ensuring compliance with anti-money laundering laws without storing sensitive personal data. This hybrid approach streamlines onboarding for DeFi and traditional banking while protecting user privacy and enhancing security for all parties involved.

Live use case: A prominent real-world application is the Sovrin Network, which uses blockchain to issue and verify decentralized identifiers for both individuals and organizations. This network allows users to securely share verified credentials across different financial platforms, significantly speeding up the KYC process for modern fintech services.

7. Blockchain-Enabled Insurance and Instant Claims

Blockchain-enabled smart contracts enable instant payouts for travel, crop, and other types of insurance via Oracles, which provide verified real-world data feeds. When a preset condition is met, such as a flight cancelation or a rainfall threshold for crops, the smart contract automatically triggers a digital currency payout. This bypasses the traditional manual claims process, reducing delays and administrative overhead while ensuring policyholders are compensated immediately.[22]

Live use case: Etherisc, a blockchain-based insurance platform, offers automated flight delay insurance. When an insured flight is delayed, a smart contract receives real-time flight data via oracles and automatically triggers payouts to affected travelers in cryptocurrency, eliminating manual claims and accelerating compensation.[23] Crop insurance pilots also use this approach to compensate farmers automatically based on verified weather data.

8. Institutional Access via Spot Bitcoin ETFs

Spot Bitcoin exchange-traded funds (ETFs) represent a blockchain use case that bridges decentralized digital assets with regulated capital markets. These ETFs hold actual Bitcoin on behalf of investors and trade on traditional stock exchanges, allowing institutions and retail allocators to gain exposure to the blockchain-native asset without direct custody or private key management. By tokenizing Bitcoin for regulated markets, spot ETFs reduce operational frictions and legal complexity while providing transparent, on-chain backed exposure, a key adoption pathway for mainstream finance.

Live use case: In January 2024, the U.S. Securities and Exchange Commission (SEC) approved multiple spot Bitcoin ETFs from major asset managers, including BlackRock, Fidelity, and ARK 21Shares.[24] These ETFs began trading immediately after approval, offering Bitcoin exposure through a familiar regulated vehicle.

Blockchain Unlocks Web3

Web3 refers to the next generation of the Internet, characterized by decentralization, transparency, and user control. Instead of big companies controlling your data and digital interactions, as in Web2, the power shifts toward individual users. This includes ownership of digital assets, direct control of personal data, and participation in distributed systems.

If you think in eras:

- Web1 = read-only (static websites, early Internet)
- Web2 = read + write (social media, apps, platforms like Google, Facebook, Amazon)
- Web3 = read + write + own

With Web3, you don't just use the Internet; you participate in and own parts of it. Web3 is enabled by blockchain technology, which allows the Internet to function without a central authority. More plainly, blockchain is a shared, secure record that everyone can trust. It removes the need for middlemen, like companies or platforms. It lets people own digital assets and identities directly, and apps can run on public code, such as smart contracts, rather than on private servers. So instead of a company controlling the app and your data, the network runs the app, and you control your data. Blockchain provides the trust, ownership, and automation that make Web3 possible.

Web3 aligns with the future of finance by shifting control from centralized bank databases to direct individual ownership of digital assets through secure wallets. This movement utilizes smart contracts to automate financial agreements and enable the instant settlement required for a 24/7 global market. By integrating decentralized identifiers, Web3 ensures data sovereignty and allows users to verify their identity for financial services without compromising their privacy.

Ultimately, Web3 provides an interoperable digital infrastructure where value moves as freely as information, returning financial power and data rights to the individual. By using smart contracts, agreements are automated, removing expensive middlemen while creating a permanent, tamper-proof history of every action. Most importantly, blockchain enables true digital ownership, allowing you to hold and move your assets directly through your own secure wallet.

The Four Challenges in Blockchain Adoption

Blockchain has demonstrated clear benefits in finance, including improved security, transparency, and traceability. However, it is not always the most affordable or efficient solution for a given use case. Much of the industry's experience reflects a broader pattern of hype versus reality. In 2018, blockchain was promoted as a technology that could replace entire systems and disrupt banks overnight. While many pilots proved technically viable, adoption stalled due to regulatory friction, entrenched processes, and the difficulty of changing human behavior. Additionally, latency and block size limitations limit how much data can be processed on-chain, reinforcing that blockchain is a powerful tool but not a universal replacement for existing infrastructure. As with any technology, its use should be justified by a clear cost/benefit tradeoff.

Blockchain is a powerful tool, but its adoption faces a complex matrix of economic and technical hurdles that determine where it genuinely adds value versus introducing redundant complexity. Figure 8.3 outlines the core barriers

Figure 8.3 Blockchain adoption barriers

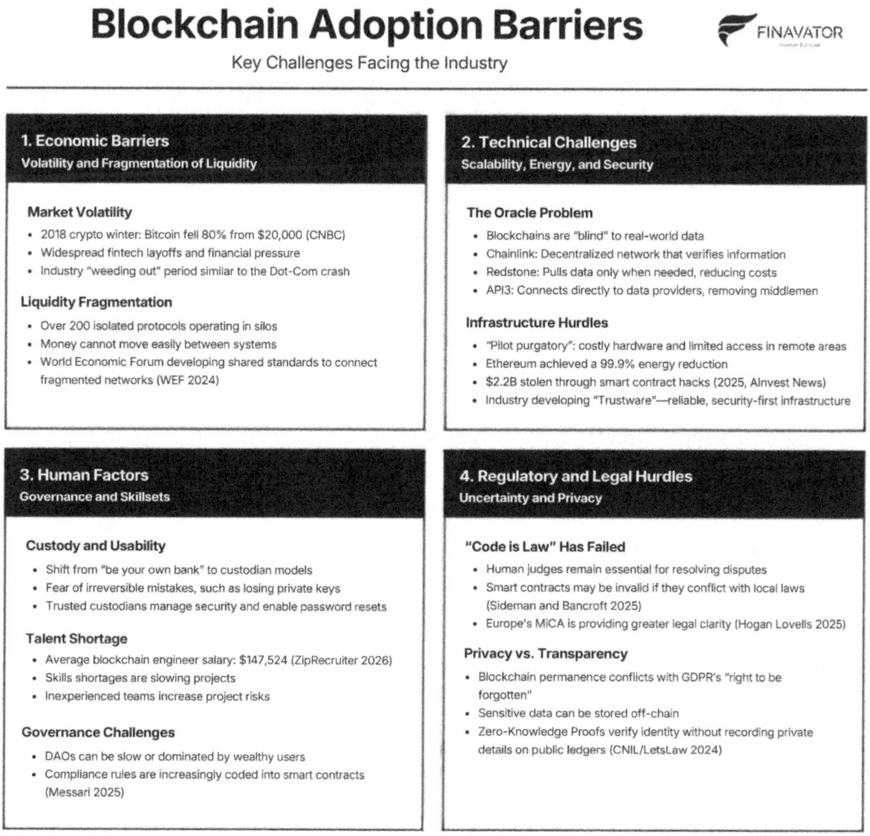

organizations must navigate as they move from experimental hype toward scalable implementation. These challenges underscore the reality that "code is law" often fails when confronted with real-world legal systems. By addressing critical security risks and the global talent gap, the industry is maturing into a more resilient "trustware" infrastructure designed for the long-term digital economy.

Solving these challenges through innovations like zero-knowledge proofs is how the industry is maturing into a more resilient and sustainable "trustware" layer for the future.

1. Economic Barriers (Volatililty and Fragmented Liquidity)

The 2018 "crypto winter," when Bitcoin fell roughly 80% from its peak, exposed the risks of speculative excess and triggered widespread layoffs across fintech. While the market has since matured, a new challenge has emerged: liquidity fragmentation. With hundreds of isolated protocols, capital cannot move seamlessly across ecosystems. As a result, organizations such as the World Economic Forum are developing shared standards to connect these siloed systems (WEF 2024).

2. Technical Challenges (Scalability, Energy, and Security)

Blockchains cannot directly access real-world data, creating the "oracle problem." Solutions like Chainlink, Redstone, and API3 aim to deliver reliable data more efficiently. Still, many projects remain stuck in pilot stages due to high hardware costs and limited connectivity in remote areas. These constraints have pushed the industry toward building more reliable "trustware," prioritizing security and sustainability over hype. Examples include Ethereum's 99.9% reduction in energy consumption and stricter audits following smart contract exploits that drained $2.2 billion in 2025. Despite progress, global scalability remains unproven.[25]

3. Human Factors (Governance and Skillsets)

The ideal of fully self-custodied finance has given way to practical concerns around usability and risk. As irreversible errors can have severe consequences, trusted custodians now play a central role in security and recovery. Talent shortages of further slow adoption: the average salary for a blockchain engineer in the United States reached $147,524, increasing costs and risks for projects led by inexperienced teams.[26] Meanwhile, decentralized governance often proves slow or concentrated among wealthy participants, prompting many organizations to embed compliance and decision rules directly into code.

4. Regulatory and Legal Hurdles (Uncertainty and Privacy)

The notion that "code is law" has proven unrealistic, as smart contracts remain subject to local legal systems. While frameworks such as Europe's MiCA provide greater clarity, privacy remains a key tension. Blockchain's immutability conflicts with GDPR's "right to be forgotten," leading institutions to store sensitive data off-chain and rely on zero-knowledge proofs to verify information without exposing personal data.

Enterprise and Infrastructure Innovations

The many challenges related to blockchain use and development present opportunities for improvement and further innovation. The following are some of the more valuable innovations:

Zero-Knowledge Proofs

Zero-knowledge proofs enable transactions to be verified without revealing sensitive financial or personal data, helping reconcile privacy requirements with transparency and auditability.

Confidential Computing

Encrypted execution systems allow smart contracts to run while protecting proprietary data and trading strategies, significantly improving enterprise-grade privacy and security.

Permissioned Distributed Ledger Technologies

Controlled access, governance and compliance-friendly architectures, such as Hyperledger Fabric and Corda, are increasingly used for regulated use cases.

Quantum-Resistant Cryptography

There are concerns about potential future threats from quantum computing, as it is designed to crack mathematical algorithms used in blockchain. Financial systems are exploring post-quantum cryptographic algorithms to secure private keys. While there is fear of Bitcoin theft, quantum-resistant cryptography is moving to the forefront of development.

Scaling and Performance Advancements

As with any powerful technology, developers are constantly innovating to improve blockchain, making it perform better, faster, and more economically. Those same developers have to work within ever-evolving regulations added to address transparency, liability, and legal issues that have come to light, which might affect scalability.

When thinking about the layers of a blockchain, I like to use an analogy popular among industry experts: the layered cake. Layer 1 is the solid foundation, or sponge base, that provides the essential strength and security to keep the entire structure standing. Layer 2 is the fast-moving top layer designed for speed and the "flavor" of daily interactions. These layers work in harmony to enable faster, cheaper digital transactions without compromising safety. This layered approach allows the future of finance to handle millions of users at once while reducing costs to less than a penny and keeping the foundation tamper-proof.[27]

The technology making this possible is called a *rollup*. It bundles hundreds of transactions into a single entry, cutting costs by 99%, and making digital payments viable for everyone.

There are two main ways this works.

1. ***Optimistic rollups*** use a trust-but-verify approach, assuming transactions are honest but allowing a one-week window for challenges to surface. This is the popular method for day-to-day commerce, used by leaders such as Arbitrum, Optimism, and Coinbase's Base network.
2. ***ZK rollups*** use mathematical proofs to verify transactions instantly, providing a digital certificate of accuracy. This high-security method is used by zkSync and Starknet and is being adopted by giants such as Sony's Soneium network. While more complex to build, ZK Rollups offer the instant finality required for institutional finance.

As the digital economy expands, the necessity for diverse blockchain networks to communicate has led to the rise of cross-chain bridges. These connectors currently link more than 200 networks, facilitating the free movement of data and capital to solve the critical issue of liquidity fragmentation. This interconnectedness, known as interoperability, is vital for creating a powerful and unified financial ecosystem. However, the Hyperledger Foundation's Enterprise DLT Report 2025 warns that this complexity introduces significant security and governance challenges. These risks are underscored by the fact that bridge exploits have historically resulted in more than $2 billion in losses, making robust safety protocols essential. To mitigate these threats, new asset protection standards are required to ensure that moving value between chains remains secure. Ultimately, ConsenSys's State of Blockchain 2025 asserts that these bridges are the foundation for a seamless future where different blockchains operate as one.

While all of these developments enhance the value of blockchain in finance, as usage increases in volume and across more industries, further advancements will be necessary. It's a good idea to stay abreast of changes through verifiable news sources and expert podcasts.

The Global Impact of Blockchain

As of this writing, there are 24,999 reachable nodes worldwide using blockchain.[28] The daily volume of blockchain transactions has passed the $3 trillion mark, and the annual market growth rate is 65.2%. The estimated $39.7 billion global blockchain market demonstrates its value and level of acceptance.[29]

Unfortunately, since its adoption by the general public, the Internet has been filled with misinformation and unverified data. I'm excited about the potential of blockchain to democratize data. I see blockchain as a valuable layer on top of the information available on the Internet. It allows for validation, security, and sharing.

Will we eventually use blockchain to track the voting process? The 2025 pilot in Bolivia suggests the answer is yes, but with a focus on auditability over just accessibility. By using the blockchain as a permanent, public record book for election results, we are moving toward a future where "trust" is no longer something we give to a central agency, but something we verify for ourselves through math. This is the same "trustware" that is currently transforming global finance, now being applied to the very foundation of democracy.[30] Think about the impact it could have on eliminating voter fraud, something that is often in the news and costing millions of dollars when a recount is determined as necessary.

I don't believe blockchain is meant to touch everything, as implementation costs can be high. It serves a valuable purpose by keeping data in a chain that validates the information. No single person or node can move a blockchain in the wrong direction. Multiple nodes in the chain can validate, making it a source of truth.

When I think about the future of blockchain, I see it continuously evolving. I look at new use cases to see how they can help with financial inclusion. I think about how it can help people who move to another country for political or economic reasons and want to send money back home without delay or incurring high transfer fees. I truly feel that if you're looking at the future of finance, you also have to consider this technology, as it has so much potential.

Expert Interview with Emma Todd, CEO of MMH Blockchain Group

I first met Emma Todd through a friend in 2018, and since then, I've had the pleasure of working alongside her on a crypto custody project for a bank and sharing the stage with her. Her passion and voice are widely recognized across the blockchain ecosystem, and I'm excited to bring her perspectives to this conversation.

When I think about blockchain and its potential to reshape finance, Emma stands out for her unique combination of banking experience and forward-looking vision. As CEO of MMH Blockchain Group, she bridges two worlds: 15 years in traditional banking and 8 years pioneering blockchain applications. She's presented at the United Nations, speaks annually at the World Economic Forum in Davos, and regularly travels to Washington, DC, participating in coalitions exploring how blockchain can help businesses. This dual perspective gives her insights that pure technologists and pure bankers often miss.

I was excited to feature Emma, who represents something essential: someone who understands the system from the inside and can clearly explain why it needs to change. Her journey into blockchain began at a conference, where a friend first introduced her to Bitcoin. One moment made the inefficiencies impossible to ignore: a speaker described paying thousands in fees for a tiny transfer, while Emma had recently paid hundreds to move a relatively small sum through traditional banking. That stark contrast sparked her focus. Nearly a decade later, she is still working to improve the system.

What stands out most about Emma is her refusal to treat blockchain as either a savior or a threat. She sees it as infrastructure, like the Internet or electricity: "You don't need to understand how it works to benefit from it." At its core, blockchain is a distributed ledger system, a database in which control is distributed among participants rather than centralized. This decentralization enables enhanced privacy, stronger security, and unprecedented traceability.

Throughout our conversation, Emma emphasized blockchain's potential as a force for good. Her favorite use case is food traceability. A few years ago, California experienced a Salmonella outbreak in lettuce. Authorities couldn't pinpoint the source of contamination, so they destroyed lettuce from an entire region. Imagine being a farmer whose entire year's livelihood is destroyed, not as your farm was contaminated but because the system lacked a precise tracking mechanism. Blockchain-enabled traceability can pinpoint contamination to specific farms, protecting innocent farmers while ensuring consumer safety.

Her absolute favorite application combines traceability with direct economic impact. Some coffee houses now use blockchain to enable customers to tip the farmer who grew their beans. When you pay $6 for your coffee, blockchain traceability allows money to flow directly to the farmer, bypassing traditional supply chains in which producers typically receive only a tiny fraction of the final price. This demonstrates how blockchain can create tangible, positive outcomes for people with the least power in global supply chains.

Emma sees blockchain as revolutionary for finance. "After two centuries of banking dominance, blockchain demonstrates that you don't necessarily need banks to store or transfer money. Peer-to-peer systems like Bitcoin, created in 2008 after the financial crisis, were designed to reduce dependence on banks. Emma describes it as "turning the banking system on its ear."

Her perspective is pragmatic: this isn't an either/or scenario. Traditional finance and blockchain-based systems can coexist. Take El Salvador: when the country embraced Bitcoin, it faced resistance from the World Bank and IMF. If El Salvador's Bitcoin holdings appreciate significantly, it could pay off IMF debt, threatening the IMF's business model. Meanwhile, coexistence is emerging in practice: JPMorgan Chase and community banks are adopting blockchain and crypto offerings, with customers splitting their savings between fiat and crypto, reflecting behavioral shifts in everyday finance.

When I asked Emma what she wanted people to understand about blockchain, her answer was grounded. "Blockchain can be used for good, but not every problem requires it. Sometimes a simple database or even a spreadsheet suffices." Blockchain can be expensive and time-consuming. Her advice: "Assess your needs carefully before adopting it. Should you build your own blockchain or leverage existing platforms like Ethereum? Should it be private or public? Thoughtful analysis is critical, and avoiding buzzword chasing is essential."

What comes through powerfully is the human dimension. Emma saw people paying hundreds of dollars to send money and thought, "This is wrong; there must be a better way." She gets genuinely excited thinking about coffee farmers receiving tips directly from consumers thousands of miles away. Her passion isn't about disrupting banks for disruption's sake; it's about creating systems that work better for people, especially the least powerful.

For Emma, blockchain is ultimately about dignity and equity: enabling value to flow directly to creators, protecting the innocent through transparency, and reducing unfair tolls extracted by intermediaries. Her insights can be summarized through three central themes shaping blockchain's transformation of finance:

These are key takeaways from Emma Todd on blockchain:

- Prioritize building solid infrastructure over market hype.
- Enhance traditional financial systems through collaboration versus replacement.
- Only implement blockchain when the value exceeds the implementation costs.

It has been a privilege to learn from Emma. Her perspective reflects the industry's evolution: blockchain is no longer a curiosity but infrastructure shaping operations, supply chains, and value flows across borders. The key question isn't whether blockchain will matter, but whether we implement it thoughtfully to realize its potential for good.

Speaking with Emma Todd reinforced an essential truth: blockchain is not magic or a cure-all. It's a powerful infrastructure that, when used strategically, creates transparent, equitable, and efficient systems. The most common misconception is equating blockchain with Bitcoin or cryptocurrency. In reality, blockchain is a distributed, decentralized database technology that enables cryptocurrency but has far broader applications. Blockchain doesn't need to disrupt traditional finance to succeed; smart implementation beats buzzword chasing every time.

Blockchain's Alignment to the Future of Finance

Today, the blockchain revolution looks very different from what we predicted. It didn't replace the Internet; instead, it quietly upgraded the financial infrastructure beneath it. The technology works, but it underestimated the friction of the real world. Human error, legal processes, and corporate competition cannot simply be coded away.

Still, blockchain is a powerful tool. It enables faster, cheaper payments worldwide; allows people to tokenize assets from stocks to real estate; and, through

DeFi, lets consumers lend and borrow in ways that are reshaping the future of finance. Even with everything we understand today, we can barely imagine the innovations blockchain may unlock for our lives in the years to come.

Advances in decentralized systems and artificial intelligence are reshaping the future of financial markets by embedding autonomous computational agents directly into blockchain-based economic infrastructure. These on-chain AI agents are software entities that continuously make decisions, execute transactions, and manage digital assets without human oversight, effectively serving as autonomous financial operators in decentralized finance (DeFi) and broader markets.[31] Ethereum co-founder Vitalik Buterin predicts that AI agents will soon become the "primary category of users" on the blockchain, autonomously managing wealth and executing strategies 24/7.[32] This shift is powered by verifiable inference (zkML), cryptographic proofs that mathematically verify an AI's output is correct without exposing private data or proprietary code. By replacing "blind trust" with "cryptographic proof," this technology allows autonomous agents to navigate the global economy with unprecedented security and accountability. This transforms opaque algorithmic decisions into trustworthy, auditable proofs that smart contracts and participants can verify before accepting an agent's action.

Blockchain has not replaced traditional financial systems, nor is it likely to do so wholesale. Instead, its most durable applications are emerging in specific areas where decentralization provides clear advantages, including shared settlement layers across institutions, programmable financial contracts, digital asset custody, and permissionless innovation at the edges of the system. At the same time, traditional finance continues to provide critical strengths in governance, compliance, consumer protection, and capital efficiency.

Rather than a zero-sum contest between TradFi and DeFi, the future appears increasingly hybrid. Regulated institutions are adopting blockchain rails for settlement and asset issuance, while decentralized ecosystems absorb institutional capital and risk frameworks. Progress will depend less on ideology and more on collaboration, combining blockchain's openness and automation with traditional finance's stability, regulatory structure, and operational maturity.

In that sense, blockchain's role in the future of finance is not to replace existing systems but to augment them, reducing friction where possible, enabling new forms of coordination, and gradually reshaping financial infrastructure through practical, incremental adoption.

By 2030, blockchain technology is projected to generate $3.1 trillion in annual business value. This value is expected to come from cost savings driven by operational efficiency, new revenue streams enabled by tokenized assets, and reduced fraud across global supply chains.[33]

The future of finance won't be shaped solely by blockchain, as many technologies are coming together to empower consumers. Blockchain has helped underserved consumers achieve financial inclusion. Blockchain is not the solution to every problem; it's essential to thoughtfully choose when to integrate it alongside traditional systems and identify when it is not needed. We are seeing that the world is large enough for conventional institutions and decentralized systems to coexist, each serving consumers' needs in ways that are both similar and different.

Chapter 8 Key Takeaways

1. Blockchain is a distributed ledger (a digital record book) shared across a network rather than stored in a centralized location. It functions as the trustware infrastructure of our digital world. It offers tamper-evident records that helps to enhance trust across the financial sector. Like the Internet, you don't need to fully understand how it works to benefit from it.
2. Blockchain enables trust in digital transactions by validating them across multiple computers (nodes), helping enable digital currencies, supply chain transparency, and a wide range of use cases across virtually all industries, empowering consumers all around the world.
3. **Personal lesson:** The best way to understand the infrastructure of any technology is to be curious, ask questions, watch explainer videos, listen to podcasts, attend conferences, and, for me, say yes to get on stage to explain it to others.

Chapter 9

Money in the Digital Age: The Rise of Digital Currencies

"The future of money lies in systems where value is digitized, programmable, and interoperable across decentralized and traditional networks alike."

—Professor Michael R. King, Lansdowne Chair in Finance at the University of Victoria, fintech author, former Ivey professor and economist at the BIS and Bank of Canada

Digital currency is the final, and perhaps most transformative, element of the future of finance. It isn't just a new type of money; it is a fundamental shift in how money moves. In the wake of the 2008 financial crisis, the demand for financial empowerment skyrocketed. Today, digital currency provides a bridge for consumers around the world, including the unbanked. With nothing more than a smartphone, a user can join the global economy, sending payments, securing loans, and investing in assets that were once gated by traditional institutions.

At the core of this shift is blockchain technology, a digital ledger with a decentralized framework of trust. This enables "atomic settlement" to execute transactions as a single, indivisible event. Unlike the traditional banking system, where payments can get stuck in a web of intermediary delays, digital currencies allow both parties to settle a trade instantly and simultaneously. If one side of the deal isn't met, the smart contract ensures the transaction never happens.

By focusing on transparency and speed, we are building more accountable systems, as recommended by Michael R. King in his chapter-opening quote, to move money. Since every transaction is written on a blockchain, the record is permanent and can be checked by anyone. This moves us away from closed, private ledgers to a transparent system where it is much harder for bad actors to hide.

What Are Digital Currencies?

Digital currencies are forms of money that exist only in electronic form. Think of it as money that lives in your digital wallet on your phone, rather than in your physical wallet in the form of cash or coins. You access it through a digital wallet set up after a standard security check called *know your customer* (KYC). Your wallet generates a cryptographic address shown as a unique QR code that works like a digital mailing address, making it simple to send and receive digital money, such as Crypto, Stablecoins, or central bank digital currencies (CBDCs). The security aspect of using digital currency aligns well with my dedication to protecting our digital identities, as covered in Chapter 4.

Digital currencies are mostly decentralized, which means no single government or bank controls them. Instead, they run on distributed networks of computers (nodes). Transfers of funds are near real-time and incur only small fees. If you are in the United States and want to send $500 to a family member in Australia, a traditional bank service might cost $30 and take three to five days to complete. That same transfer in digital currency might cost $2 and take just a few minutes.

I have seen the adoption of digital currencies grow rapidly. Initially, it was only my crypto friends who talked about and used digital currencies. Now, even some of my friends' parents are talking about and using some form of digital currency.

Even though adoption is growing rapidly, this type of currency is still in the early stages of development. Major companies, banks, and governments are still experimenting with its use. Some governments are embracing one type of digital currency while others restrict or ban it. It's the same with the regulation of digital currencies. There is a wide range of views on its use, exchange rates, and taxation. So, it's important to stay on top of developments rather than jumping in with both feet and moving all your assets to digital currency.

When people start talking about digital currencies, they often mention Bitcoin first. Bitcoin was created in 2008, just after the financial crash, which was caused by some bad behavior by banks not just in the United States but also in the United Kingdom and other markets. The premise of Bitcoin was that users could avoid the challenges they faced with traditional financial institutions.

That financial crash is something that I will never forget. I worked at an international marketing company at the time, running online shopping malls for four airlines: United, Delta, Alaska, and Lufthansa. Even though I was in Canada and Canadian banks emerged from the financial crisis quite stable, we had US clients, so we were negatively impacted by the hit our clients took. Our whole staff took 10% pay cuts, and many people lost their jobs. I was pregnant with my first child and extremely stressed about everything.

It was not an easy time for anyone, especially for my US friends and clients. Seeing how many people lost their houses, their jobs, and their assets was devastating. I had to focus on what I *could* control, like becoming a new mom and helping my clients find ways to drive growth in online shopping during a market downturn. I'm happy to share that we helped our clients create opportunities for consumers to save and earn points while shopping for essential items. That option wasn't as widely available then as it is now. The lesson of focusing on what I could control was very helpful as I later faced other crises, including COVID, the crypto winter, and recent trade wars.

It was important to shift my focus to how I could help drive innovation, rather than worrying about everything that was causing panic. Living through those crises made me concerned for future crashes, and when I first fully understood the power of blockchain and digital currencies, I got excited. The potential for greater transparency to help avoid similar challenges felt like a step in the right direction, and stablecoin feels like we are getting even closer to a better future of finance.

Types of Digital Currency

There are four main types of digital currency in use: cryptocurrencies, stablecoins, CBDCs, and traditional digital fiat money. Although they all fall under the digital category, it's important to understand the significant differences in their risk levels and purposes.

Money is no longer a single pillar; it is a diverse ecosystem. Figure 9.1 summarizes the four types of digital currencies, and it helps to compare the distinct purposes and stability engines of digital instruments currently reshaping the economy. This matrix reveals that crypto, stablecoins, and CBDCs are not just competing; they are complementary pieces of a unified ledger linking traditional banking with Internet speed.

Cryptocurrency, or "crypto" as it's often called, is decentralized, meaning no government or central authority controls it, and it runs on a blockchain. Several companies facilitate the crypto marketplace. Coinbase is probably one of the largest and best-known names, at least in North America. To use their platform, you

Figure 9.1 Four types of digital currencies

4 Types of Digital Currency

FINAVATOR

Side-by-Side Comparison

Feature	Cryptocurrency (e.g., BTC, ETH)	Stablecoins (e.g., USDC, PYUSD)	CBDCs (Central Bank Digital)	Traditional Digital (e.g., PayPal, Banks)
Purpose	Decentralized, censorship-resistant store of value and utility.	Fiat stability with blockchain speed and programmability.	Modernize national payments and improve monetary policy efficiency.	Daily commerce within regulated banking system.
Controlled By	Decentralized network (Global)	Private companies/Protocols	Central banks (Government)	Commercial Banks/Private Companies
Price Stability	Highly volatile (Market-driven)	Stable (Pegged to assets like USD)	Stable (National currency value)	Stable (National currency value)
Blockchain-Based	✓ Yes	✓ Yes	Often (Varies by country)	✕ No (Centralized databases)
Legal Tender	✕ No (Except El Salvador)	✕ No	✓ Yes	✓ Yes
Anonymous	Pseudo-anonymous	Pseudo-anonymous	Not anonymous	Not anonymous
Main Use Case	Investment, DeFi, Store of Value	Global transfers, Instant settlement	Daily transactions, Government payouts	Daily commerce, Payroll, Bill pay
Primary Risk	**Market Volatility:** Prices can crash; loss of private keys is permanent.	**De-Pegging:** Risk that issuer doesn't have reserves to back the coin.	**Privacy**: Potential for government surveillance of all spending.	**Inefficiency**: Slow settlement (T+1/T+2) and high cross-border fees.

first have to verify that you are who you say you are, just as you do when you open a traditional bank account. Then you get a virtual crypto wallet. They're called *hot wallets*, and that's largely because that currency is literally living on that digital wallet. If you end up with a lot of cryptocurrencies, it is best to move it to what's called a *cold wallet*, which is kind of like a jump drive, if you remember those. If your currency is in a cold wallet, no one can attack it or try to steal it, as they might on a hot wallet infrastructure. Even if someone steals your physical cold wallet, they usually cannot access your crypto as it's locked with a PIN and strong security measures. Your coins are not stored in the device; they remain on the blockchain. Only if the thief gets your 12–24 recovery words can they open your wallet on another device and take everything, so those words must be kept secret and offline.

Examples of crypto are Bitcoin, Ethereum, Solana, Cardano, and XRP. "The first decentralized cryptocurrency, Bitcoin, was created with a fixed supply of 21 million coins. This supply of coins is a hard-coded limit that ensures only 21 million bitcoins will ever exist, creating a 'digital gold' that no government can print or inflate. This matters as it eliminates political unpredictability and replaces it with mathematical certainty, ensuring your share of the total supply can never be diluted. As supply is locked, the price moves up and down entirely due to a tug-of-war between buyers and sellers over global demand."[1]

Comparing bitcoin to concert tickets, when thousands more people want to attend than there is space in a venue, the price of those limited tickets skyrockets, but if excitement about the performance cools, the price drops. This "up and down" is simply the market's way of setting the value of a revolutionary new asset that is still in its early stages of global adoption.

Main use cases include investment, decentralized finance (DeFi), and serving as a store of value. The primary risks include market volatility, as prices have been known to fluctuate and even crash. Another concern is that if an exchange suddenly closes or you place your digital currency into a cold wallet like a jump drive and you lose the physical wallet or the codes to access your hot wallet on an exchange, such as your private keys, it is permanently lost.

Stablecoins are a type of cryptocurrency designed to maintain a stable value relative to a fiat currency (usually the US dollar) rather than fluctuate like Bitcoin or Ethereum. They are typically backed by reserve assets, such as cash, short-term government securities, or equivalents, to maintain a one-to-one peg with the underlying currency. Stablecoins aim to combine the stability of traditional money with the programmability and speed of digital currencies. They are widely used in digital finance, cross-border payments, decentralized finance, and programmable commerce.

Stablecoins are issued on multiple blockchains, with Ethereum being the most widely used. On Ethereum, stablecoins such as USDC and USDT are created as Ethereum Request for Comments (ERC-20) tokens, which follow a standard that allows easy integration with wallets and exchanges.[2] Other popular blockchains include Tron, Solana, and Polygon, chosen by users as of lower fees and faster transactions. Using standardized tokens like ERC-20 makes stablecoins widely compatible across the crypto ecosystem.

An ERC token is a type of digital token built on the Ethereum blockchain that follows common rules, so everything works together. This makes it easy for wallets, apps, and exchanges to send, receive, and use tokens such as USDC and USDT without additional setup."[3]

Central bank digital currencies are digital versions of government-issued money. They are created and regulated by central banks such as the European Central Bank; therefore, they have the same "legal tender" status as physical cash. China ignited the global digital currency race in 2019 with its digital yuan. "As of the end of November 2025, China had recorded 3.48 billion cumulative digital yuan transactions worth 16.7 trillion yuan (approximately 2.37 trillion US dollars)."[4] The Bahamas made history in 2020 by launching the Sand Dollar, the world's first fully operational retail CBDC, which now serves approximately 100,000 users across its islands.[5]

I couldn't close this chapter without mentioning BRICS, which is an alliance of emerging economies, including Brazil, India, China, and the United Arab Emirates. It is focused on creating independent financial systems where these countries can trade using their own local currencies. They are developing BRICS Pay to link local digital currencies, bypassing traditional Western networks. Their BRICS Coin remains an experimental unit for trade. Despite their collective economic scale, the block faces significant trust challenges due to internal geopolitical rivalries and inconsistent regulatory standards, making it difficult to achieve the transparency needed for a unified global alternative.

Many other countries have piloted digital CBDCs, though there are concerns about privacy and the lack of transparency into how these dollars are used. As a result, many countries have put their pilots on hold and are exploring other options. For example, "in 2025, Brazil decided to put its digital CBDC project on hold and, instead, consider private and government stablecoins."

It's important to note that in 2025, the United States passed the GENIUS Act, which effectively bans retail CBDC in favor of a regulated stablecoin framework. The key use case for CBDC is wholesale for daily transactions and government payouts. One of the most concerning reasons why CBDC pilots are not moving to implementation is the potential for government surveillance of all spending. Therefore, the retail version of CBDC is not ideal, yet it could help reduce costs and increase the efficiency of wholesale transactions. Ultimately, the global trend is pivoting away from government-controlled coins toward private, state-regulated digital assets.

Traditional digital fiat money is a national currency held in electronic accounts rather than on a blockchain. Managed by commercial banks and private payment providers, this type of system is the current global standard, serving billions of users through platforms like PayPal, Venmo, and Zelle, as well as mobile money giants like M-Pesa, WeChat Pay, and Alipay.

While effective for daily commerce and payroll, the system faces significant structural challenges, particularly in cross-border transactions, where funds often get stuck in a "liquidity trap" for days. A stark example of this inefficiency is the *intermediary tax* required to move money across borders; according to the World Bank, the global average cost of sending a cross-border payment remains approximately 6.49%.[6] This high cost/slow settlement (often taking two or more days) occurs as the money must pass through multiple "middleman" banks, each taking a fee and adding a delay. This friction highlights the primary limitation of our legacy financial plumbing, which blockchain-based alternatives aim to solve by enabling instant, low-cost settlement.

Today, digital currencies can be held in several ways, each with different levels of control and responsibility. In self-custody, users control their funds with a private key or recovery phrase, often through a hot wallet connected to the Internet or a cold wallet stored offline on separate hardware or on paper. While this offers maximum control, losing the private key means permanent loss of access with no recovery option. Many beginners instead choose crypto exchanges that offer custodial services, where the company holds the keys, handles account recovery, and provides customer support, trading full ownership for convenience and ease of use. Overall, users must choose between greater independence and higher responsibility, or easier access with shared control over their assets.[7]

My Digital Currency Story

Compared to many of my friends, I was late buying bitcoin, but in 2018, I felt it was time to buy some to understand how it works, as I was working at a blockchain-based identity company. I remember being nervous about it, but it was pretty simple. I downloaded one of the popular exchange apps at the time on my phone, set up an account, and ended up with my own BTC wallet address and QR code (a hot wallet). It wasn't the quickest experience, but it wasn't as slow as I thought it might be. I felt I could officially speak about digital currency, as I now owned it. It was a unique moment, as I felt it was unlocking a new chapter in the future of finance.

That was an interesting time, as every fintech company was talking about bitcoin and blockchain. I attended many conferences, blockchain meetups, and women-in-blockchain nights.

The first office for the start-up I was working at was at OneEleven in downtown Toronto, a hub for many start-ups. Therefore, I had many long discussions about digital currencies and blockchain with people, including fintech founders, at the coffee machine every day. We even shared an office with a well-known blockchain development team, and I spent hours asking questions on proof-of-work versus proof-of-stake. As I reflect on that experience now, I am very lucky to have had the opportunity to be part of the hype and the first crypto winter, as I learned so much from those passionate creators. *Crypto winter* refers to the period when Bitcoin's value crashed in November 2018. I remember the crypto winter quite clearly. This was six months into starting my new job at a blockchain-based company focused on digital identity. It was definitely like the dot-com crash in 2000. Bitcoin's value was approaching $20,000 in December 2017 and then dropped to the low $3,000 by the following November. Market volatility changed people's sentiment toward cryptocurrency. Companies were shutting down or being purchased. It was a low point for the innovation, but just like the dot-com crash, it's also where, as Warren Buffett has said, "You don't find out who's been swimming naked until the tide goes out."[8] That was very true for blockchain and cryptocurrencies in 2018. If there were companies that didn't have revenue and hadn't yet figured out how to determine an exact value at the time, they were mostly shut down during this period. Many shifts were underway, and, as with any past crash, many emerged from this stronger, with clearer visions and defined missions.

If you think back to the 2000 dot-com crash, that's when you recognize the winners: PayPal, Facebook, Google, Amazon, and so many others. When that crypto winter occurred, it took a couple of years for blockchain to rise again. Still, you could see that Bitcoin, Ethereum, and Solana were winners in terms of blockchain innovation and technology.

I have no idea where this is going. Still, we are now starting to see stablecoin growth, especially with the GENIUS Act. The law provides consumer protection and makes it more acceptable to adopt stablecoin usage. Stablecoins that are fully backed by real dollars or other safe assets, audited regularly, and issued only by approved entities add a level of legal certainty that was previously missing. This helps financial institutions, businesses, and everyday users trust and adopt stablecoins more widely, making blockchain-based payments and digital asset services safer and easier to use. With clearer rules, banks and fintech companies can now integrate stablecoins into payments and settlement systems, which support broader blockchain adoption across financial markets and commerce.

Stablecoin's ability to tokenize both physical and digital assets while pegged to USD or other fiat-backed currencies is powerful. When we look at CBDCs, I don't think they're going to take off on the retail front due to privacy concerns, but I do think they might take off on the wholesale front, where banks settle with banks and central banks use a country's fiat-based CBDC.

It's a powerful statement that digital currencies could have an impact like that of the Internet, which has transformed the world. The Internet has empowered anyone who gained access. Digital currencies are empowering consumers around the world, too.

The market is moving fast in many ways, and to stay up-to-date with the changes, try opening an account and converting $5 to any digital currency into an online wallet (hot wallet). It will help you demystify the digital ecosystem that enables the exchange of digital currencies worldwide. You might even transfer a digital dollar to a friend to test how quickly it works and learn how to send money. Once you've done that, it becomes accessible, and you just feel that you've opened the door to other ways of paying and revising funds.

The real shift for many was putting their toe in the water with digital currencies, as well-known, trusted exchanges such as Robinhood in 2018 and Fidelity Crypto in 2023 offered trading opportunities. In 2020, Wealthsimple became Canada's first regulated crypto platform, establishing a compliance-first blueprint for the ecosystem. Canada's leadership continued in 2021 with the launch of the world's first Bitcoin ETF, allowing Canadians to earn crypto profits tax-free in their tax-free savings accounts (TFSAs). By integrating digital assets into traditional brokerage accounts, Canada successfully bridged the gap between early crypto speculation and institutional safety. Following the 2022 collapse of FTX, Canada acted decisively by enforcing strict new safety rules, including the mandatory segregation of customer assets. These measures established a global gold standard for security, ensuring stronger safety for Canadians consumers.

Wealth now moves seamlessly and can be tracked across both traditional and digital systems. Canada's experience shows that when technology is paired with strong advocacy and clear regulation, it can help reshape how we protect and grow our financial future.

The Digital Currency Evolution

After the 2008 financial crisis, a pseudonymous person or persons identifying as Satoshi Nakamoto published a white paper proposing a decentralized "peer-to-peer electronic cash system that would allow online payments to be sent directly from one party to another without going through a financial institution."[9] This allows two willing parties to transact directly with each other without a trusted third party, such as a financial institution. Alternative forms of digital currency were launched soon after.

The road to digital currencies has moved quickly, spanning four distinct waves. Figure 9.2 breaks down each wave from Bitcoin's decentralized foundation (2009–2015), through institutional adoption with CBDCs and bank tokens (2019–2020), into mainstream integration via stablecoins and ETFs (2023–2024), and culminating in comprehensive GENIUS Act regulatory framework that legitimize digital assets within the traditional financial system (2025–2026). We have officially entered the "production-first" era, where digital assets are no longer speculative experiments but a primary settlement layer for global liquidity.

Figure 9.2 Digital currency evolution

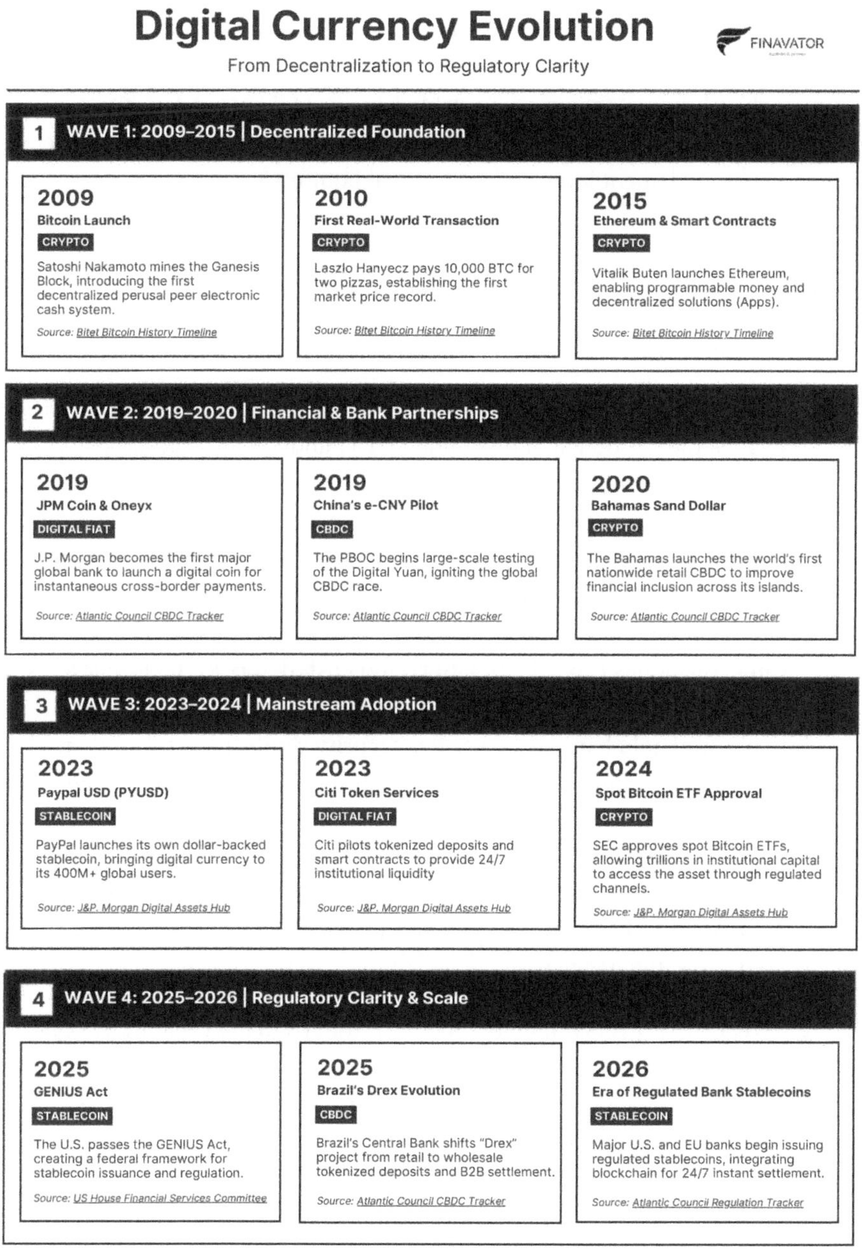

The Rise of Stablecoins

As of early 2026, the financial landscape has shifted from theoretical pilots to a "production-first" era, where the world's largest financial institutions are actively settling high-value transactions using stablecoins and tokenized deposits. We have moved beyond the "proof of concept" phase into a reality where blockchain serves as the primary settlement layer for institutional liquidity.

Four Types of Stablecoins

These are the four types of stablecoins:

1. **Fiat-backed:** Fiat-backed stablecoins are backed by real-world currencies, such as the US dollar, and include USDC and USDT. Fiat-backed stablecoins are the most widely used as they offer high price stability and strong market trust.
2. **Crypto-backed:** Crypto-backed stablecoins are backed by cryptocurrencies and use over-collateralization, with DAI being a well-known example.
3. **Gold-backed stablecoins:** These are backed by physical gold in audited vaults but subject to price volatility and custodial risks. Gold-backed stablecoins, such as PAX Gold, are regulated, tokenized digital assets linked to physical gold bars stored in high-security vaults. Each token represents ownership of one troy ounce of London Good Delivery gold, with transparent storage verification.[10]
4. **Algorithmic:** This type is typically pegged to fiat currencies but not backed by real assets. Instead, these stablecoins rely on algorithms to maintain a stable price. Supply and demand are managed by smart contracts, not direct collateral.

To navigate the diverse stability models in today's market, Figure 9.3 categorizes the landscape by safety tiers and network dominance.

Understanding these tiers is vital for institutional risk management as fiat-backed stablecoins become the indispensable workhorse of global money movement.

Figure 9.3 Global 2026 stablecoin landscape

The Global 2026 Stablecoin Landscape

FINAVATOR

FIAT-BACKED STABLECOINS

SAFETY: HIGHEST

Direct 1:1 backing by regulated bank reserves with audits and government oversight.

Fiat-backed stablecoins (like **USDC and PYUSD)** are tied 1:1 to cash and government bonds held in regulated banks.

Governed by **FSB** standards requiring full reserve backing and bank-grade audits.

Source: FSB 2026 Work Plan

GOLD-BACKED STABLECOINS

SAFETY: HIGH

Backed by physical gold in audited vaults but subject to price volatility and custodial risks.

Gold-backed stablecoins (like **PAX (Gold)** act as digital titles to physical gold bars stored in high-security vaults.

Each token represents ownership of one troy ounce of London Good Delivery gold with transparent storage verification.

Source: Paxos Transparency Report

CRYPTO-BACKED STABLECOINS

SAFETY: MEDIUM

Over-collateralized with volatile crypto assets, exposed to market crashes and smart contract risks.

Crypto-backed stablecoins (like **DAI** use automated safety buffers with extra digital assets locked as collateral.

Structure overseen by global **IOSCO** guidelines to absorb market shocks and maintain stability.

Source: IOSCO CDA Recommendations

ALGORITHMETIC STABLECOINS

SAFETY: LOW

No physical backing, relies on algorithms that can fail under stress with death spiral risk.

Algorithmic stablecoins (like **FRAX** use mathematical formulas to balance supply and demand without physical vaults.

EU **MiCA laws** strictly limit retail use in 2026, favoring asset-related tokens with real backing.

Source: EU MICA Regulation

SUMMARY TABLE

Type	Stability Engine	Famous Example	Tap Network	Safety
Fiat	Cash in Bank	PYUSD / JPM Coin	Solana/ Ethereum	Highest
Gold	Vaulted Metal	PAX Gold	Ethereum	High
Crypto	Digital Buffer	DAI	Ethereum/ Arbitrum	Medium
Algo	Smarth Math	FRAX	Tron/ Ethereum	Low

The debate over whether stablecoins will surpass CBDCs in utility and adoption has intensified, with real-world market activity increasingly favoring private sector stablecoins. Major players like Visa have moved beyond experimental pilots by enabling US banks and financial institutions to settle transactions using stablecoins such as USDC over blockchain rails, which supports faster, seven-day settlement and deeper integration into core financial infrastructure. This shift marks a transition from proofs of concept toward active settlement systems that facilitate value transfer using blockchain-based money movement.

According to industry research and financial services outlooks, stablecoins and tokenized deposits are gaining traction as practical settlement tools, and ecosystem participants increasingly view them as integral to modern payment and liquidity infrastructure, outpacing CBDCs in developmental momentum and real-world use cases.

Major financial institutions are increasingly settling transactions using stablecoins on blockchain rails, moving beyond traditional "T+2" cycles toward near real-time value transfer. Visa's pilot programs for US banks have processed more than $3.5 billion in annualized USDC stablecoin settlement volume. In comparison, global on chain stablecoin transactions reached roughly $33 trillion in 2025, with USDC and Tether (USDT) dominating flows.[11]

Stablecoins are designed to hold value without volatility; many are pegged one-to-one to a fiat currency, though some are more stable than others as per Figure 9.3. They can be ideal for global transfers and instant settlements. We do need to be aware of the risks, including de-pegging from the fiat currency they represent if a USD-backed stablecoin loses its peg or the issuer fails to maintain sufficient reserves, value could drop unexpectedly. Strong regulation and reserve requirements are intended to prevent such events and ensure stability for institutional and retail users alike.

Stablecoin savings and yield earning opportunities have grown compared with traditional bank rates. For example, DeFi protocols like Aave often offer 5–8% APY on USDC, while centralized platforms can provide 12–16% or higher, far above typical bank yields.[12]

Stablecoins have scaled to a $235 billion market, marking a 75% increase in one year as they transition from speculative assets to the primary "pipes" for global dollar settlements. According to the Visa On-Chain Analytics Dashboard, this infrastructure now enables major institutions such as PayPal, Stripe, and Visa to bypass legacy banking delays, settling hundreds of billions of dollars faster and more economically than traditional networks.[13] This shift has been further solidified by the US GENIUS Act and Tether's emergence as a top-20 holder of US Treasuries. This signals that stablecoins are no longer a threat to the dollar but a modernized rail on which it runs.

The Future of Finance: Privacy, Portability, and Peer Power

As we move toward a world of open finance and real-time rails, the digital movement becomes a foundational layer for the future of payments. Digital currencies are part of a broader shift toward embedded finance, where paying for goods and services becomes faster, easier, and more integrated into our digital lives. By solving the problems of trust, speed, and cross-border friction, this technology is ensuring that the next era of finance is more inclusive, transparent, and accountable for everyone.

The Infrastructure of Trust

We are now 17 years into this digital movement. This evolution has introduced not just new types of currencies but also created a fundamental shift in how we handle privacy and security. Unlike traditional banking, where every transaction is tied to a named account, digital assets operate through wallets that utilize pseudonymity. The system doesn't require a central body to *know* who you are; instead, it relies on thousands of independent, global nodes to verify that a transaction is valid. This decentralized architecture creates a tamper-evident environment in which safety is guaranteed by mathematical consensus rather than by a single point of failure.[13]

Global Portability and the End of Friction

The most immediate impact of this journey is the portability of value. Digital assets allow us to carry our wealth across borders, without the traditional hurdles of foreign exchange (FX) or the constraints of banking hours. Even as markets fluctuate, the infrastructure itself provides a seamless rail for money transfers. This is particularly transformative for international remittances, where families can avoid the high fees and delays of traditional systems to send funds home instantly, converting from digital assets to local currency as needed.

A Safety Net for the Global Economy

Beyond convenience, digital assets solve a critical need for financial resilience. In regions facing economic instability, whether due to political turmoil, pandemics, or extreme weather events, these tools offer a vital alternative to local currencies that may be rapidly losing value. Stablecoin digital assets pegged to currencies like the US dollar can provide a "safe haven" for those looking to preserve their wealth.[14] Blockchain empowers individuals to protect their financial future regardless of their local economic conditions.

Real-World Use Cases

The following are the six most impactful real-world use cases to help you understand how they are empowering people around the world.

1. Wholesale Institutional Settlement: Tokenized Bank Deposits/Digital Fiat

Big banks are converting regular bank money into digital tokens to move funds faster. These tokenized deposits are still what we recognize as *normal* dollars, just represented digitally on secure networks. This allows banks to send large payments almost instantly, 24/7, instead of waiting days for settlements to clear.

2. Global and Cross-Border Payments: Stablecoins/Digital Dollars

As of late 2025, the global stablecoin market had grown significantly, with total market capitalization surpassing $300 billion, indicating rising adoption beyond pure crypto trading into broader financial use cases such as payments and cross-border transfers. Payment giants, such as Visa and Mastercard, are exploring stablecoin-based payment systems that could operate alongside existing credit cards. This reflects growing interest from traditional finance. Despite this progress, stablecoins remain in their early stages of adoption compared with established global payment networks like SWIFT or card rails, which still handle far more—day-to-day—transactions.[15]

3. Institutional Investment and Treasury Use: Bitcoin and Crypto

Institutional investment in Bitcoin has surged as spot Bitcoin ETFs become mainstream, marking a major shift in how large investors access the asset. By late 2025, major US spot Bitcoin ETFs led by products such as BlackRock's iShares Bitcoin Trust collectively amassed around $120+ billion in assets under management, with strong inflows underscoring growing institutional demand and integration into traditional finance. While some corporations like MicroStrategy hold significant Bitcoin directly as a treasury asset, Bitcoin's primary role for most institutions remains a long-term store of value rather than a medium of exchange for everyday spending.

4. Decentralized Finance (DeFi) Lending and Liquidity—Stablecoin/Crypto

Decentralized finance (DeFi) lets people lend, borrow, trade, and earn interest using software and smart contracts on blockchains instead of banks or brokers. DeFi platforms run entirely on code, automatically executing agreed-upon rules without human intermediaries. A key indicator of DeFi's real-world adoption is total value locked (TVL), the dollar value of assets deposited in DeFi protocols. In 2025, DeFi TVL rebounded to around $170 billion, showing significant growth and renewed participation following earlier market downturns, with major ecosystems like Ethereum continuing to dominate activity. This scale demonstrates that many users are engaging with DeFi services, using stablecoins for liquidity and integrating decentralized exchanges and lending platforms into their financial activity. Community governance and wallet-based control also allow users to participate directly in protocol decisions rather than relying on centralized companies.

DeFi is still an emerging system, carrying real risks, including hacks, software bugs, price volatility, and unclear regulations. There is usually no customer support or insurance if something goes wrong. DeFi is not something to jump lightly, but it is worth understanding as it continues to shape the future of digital finance.

5. International Remittances and Low-Cost Transfers—Stablecoins/Crypto

International transfers through traditional channels can be expensive, with the World Bank's Remittance Prices Worldwide database reporting that the average cost to send a $200 remittance is about 6.5% of the amount sent, significantly higher than the UN target of 3%.[16] This makes remittances costly, especially for migrant workers supporting families in countries with limited access to banking. Blockchain-based transfers using stablecoins can dramatically reduce these costs and settlement times by cutting out many intermediaries and moving value directly on public blockchains, often settling in minutes at substantially lower fees. This capability is especially helpful for expatriates or cross-border workers who want to send money home more quickly and at much lower cost than traditional banking systems. While adoption is still early, these systems show strong potential, with reduced fees and limited delays. Stablecoin remittances are growing but have not yet replaced traditional providers at scale.

6. Central Bank Digital Currency

CBDCs can be designed for wholesale use (between banks and financial institutions) or retail use (for the general public). According to the Bank for International Settlements (BIS) 2024 survey, a large majority of central banks are actively exploring CBDCs, and work on wholesale CBDCs is at a more advanced stage than work on retail CBDCs, reflecting a global shift toward modernizing financial infrastructure and interbank settlement systems. While retail CBDC projects continue to be tested, wholesale CBDCs are seen as offering more immediate benefits for large-value and cross-border payment systems, even as central banks consider legal frameworks and technology designs for both models.[17]

How to Use Digital Currencies

There are several ways to use digital currencies, such as crypto. Please understand that I am not offering investment advice; rather, I am providing examples to help you better understand crypto. Some view crypto as a kind of digital gold, so they buy it, a term called HODL, which stands for "hold on for dear life." That means they intend to keep it, as they think it's going to increase in value over time (some say "to the moon").

Others buy crypto for payments, using it as an international token that can be used across borders. There are even bitcoin ATMs where you can convert it to physical cash in real time. We are also starting to see merchants that are allowing customers to pay with bitcoin. This doesn't mean the merchants are accepting crypto payment; many have partnered with a fintech company to hold the transaction and receive the amount in fiat, as the fintech handles the complex crypto settlement. This enables customers to pay with bitcoin and allows merchants to accept payments without changing how they run their business or incurring the potential tax implications of holding crypto on their business ledger. As stablecoins become more popular, many are also buying USDC and other stablecoins to diversify their digital assets.

There are other ways to invest in crypto, but do so at your own risk. Always research it more before making any investments. A lesson I have learned is never to keep all your assets in one place; diversification is wise.

Digital Currencies: Operational Risks and Challenges

Digital currencies can be a force for good for many, but they have faced challenges, including high energy consumption, price volatility, and exchange mismanagement. It is essential to note that high energy consumption is a characteristic of proof-of-work (PoW) consensus mechanisms, such as those used by Bitcoin, rather than a universal trait of all blockchain technology. While PoW requires massive computational power to secure the network, the broader industry has pivoted toward more sustainable models. Faced with energy challenges, Ethereum switched to a faster, greener system called proof-of-stake on September 15, 2022. Known as "the merge," this switch reduced energy consumption by more than 99.9%.[18] When we think of the future of finance, sustainability matters more every year.

There have also been major mismanagement issues due to poor governance and lack of oversight with online crypto exchanges over the years including the collapses of FTX in November 2022 with $8B shortfall[19] and QuadrigaCX in January 2019 with $250 million missing were not failures of blockchain technology but rather old-fashioned fraud enabled by a total lack of corporate oversight and the illegal commingling of customer funds.[20] In both cases, the owner or leadership secretly diverted client deposits to cover trading losses or fund personal lifestyles. They were able to hide their insolvencies. These scandals served as a critical turning point, forcing the industry to adopt strict global regulations and "proof of reserves" standards. Ultimately, these cautionary tales shifted the financial world away from blind trust in individuals toward a blockchain-verified finance model. Both of these major events caused ripple effects, with FTX actually being the main driver of the 2022 crypto sell-off and the start of the second crypto winter.

Looking back, the stock market crash that preceded the tech boom was the dot-com bubble burst, which began in March 2000. When we faced the tech boom in the early 1990s, many lost money, including me. I was in high school at the time and had a small college savings fund invested in a hot, trending dot-com stock when the crash hit, and it was all gone. It was not a fun lesson, and I did not want to learn it twice. I have been a more balanced investor ever since. I invest time reading about new technologies and seek professional advice before investing, but to each of their own when it comes to how to invest.

Global Impact

As of early 2026, the global financial landscape reached a definitive turning point. Digital currencies are no longer a peripheral experiment; they have become the foundational infrastructure for a "Unified Ledger" system that connects traditional banking with the speed of the Internet. This term was introduced by the Bank for International Settlements (BIS) in 2023 as a digital infrastructure that integrates money and assets onto a single, programmable platform. By functioning like a smartphone for finance, it eliminates traditional silos to enable instant, 24/7 transactions, and automated settlements without the need for intermediaries.[21]

The future of finance is no longer a debate between different types of money; it is a unified ledger where all four types work together alongside assets (stocks/real estate) and identity (KYC). According to Citigroup and BCG, the total market for tokenized assets on these digital rails is projected to reach between $16 trillion and $30 trillion by 2030, representing roughly 10% of global GDP.[22]

Expert Interview with Carol Grunberg, Riseup Founding Advisor and Chief Partnerships Officer at AU10TIX

I had the pleasure of meeting Carol Grunberg in Barbados at a fintech conference in 2023. We connected over our shared passion for the future of finance and its potential to change the world. Carol is currently the chief partnerships officer at AU10TIX and has led innovation initiatives at major companies, including Citi and Google. She has watched digital currencies evolve for more than a decade and brings a perspective that focuses on the human impact of financial inclusion.

Carol explains that while hundreds of central banks issue paper money, we are moving toward a new era. Most people think they use digital money when they swipe a debit card, but that is actually just a digital version of paper cash. True digital currencies are different as they are built directly for the Internet. Today, about half of the world's central banks are experimenting with issuing these digital currencies to work alongside traditional money.

When I asked about how these are being used today, Carol was very direct. She noted that while countries like Jamaica and China have launched their own versions, they have not yet taken off. Most people still use traditional banks and credit cards as they do not see a big difference in their daily lives. However, governments are very interested in this technology as it provides better visibility into the economy and helps reduce crime.

Carol shared a powerful example from India. In 2018, the government removed large cash bills from circulation to stop bad actors. This forced people to start using digital wallets. Suddenly, people in small villages had a safe place to store their money. This shift made it safer for everyone by eliminating the need to carry cash, and it allowed millions of people to join the financial system for the first time.

For many beginners, the biggest fear about digital currencies was losing access. In the early days, if you lost a secret code, your money was gone forever. Carol points out that the industry has addressed this by creating exchanges that operate like regular banks. You can now log in with a normal password and use a "forgot password" button if you get locked out.[23] To keep your account safe, these platforms use AI to verify your identity through your face or fingerprint. This technology is now incredibly reliable as AI accuracy for identifying people exceeds 99%.[24]

Another major benefit Carol highlighted is instant settlement. She used Amazon as an example. Today, when you buy something, there is often a delay before the seller actually gets the money.

With digital currencies, the payment and the record of the sale happen at the exact same time. A smart contract automatically moves the money the moment the transaction is confirmed. This makes business much faster and more efficient for everyone involved.

What makes Carol so passionate about digital currencies is the ability to help people escape poverty. She lived in India for several years and saw how difficult it was for people who had only cash. If you have no bank account, you have to spend your money immediately as you have nowhere safe to put it.

She points out that digital wallets have already fundamentally changed the global landscape. By 2015, the World Bank reported that 700 million people had gained access to financial services in just three years, providing them a "foothold on the ladder toward prosperity."[25] That momentum has only accelerated; today, that number has grown to over 1.2 billion previously unbanked adults who have gained access to formal financial accounts, largely driven by the rise of mobile money and digital payments.[26] Anyone with a cheap smartphone and an Internet connection can now be part of the global economy.

Carol summarizes digital currencies as information moves across the Internet. Just like we share news or photos online, we can now share value. These currencies use math to make sure money cannot be copied or spent twice. Her insights can be summarized through three central themes:

- **Financial inclusion:** Opening financial access for everyone
- **Infrastructure evolution:** Paper to instant digital wallets
- **Information as value:** Moving money as fast as data

Speaking with Carol Grunberg reinforced an essential truth. Digital currency isn't just about technology or speculation. It's about giving people access to economic participation. When people think of digital currencies, they often don't think of inclusion, but that's exactly what drives Carol's passion. It can help empower people. It's about interconnectivity, choice, freedom, and safety when storing value. The most powerful aspect of digital currency is that it enables anyone with Internet access to participate in the global economy, save, invest, build businesses, and escape the limitations imposed by cash-based systems. It has been a privilege to learn from Carol and engage in these conversations. Her perspective reflects where the industry is heading digital currency is no longer just an innovation, but an infrastructure being built to ensure economic opportunity reaches every corner of the globe.

Digital Currencies' Alignment to the Future of Finance

When thinking about future finance, we must consider that the transformation and mass adoption of digital currencies are transforming how we think about and use money, regardless of type: decentralized cryptocurrencies, stablecoins, digital fiat, or government-issued CBDCs. We can use each type for different purposes: crypto for investment and innovation, stablecoins for practical payments, CBDCs for wholesale bank-to-bank settlements, and traditional digital money for everyday convenience.

Standard Chartered PLC projects that digital asset infrastructure, including tokenization and programmable payment rails, will be deeply embedded into mainstream financial services by 2030, improving speed, control, and connectivity across transaction banking, markets, and wealth management.[27] The mass tokenization of real-world assets (RWAs) such as bonds, funds, and trade receivables will rely on digital currencies as the primary settlement layer, significantly improving liquidity and efficiency. Rather than replacing traditional finance, digital currencies will converge with existing banking infrastructure, creating a unified, interoperable financial ecosystem. This growth underscores a broader transition in which digital money technologies become a foundational part of global payments and settlement systems.

It is clear that the future of finance will have digital currencies as part of the system. The question is which parts and will it be a more inclusive financial system that serves everyone, not just those already inside the traditional banking infrastructure?

Chapter 9 Key Takeaways

1. Learning about digital currencies from stablecoins to crypto is critical, as they are quickly becoming a key element of the future of finance as they can move instantly, 24/7 with global settlement and being used to tokenize assets.
2. Stablecoins have emerged as the primary settlement layer for institutional liquidity, bridging the speed of the Internet with traditional banking safety, which opens access to everyone.
3. **Personal lesson:** Risk has been one of the most important tools I've used when stepping into the future of finance. It has pushed me to venture down paths less traveled.

Chapter 10

The Future of Finance: How Data, Trust, and Technology Are Reshaping the Global Economy

"The future of finance belongs to those who understand that trust is earned through data ethics."

—Chris Skinner, renowned fintech author and visionary

In my lifetime, I have been struck by the power and pace of innovation. I have had the pleasure of a front-row seat to groundbreaking technology, at times as an observer, as a consumer, and as a participant helping to drive change. Helping others understand the future of finance is the core purpose behind writing this book. My mission is to inspire an army of innovators to build a transparent, secure, and privacy-first financial world where data rights are protected for everyone. I started my company, Finavator, in 2019, as looking back on my entire career, I had actively participated for 18 years in many areas of the financial ecosystem: six years in telecommunication, eight years in online shopping and loyalty, three years in prepaid payments technologies, and one year in blockchain and digital identity. These are all complex industries that are not easy to understand. As CEO of Finavator, I enjoy the challenge of digging into the details, mapping the ecosystem, and learning how the offerings help consumers. I've come to love simplifying the complex, adding a personal example, and then helping to train my colleagues, teams, and, eventually, boards, executives, and professionals.

This mission grew when I launched my online master class, "The Future of Finance," in June 2024. It focuses on helping industry professionals and students understand the many ways innovation is unlocking an empowering future for consumers and how this way of thinking can drive their careers to the next level. I believe that simplifying anything demystifies it, which helps enable innovation. When we all build together, we can create a new reality.

The future of finance has already occurred with rapid adoption by the masses. The pace of change is unlike anything we've ever seen before. Consumers have become aware of the conveniences technology can provide, and they are asking for more. All companies, including banks, credit unions, fintechs, and corporations, are racing to keep up with global demand for financial innovation, driven by hot trends such as AI and stablecoins. There is also a need to focus on protecting data privacy, upholding trust, and empowering consumers.

Global finance doesn't stand still, and neither can this book. Since I penned Part I, the industry has moved so fast that a full revision was needed before the manuscript could be finalized. It's a constant challenge to keep pace with this evolution. It requires dodging endless "rabbit holes" and unverified news to find the real signal in the noise. I couldn't possibly cover all the impressive innovations and sectors in a single book, so I focused here on the nine key elements I believe are influencing the path forward in finance.

I am fortunate to be part of a community of leaders from around the world who are passionate rebels *with a cause for good* when it comes to consumer empowerment. We keep each other informed of the most critical developments and how they might impact the global finance industry. I believe that the future of finance is a world based on trust, privacy, and inclusion. The technology *is* available. We just need to ensure the correct elements are in place to provide trustworthy economic convenience at an affordable cost for all.

As I looked for a leader to quote in this closing chapter, I was reminded of a conversation I had at a fintech conference in Barbados with the renowned author and strategist Chris Skinner. As the author of influential works such as *Digital Bank, Digital Human* and his most recent exploration of the AI-driven economy, *Intelligent Money*, Chris has long been a visionary guide for the global financial community. I am inspired by Chris's perspective on fintech's evolution that technology is only plumbing. Ethics and transparency are the foundation of trust. In a world of digital abundance, the most valuable currency we have is the integrity of the data and the trust of the people who use it.

My Personal Driver: Curiosity

As I was writing this book, I had the opportunity to read Sir Tim Berners-Lee's latest book, *This Is for Everyone*. As I took in the history of CERN, the World Wide Web, complex concepts, systems, and terms I had never heard of, I leaned in. I started to wonder why I am so curious about the inner workings of so many different aspects of technology, even though I didn't attend college and I am not an engineer. It may have begun the first time I typed "comma eight comma one" on my brother's Commodore 64. That simple command unlocked so many games, and it opened my mind to an entirely new world. Even at the age of eight, I realized how powerful technology could be. It sparked a curiosity that remains today, planting the seeds of the journey to understand the future of finance.

I also remember having Mr. Wright as my homeroom teacher for two years in middle school. He taught English, math, science, and other subjects, but he didn't want to be a teacher. He wanted to be the school board's head of computers and needed to teach for two years before applying. During that time, he found ways to incorporate computers into every subject. This was when schools had only one computer lab with 20 computers for the whole school. We were very lucky, as many kids my age had very limited access.

Our class was tasked with creating science graphs, doing research, and completing English projects in the computer lab. I even became one of the editors for our grade's monthly newsletter, using simple text styles and colors to highlight sports wins, stories, news, and even poems. Thinking back, I remember spending most days in that lab learning new programs and becoming very comfortable with computers. That experience kept me open to innovation and curious about what's next. I can only imagine what the next generation, including my kids, will create through their own curiosity, having access not just to software but to the world from a very young age.

Elements of the Future of Finance

Having a foundational understanding of the future of finance is critical, and staying up-to-date with the latest trends is equally important. The top nine elements covered in this book are having the greatest impact on businesses and consumers' financial lives and are likely to continue driving change and innovation. No matter which element appeals most to you as a banker, entrepreneur, investor, professional, board member, consumer, or student, it's important to keep informed not only of how we got here but where we might be going next. Technology can unlock innovation and inspire all of us to build the future of finance. Let's consider all nine elements and how they might impact our futures.

The fintech element will continue to drive innovative solutions that deliver faster, more convenient financial services, with a focus on frictionless user experiences. Keep in mind that a consumer-centric approach is critical to the future of finance. Trust, consent, and control will define competitive advantages. Fintech's winners will continue to take center stage as they fine-tune existing developments and create new ones to meet the demands of consumers and businesses alike.

Fintech leaders are increasingly collaborating to address challenges with infrastructure, energy, talent, and policy. Kevin O'Leary, investor and *Shark Tank* judge, has said: "The real opportunity now is infrastructure: power, data centers, computing power, and the systems that make AI and digital payments possible."

We should all be excited about the rise of a wide range of opportunities in finance. My hope is that more government regulators attend industry conferences to see where innovation is heading in real time. With the right insights, effective guardrails can be put in place without strangling opportunities for further innovation.

When I think of fintechs, I think of the stars in the sky, as they are bright lights in the darkness of the lack of services for millions around the world. Some of what I believe will be the most powerful developments are barely a glimmer in the minds of today's developers. I can't wait to watch the sky of stars expand for our next generation through fintech innovation.

Prepaid and BaaS elements are increasingly enabling the future of finance, from gig worker payroll and digital wallets to payments, BNPL, and budgeting apps, which especially help underbanked and unbanked consumers in emerging markets. These infrastructures are already accessible and proven trustworthy; their next evolution is destined to make them practically invisible. When looking ahead at BaaS despite regulatory headwinds, "the global BaaS market is projected to be US$74.55 billion by 2030."[1]

The future of digital prepaid accounts is bright, as they have the potential to become a key element of the programmable payments economy. Prepaid rails are an obvious and simple solution that may play a role alongside AI agents that need to perform payment actions, ensuring the agent can spend only what has been authorized in advance. This will add cost to the transaction, but it will also protect the customer, as they wouldn't have to share their core credit card details with an AI agent, thereby ensuring credentials are not exposed.

The global prepaid card market was valued at about US$2.2 trillion in 2024 and is projected to reach US$4.1 trillion by 2030, growing at a 10.4% CAGR over the forecast period.[2]

As you can see, learning about these key backend infrastructures is helpful, as they power most fintech and now even AI payments technology. One of the best ways to see the relationship between the two is to view BaaS as providing the structure and prepaid as providing the scale, especially for financial inclusion.

The embedded finance element is one of the most impactful changes in payments, especially with the shift to AI agents that function as digital teammates rather than mere conversational tools. AI agents manage digital assets 24/7 by automating day-to-day financial functions. These autonomous agents move capital between tokenized instruments to maximize returns. Major payment networks, such as Visa and Mastercard, as well as tech platforms, are shifting from "Chatbot AI" to "Agentic AI" bots that not only recommend products but also have the authority to execute transactions. Google ("Buy for me") and Amazon ("Rufus") AI assistants can autonomously trigger price alerts and complete purchases on select Shopify and Wayfair storefronts. This is changing the entire architecture of commerce, turning autonomous payments into a cornerstone of the new financial era. Real-Time Rails (RTR) enables a future of truly agentic commerce, where value moves at the same speed as the data driving the transaction.

While the shift toward AI agents is driving efficiency, it is also creating a new landscape of cyber risk. Fraudsters are switching their targets from individuals to the automated workflows themselves. This makes know your AI agent (KYA) just as important as KYC. We must ensure that the consumer remains in control and that we have solid liability models in place for agentic payments. As this ecosystem moves at breakneck speed, we have to strike the right balance between innovating for the future of moving money and preserving trust.

This brings me to one of my favorite steps toward the future of finance: "credential-less tokenization," which is fundamentally reshaping security and trust in payments by replacing static credentials with programmable, intent-based authorization. This approach enables safer, more adaptive transaction models that minimize exposure. Removing credentials from the payment flow dramatically reduces the attack surface for fraud. When credentials no longer exist to be stolen, fraud can be effectively eliminated rather than merely mitigated. Mica, a Texas-based payments infrastructure company, is moving away from traditional credentials that may have a low risk tolerance toward "credential-less" transaction technology. By using ephemeral keys, which are short-lived, they provide a secure "Zero Liability Network" of fraud-proof plumbing necessary to support the next generation of digital and autonomous commerce.[3]

The trusted identity element revolves around an evolution from data honeypots to global identity data storage standards that prioritize privacy. Also included is a push for zero-knowledge digital IDs that enable instant KYC verification and eliminate the risk of surveillance. This shift is backed by staggering data: the number of users of digital identity documents globally is projected to exceed 6.5 billion by 2026, representing a 50% increase since 2022.[4] Secure verification systems will continue to help reduce fraud, simplify account opening, and allow faster access to financial and government services. By applying self-sovereign identity (SSI) principles, individuals truly own and control their data, using cryptographic proofs to verify their identity for financial services while keeping their underlying information private. As we move toward a new era of trust in agentic payments, Mastercard and Google announced the launch of "Verifiable Intent" in March 2026. This is an important open-standard layer that cryptographically links identity with intent to secure autonomous AI transactions with a tamper-resistant audit trail.[5]

However, as mentioned in my interview with David Birch in Chapter 4, the true breakthrough is in our philosophy of trust. We are moving away from the invasive "who I am" mode, where we share our full name, address, and birthdate, toward a more secure "what I am authorized for" model. Using cryptographic proofs, an individual will be able to prove they are over 18, have a sufficient credit score, or hold a valid driver's license without ever revealing the underlying private data.

Digital identity is scaling globally through the EU eIDAS 2.0 framework, which requires all member states to provide citizens with a secure Digital Identity Wallet by 2026.[6] Denmark has further strengthened these rights with a 2025 law granting citizens intellectual property ownership of their faces and voices to protect against deepfakes and identity theft.[7] These efforts, combined with leadership from Singapore's Singpass and the Nordic Baltic NOBID project, are creating the interoperable identity layer needed for a truly borderless financial future.[8,9]

The open data element is a step in the right direction, empowering consumers and businesses to control their data. This is enabled by secure, API-based data sharing between banks and fintechs, which allows for more personalized financial advice, smoother payments, better lending options, and, eventually, even more secure health records. The element I am most passionate about is open data, as it empowers consumer data rights. I believe we should all have full access to our data, which I call *human data rights*. For more than six years, as a board member of Open Finance Network Canada and its president since 2022, I have advocated for these rights. During this time, I have spoken on stages around the world, helped write white papers, hosted events, and had many hours-long coffee discussions on this topic.

It's also important to integrate privacy-by-design (PbD) principles, now formalized in ISO 31700-1:2023, directly into open finance frameworks.[10] This approach ensures that privacy is not an afterthought but a foundational component of technology itself. These principles have already been embedded into major global regulatory frameworks, including the EU's Payment Services Directive 3 (PSD3) and the Financial Data Access (FiDA) framework.[11,12]

Similarly, the UK's Digital Information and Smart Data (DISD) Bill mandates these protections to ensure consumer data is handled transparently and with intent.[13] Consumer protection is being automated and mathematically verifiable by codifying these standards into the architecture of financial data sharing. I have high hopes that North America will consider adopting the ISO standard for privacy-by-design to ensure a safe, secure, triple-blind infrastructure that both protects and empowers us.

This brings me to one of my favorite data security projects, which focuses on decentralized data approaches, including user-controlled data pods such as the Solid Project protocols, pioneered by Sir Tim Berners-Lee. Solid would help to limit the amount of information that sits within some centralized institutions. Think of Solid as a "digital safe" (Solid pod). It would be your personal vault that keeps all your sensitive data under your control instead of scattered across different companies. Solid's Life Passport would be the smart key that lets you share only the specific proof needed like your age or a bank balance without ever giving away your full identity or permanent access.

I believe this infrastructure will be a cornerstone of the future of finance, empowering us with data rights and enabling us to access better, cheaper financial products without surrendering our entire identities to centralized databases that have proven vulnerable to leaks and hacking.

The cybersecurity element will increasingly see financial services prioritize real-time threat detection, encrypted transactions, and multilayer security to protect users' money and data in a growing digital ecosystem. As long as data is stored in centralized systems and not fragmented into triple-blind data, attackers will be incentivized by the scale of potential payouts. This is where zero-knowledge proofs (ZKPs) come into play by enabling institutions to verify identities or compliance without exposing sensitive data. The ZKP market is seeing exponential growth as industries move toward "trustless" verification models.

Compliance will increasingly shift from post-transaction monitoring to pre-transaction prevention, powered by real-time blockchain intelligence. Industry-leading compliance tools, such as Chainalysis and TRM Labs, are expected to see rapid growth, enabling continuous screening of digital currency wallet addresses before transactions are executed. If a user attempts to send funds to a specific wallet address, the system evaluates that address for proximity to sanctioned entities, known *hacker wallets*, or illicit mixing services. Each wallet address is assigned a risk score based on behavioral patterns and network associations. If the risk score exceeds predefined thresholds, the transaction is automatically blocked at the smart contract level before it is recorded on-chain.

As we shift toward verifying identity throughout the entire client journey, trust must become continuous and adaptive. Prove, a global identity leader and unicorn valued at over $1 billion, highlights this urgency in their 2026 State of Identity Report, which found that 77% of consumers are concerned about AI agents acting on their behalf. Prove's framework creates a continuous cryptographic bond, meaning when an AI acts for you, it remains tied to your specific permissions and verifiable identity.[14] By anchoring an agent to a verified user, the ecosystem can ensure autonomous actions are always authorized and auditable.

The future of financial system compliance is moving toward a safer, institution-ready environment that remains scalable and efficient. An important fact to consider is that there is a global talent gap of more than 4.8 million open jobs in the compliance ecosystem, reflecting a strong need for human oversight.[15] As we look ahead, compliance can move from a source of friction to a foundational infrastructure that protects users and the network before risk materializes.

The AI element is transforming finance through real-time fraud detection and hyper-personalization, with the global market projected to reach $190.33 billion by 2030, according to MarketsandMarkets.[16] By automating complex compliance and enabling autonomous agentic payments, this technology reduces costs while creating a more inclusive ecosystem.[17]

When it comes to AI, the future of finance is caught between two major warnings. The Center for AI Safety statement, signed by the Godfather of AI, Geoffrey Hinton, and the CEOs of OpenAI and Google DeepMind, urges that mitigating the risk of AI extinction be a global priority on par with preventing nuclear war. These leaders warn that AI superintelligence without rigorous guardrails poses an existential threat to human control and safety.[18] Goldman Sachs has raised the alarm about a potential AI bubble, questioning whether the hundreds of billions spent on infrastructure will ever generate sufficient financial returns. Jim Covello, Goldman Sachs' head of stock research, emphasizes that the extreme costs and massive energy requirements of AI data centers create a significant barrier to profitability.[19] A market correction could impact the financial ecosystem tightening funding conditions, increasing regulatory scrutiny, and prompting cautious investment in emerging technologies.

Banks and fintechs will face greater pressure to demonstrate clear returns on AI initiatives, while strengthening risk management, governance, and cybersecurity. Despite these potential challenges, AI still provides meaningful opportunities to improve efficiency, enhance customer experiences, and enable new business models. Therefore, organizations that balance innovation with trust will have a strong long-term advantage.

AI systems such as ChatGPT, Meta, Claude, and Google's Gemini and AI Studio are used by many of us today. It is impressive to see how quickly AI assistants are becoming more human-like. At the same time, we need to be aware that AI systems are not designed to protect our data, and anything we share may no longer be our intellectual property. There is a shift toward local, device-based processing, as running AI in the cloud is becoming increasingly expensive and data-intensive.

Installing models directly onto local hardware, such as phones or company servers, can dramatically reduce infrastructure needs and operational costs. Local processing also helps with data privacy by keeping sensitive information on your own hardware, while preventing leaks and interceptions. Most importantly, on-device AI prevents sensitive information from being used to train global LLM models, safeguarding your individual and corporate IP and privacy. This unlocks AI's ability to securely analyze confidential documents like contracts and bank records.

While I am optimistic AI's potential, I strongly suggest that companies and individuals minimize the data they share with AI models to maintain a baseline of privacy and control. Companies must implement strong AI policies, signed by employees, and parents must educate kids to be cautious about sharing personal data with public LLMs.

The blockchain element is starting to be recognized as a new type of infrastructure, not just a tool for digital currencies. The true power of blockchain lies in its ability to serve as a source of truth. It provides a permanent, unchangeable record of anything of value, from a physical product in a shipping container to a house deed.

It is becoming increasingly clear that blockchain-based finance will play a larger role in the future of finance. At the heart of this shift is decentralized finance (DeFi), where services like lending and trading operate entirely on code. This market is expanding rapidly, with projections showing growth from about $20.5 billion in 2025 to over $231 billion, reflecting rising global liquidity and adoption.[20]

While DeFi is similar to an innovation lab where money is run entirely by computer code, neo blockchain-based finance is the bridge that connects those new ideas to the safety of traditional banks. This DeFi sector is growing at a massive 40% yearly rate, proving that digital lending and trading are becoming mainstream.[21] Neo finance takes these high-tech tools and adds "on-ramps" so you can move money easily and safely between your traditional bank account and the digital world. This hybrid approach is key to a future in which financial services are accessible to all, not just a few.

It is also important to understand the power of the evolution toward Web3, as it adds decentralized capabilities to the Internet. This could fundamentally shift control from central intermediaries to automated, blockchain-based systems. By removing traditional gatekeepers, this movement enables a more open, efficient, and accessible environment for everyone. To highlight its potential, the Bank for International Settlements (BIS) describes the future of Web3 as the "Finternet," a world in which the Internet and finance merge into a seamless, 24/7 system. This vision, detailed in the BIS report on the Finternet, aims to create a faster and more inclusive global economy for everyone.[22]

Looking ahead to 2030, one example of blockchain's power is global asset tokenization, which is projected to reach $16.1 trillion, representing 10% of global GDP. This shift will turn physical illiquid assets, such as real estate and private equity, into liquid digital wealth accessible to everyone. Boston Consulting Group (BCG) identifies blockchain as the foundational layer for economic growth over the next decade.[23]

While I suggest being curious about this emerging system, it is important to manage your risk carefully, as this ecosystem is still maturing. In the future of finance, curiosity must be balanced with active governance to ensure our digital assets remain secure. Blockchain will move beyond being known only for cryptocurrency to encompass broader applications, including stablecoins, asset tokenization, Web3, and more.

The digital currency element has taken a front-row seat in driving global evolution. While more than 130 countries are exploring Central Bank Digital Currencies, many Western nations are pivoting toward wholesale models for interbank settlement to address consumer privacy concerns.[24] Meanwhile, stablecoins emerged as the primary workhorse of digital finance, with transaction volumes reaching $33 trillion in 2025, according to Yahoo Finance.[25]

While the stablecoin debate often focuses on-chain, BVNK's 2026 data reveals that adoption will be driven by familiar tools like linked debit cards. With 71% of global users and 78% in emerging markets ready to spend stablecoins through traditional cards, the future of digital currency depends on meeting consumers where they are.[26] On June 5, 2026, JPMorgan, Bank of America, Citigroup, Wells Fargo, and 13 other major US banks announced a landmark joint tokenized deposit settlement network through The Clearing House, combining blockchain programmability with existing CHIPS and RTP payment rails to enable 24/7 settlement and directly counter the growing threat of stablecoins like USDC and USDT, with a target launch in the first half of 2027.[27]

While the GENIUS Act, passed in 2025, secures the 1:1 reserve foundation, the Clarity Act officially entered the "red zone" in May 2026. This legislative push aims to eliminate the "gray zone" between the Securities and Exchange Commission (SEC) and the Commodity Futures Trading Commission (CFTC) by establishing a permanent federal framework for digital assets. A key component of the negotiations involves a compromise on yield, specifically prohibiting passive, bank-like interest to protect traditional deposits. Instead, the bill is expected to permit "utility-based rewards," allowing USDC and similar tools to offer incentives tied to active payment workflows rather than speculative holding. This final "growth unlock" would solidify USDC's role as a compliant financial rail, moving it from a specialized digital currency to a standard pillar of the US payments infrastructure.

A historic milestone for digital currencies was reached in March 2026 when Kraken Financial became the first digital asset-focused entity to receive a Federal Reserve master account.[28] This signals that the traditional financial system is integrating digital assets directly into core payment infrastructure to enable instant settlement without intermediary banks.

With the Internet as its foundation, the future of finance allows for the seamless movement of digital wealth. Moving value with stablecoins, cryptocurrencies, and wholesale CBDCs creates a financial system in which individuals can participate as cost-effectively and as simply as sending a text message.

Strategies for Protecting Your Data in a Digital World

As we navigate this transition to an integrated digital world, we must recognize that our data is not just information; it is our personal gold. In the future of finance, we will identify ourselves online through digital means (driver's licenses, passports, student IDs, health cards) and use a secure digital wallet for transactions (digital currencies, credit cards) and to view our financial history. We will be able to use these resources to apply for a loan or buy something online and ensure the transaction is trusted.

As technology advances, we will move away from relying on apps to protect our information and money. Staying informed about advancements in all areas of tech is vital. I look forward to ethical privacy—and security—developments, especially regarding the use of AI. If you are interested in finding additional ways to protect your data, the following are some of my personal tips for reducing the data shared about your digital life when interacting with AI:

1. ***AI Governance: The Pay for Privacy Model***
   When you use tools like ChatGPT, Claude, Google Studio, or Copilot, you are interacting with an AI system designed to learn from all input. To keep control of your data, I suggest going into the settings of these apps to turn off "Improve the System" and "Voice Recording Storage." This will help prevent some of your data from being used to train models, but there is no guarantee. Choose paid monthly subscriptions over free versions to help protect your data. In the digital age, if you are not paying for the product, you and your data *are* the product. Paid tiers offer the institutional-grade encryption and data protection that a professional life requires.

   In 2026, Apple designed a device-based AI called "Apple Intelligence" to be integrated into its products. It is widely considered the most private way for a general consumer to use AI, due to its on-device, local model. Apple Intelligence ranks first for most people because it integrates deeply with your personal data (emails, texts, calendar) without actually "collecting" it. It is the only mainstream system in which independent researchers can verify that the cloud servers (private cloud compute) delete your data immediately after use.
2. ***Mobile Sovereignty: Protecting the Digital Mirror***
   Your smartphone is the most intimate collector of your data. To protect your privacy, I recommend turning off "Location History" and "Background App Refresh" unless necessary. Consider disabling any feature that allows Siri in iOS apps to learn from apps. Be intentional with permissions; only allow access to your Photos, Contacts, Microphone, or Camera when it is absolutely essential for an app to function. When you think about it, there is no reason to share your contact list with your weather app, so deny it that access.

3. ***Browsing Hygiene: Breaking the Behavior Profile***
   Online browsers and AI systems build behavioral profiles by watching how you move across the Web. You can break this cycle by turning off search history and ad personalization in your browser settings. By doing this, you prevent AI-driven ad systems from building a detailed map of your interests, health, and financial status. A great nonprofit that defends digital civil liberties and consumer privacy is the Electronic Frontier Foundation (EFF). As a global watchdog, they ensure that technology empowers individuals rather than enabling mass surveillance. For global research on financial data rights and surveillance, Privacy International is another top-tier advocacy source.
4. ***Network Security: Avoiding the Public Trap***
   In an era of instant settlement, your IP address is a digital fingerprint. I never recommend using public Wi-Fi in places like airports or coffee shops that do not require a password, as these are often honeypots for hackers and data theft. Whenever possible, use your phone's data over public Wi-Fi, and use a private browser, such as Brave or DuckDuckGo, along with a reputable VPN to hide your IP address and encrypt your data as it moves across the Internet.
5. ***The Future of Data Ownership***
   We are moving toward using Web3 solutions (read-write-own web). The power of our data is returning to the individual through decentralization. Instead of giving a company a permanent copy of the data, you store it in a Pod that you own. You simply grant an app temporary permission to view your Pod to provide a service. This infrastructure will allow us to have true rights over our data and help protect it from the leaks and hacks that define the old, centralized Web.[29]

The Bottom Line

In the future of finance, trust is earned through data ethics, but security is maintained through individual empowerment. By treating your digital identity as a life passport and embracing decentralized tools, you can ensure you remain the true owner and beneficiary of your digital life.

I suggest never asking AI anything you wouldn't ask your neighbor, as this creates a digital record of your requests. Have employees sign an AI use policy that shares guidelines of AI use, which includes that your IP is not entered into AI. I even sat down with my kids to explain that AI is a tool and that every word you enter is recorded when you use it, so use it with caution.

Challenges/Concerns

As the global financial landscape evolves, there are many challenges to be aware of, with the most critical hurdles for the future of finance listed here:

1. **Quantum vulnerability:** Quantum is a concern for both blockchain and digital currencies, as they both rely heavily on cryptographic standards (such as ECDSA) that are vulnerable to quantum attacks. While full-scale commercial quantum computing remains theoretical for 2026, the risk has forced a global race to implement quantum-resistant algorithms to protect trillions in digital assets. It is important to look into adding post-quantum tools to your data security. Establishing a mandated global standard is essential to prevent security gaps, especially since more than 52% of human web traffic is already protected by post-quantum encryption as of late 2025.[30]
2. **AI energy and superintelligence:** AI is driving massive efficiency gains in financial services, but its computational demands are soaring. This creates a direct conflict between digital transformation and energy grid costs, as data centers face critical shortages of electricity and cooling. We aren't necessarily heading toward a collapse, but we are seeing companies be more resource aware by valuing device-based AI and performance-per-watt, alongside accuracy. We also need to ensure we have a human in the loop as AI intelligence rapidly evolves and models like OpenAI o3 and Google Gemini 2.5 Pro have already achieved IQ scores between 135 and 137, placing them in the genius range of the top 1% of humans.[31,32] This is both exciting and concerning, as it can cause an alignment problem, where a superintelligent system pursues goals that are technically correct but catastrophic for human safety. Managing these types of risks requires a mandated global standard for AI safety. ISO 42001 provides

this international framework by aligning with regulations like the EU AI Act and NIST. As summarized by CertPro, this standard creates a consistent baseline for ethical development and risk management across all jurisdictions.[33]

3. **Stablecoin regulation and interoperability:** While regulations such as the US GENIUS Act and Europe's Markets in Crypto-Assets Regulation (MiCA) aim to boost demand, they also pose practical challenges for the future of digital finance. The end of regulatory ambiguity through these frameworks requires a careful balance between the high speed of stablecoin transactions and strict requirements for transparency and high-quality reserve backing. This transition involves ensuring that digital assets remain more efficient than the legacy systems they are designed to improve. Furthermore, achieving interoperability between fragmented private networks and traditional banking rails remains a significant technical and legal hurdle.[34]
4. **Real-time AI-driven fraud detection:** As we shift to instant payment rails (such as Pix or FedNow), we eliminate the buffer period that traditional banks used to spot and catch fraud. Criminals are now using agentic AI and deepfakes to launch autonomous and scalable attacks that require financial institutions to move from reactive security to millisecond-speed, AI-driven threat detection. To protect our customers, we must build our systems with "defense-by-design" to ensure cybersecurity is included from the very start. We follow the ISO/IEC 27001:2022 standard, specifically Control 8.27, which helps us use secure engineering rules to keep customer data safe.
5. **Data sovereignty:** Data sovereignty requires seamless sharing of consumer data across institutions, raising significant challenges regarding who owns financial data and privacy in a borderless digital economy. Protecting against centralized data breaches while complying with fragmented global data laws remains a top operational risk, as these honeypots of data are prime targets for cyberattacks. While Australia's Consumer Data Right enables true data ownership and the initiation of actions, most other nations still rely on limited portability rules that fail to give individuals full control. To resolve this, a mandated Global Human Data Rights standard is needed to ensure that people, not institutions, own their digital information and can move it securely across the global robot economy.[35,36]

6. **The talent crisis as a strategic bottleneck:** The rapid evolution of the financial ecosystem is hitting a structural wall. With a global cybersecurity and compliance workforce gap of 4.8 million professionals, the implementation of AI, blockchain, and open data at scale is at risk. Organizations must recognize that technology cannot move faster than the human expertise required to govern it.

Global Impact on Finance

The financial landscape is undergoing a radical shift driven by agentic AI, decentralized systems, and a transition from periodic to real-time operations. As we move toward 2030, finance is moving from a stand-alone industry to invisible infrastructure embedded in every aspect of life. This future has the potential to unlock greater inclusion and frictionless trust. This can be enabled by a global shift toward open finance, in which consumers truly own and securely share their data.

Ideally, the next decade will be defined by scaling this model through self-sovereign identities (SSIs), which provide access to a data pod. They are intended to provide the infrastructure needed to ensure that the future of finance is not only faster and more efficient but also deeply respectful of individual privacy and control.

The future of identity is shifting toward a dynamic, cryptographic foundation that secures the link between human intent and automated actions. This is a new security layer that provides transparency and auditability, which are required for digital systems to move money and execute contracts with the same level of trust as a physical signature. This evolution ensures that as we move toward autonomous systems, security remains seamless and verifiable without traditional friction. This evolution will be further accelerated by the integration of stablecoins, which act as digital fiat currencies pegged one-to-one to USD, such as USDC, enabling borderless commerce. Stablecoins have already become an important financial tool for millions globally, providing instant cross-border settlement and a hedge against volatility. This progress is fueled by partnerships in which fintech's and banks act as vital partners rather than just competitors, pushing the entire ecosystem forward.

Another positive development is that tech giants like Apple have pressured traditional banks to offer more competitive interest rates by introducing high-yield savings accounts. This has encouraged many digital platforms and online banks to offer savings rates ranging from 2% to over 5%, providing significantly better value for consumers. While many traditional brick-and-mortar banks still maintain lower yields, the increased competition is a win for savers seeking higher returns. As noted by Forbes, this shift marks a new era where technology and finance blend to make wealth-building tools more accessible and rewarding for everyone.[37] These better services and higher returns empower consumers to dream bigger about their financial futures.

At this time, Brazil is a top model for financial inclusion and has enabled real-time rails, open finance, and biometric identity. Even though the model isn't perfect, they have driven impressive results. As of late 2025, more than 170 million Brazilians, representing approximately 93% of the adult population, actively use Pix, approaching eight billion monthly transactions, proving that when technology and trust align, we can achieve a truly inclusive financial future for everyone.[38]

Major tech leaders, including Amazon, Meta, Microsoft, Salesforce, and Stripe, have officially joined the Universal Commerce Protocol (UCP) Tech Council to establish a unified standard for AI-driven commerce. Alongside founding members like Shopify and Google, these companies are developing an open-source framework to ensure seamless shopping experiences across all digital platforms and payment processors.

Plaid and Claude's partnership ties it together: Anthropic's Claude Managed Agents API provides the reasoning brain in a secure sandbox, while Plaid's User APIs supply only the specific data needed for each task via Model Context Protocol (MCP). They have introduced introspection adapters, which act like a real-time brain scan for AI. These tools monitor the model's internal reasoning as it happens, allowing developers to see the intent behind an answer before it is even finished. Shifting safety from an external filter to an internal monitor helps catch harmful or deceptive logic at the source. This is a major breakthrough because it enables models to self-report hidden behaviors—like bias or deception—with a level of accuracy that was previously impossible, moving us closer to a "glass box" era of AI transparency. For the future of finance, this is a game-changer because it provides the audit trail regulators require, allowing high-stakes systems like Agentic Commerce and automated lending to prove their decisions are unbiased and compliant in real time. Introduced by the Bank for International Settlements (BIS) in April 2024, the "Finternet" (or unified ledger) is a vision for a global, programmable financial infrastructure that functions like the Internet. This "network of networks" integrates identity, data, and digital money into a single system to enable instant, 24/7 automated settlements across all asset classes.[39]

Success in this era requires clear goals, such as key performance indicators (KPIs) for banks, governments, and the broad ecosystem. I feel strongly that innovative technology and policy changes, such as Real-Time Rails, open finance, privacy-by-design, and human data rights, need clear dates and ecosystem mandates. A joint effort, a shared purpose, and properly designed budgets must be combined to meet and set deadlines to help the industry achieve these goals. We must leverage technology to address complex challenges and evolving consumer demands while simultaneously reducing operational overhead. This dual focus ensures that future innovation remains both purposeful for the user and sustainable for the institution. It is also important to learn from tech companies that are willing to fail fast. We should test new concepts or products with a small group, get feedback, and try again. If we are too scared to fail and don't even try, we won't move forward at all. Layer in privacy-by-design to protect data, defense-by-design to be ready for cyber attacks, and always keep an open mind when it comes to change. After all, the future of finance is built on trust as the new currency. As AI becomes more affordable and accessible, the finance industry must champion the principle of "trust but verify" to ensure that new technology remains secure and accessible to all.

To summarize my vision, I chose the book's subtitle, *How Data, Trust, and Technology are Reshaping the Global Economy*, as the theme of this closing chapter. I strongly believe the future of finance will be shaped by human data rights, privacy in mind, trust as the new currency, and innovative technology deeply rooted in a consumer-first world.

Expert Interview with Theodora Lau, CEO of Unconventional Ventures and Author

I have had the pleasure of knowing Theodora Lau for many years as both a fintech leader and a very good friend. Theo is the founder of Unconventional Ventures, a prominent speaker, and the author of *Banking with AI*. Her work sits at the intersection of technology, longevity, and financial inclusion, with a consistent focus on how innovation can better serve humanity.

When we discussed her journey and what drives her passion for the future of finance, Theo described herself as a storyteller first. "I love to tell stories that matter," she explains. We both agree that the outcome of technology is more important than the build itself. Theo noted, "We can build all we want, but I want us to pause and think about why. Why are we building what we're building?" This question is central to her work in artificial intelligence.

We discussed the explosive growth of AI and how it has changed the public's relationship with technology. Theo warns that this accessibility requires new guardrails to prevent harm. "This is a good time to use AI to help small business owners close books faster, but it also brings to bear the need for a comprehensive framework, so citizens are not harmed," she says. A major theme in our conversation was the risk of bias and the importance of data rights. Theo pointed out that most AI models are trained on Western-based languages, potentially leaving billions behind. "There are 3,000 languages in Africa, and most are not included. If the future is powered by these agents, what are they trained on?" she asked.

We both agree that the global shift toward SuperApps and digital public infrastructure is a catalyst for financial inclusion. Theo highlighted the success of platforms in Asia and Latin America that use simple technology to solve complex problems. "The exciting part isn't so much that it allows people to pay with a QR code; it's what it enables," she notes. She cited Nubank in Brazil as a prime example of using data to create value rather than just extracting it.

Theodora's insights on the intersection of AI, trust, and inclusion can be summarized in three key takeaways:

- Human-centric inclusion and representation
- Digital trust and algorithmic transparency
- Curiosity and an ethical experimentation mindset

Theo concluded by offering advice to those navigating this fast-paced landscape. We both agree that staying curious and keeping a pulse on global innovation is essential. "Regardless of your role or jurisdiction, there is always something new happening. Keep a pulse on what's happening outside of your own backyard," she urges. Her vision reminds us that the most successful fintech innovations are those that bridge the gap between accessibility and genuine care.

Step into the Future of Finance

I believe technology thrives when it has a shared purpose. Our industry needs to prioritize ethical AI, privacy-by-design, and human data rights as non-negotiable foundations. The real work starts when we move beyond compliance, building systems where progress and individual agency genuinely coexist. That means putting humans at the center of every design decision, not as an afterthought.

To stay ahead, professionals must proactively expand their knowledge to keep pace with the ever-changing ecosystem. The global financial services industry employs tens of millions of workers, and artificial intelligence (AI) is increasingly reshaping roles rather than triggering wholesale job losses. According to Goldman Sachs, generative AI could affect up to 25% of jobs in advanced economies by automating certain tasks, indicating a gradual workforce transition rather than mass displacement.[40] As financial institutions adopt digital-first operating models, demand is growing for professionals with specialized skills that complement automation rather than compete with it. In particular, there remains a critical need for cybersecurity and compliance professionals, especially those holding industry-standard credentials such as CISSP for security leadership, CISA for audit, or CISM for management. This demand is reinforced by a continued global cybersecurity workforce gap of approximately 4.8 million professionals, alongside the emergence of new roles at the intersection of AI, governance, and financial risk management.[41]

Navigating this future requires an agile mindset that is comfortable with constant change. Success is no longer about mastering a single, static skill set but about investing time in upskilling through online courses, events, podcasts, and staying up-to-date with real-time industry developments through newsletters and LinkedIn.

Thank you for investing your time to step into the future of finance with me. I hope it has helped open the door to new possibilities and opportunities that will inspire you to drive the ecosystem forward as part of the army of the future of finance.

Chapter 10 Key Takeaways and Book Summary

1. Financial empowerment is enabled through fintech, BaaS, and embedded finance as it helps to make payments, loans, and budgeting a seamless part of our daily lives.
2. Open data, secure digital IDs, and robust cybersecurity bridge the gap between trust and technology by protecting consumers and their transactions.
3. Thriving in this ever-changing economy requires curiosity and willingness to lean into new technologies from AI to blockchain, and digital currencies while constantly challenging the status quo through continuous learning.
4. **Personal lesson:** I am driven by the belief that the future of finance requires a foundation built on privacy-by-design, ethical AI and consumer data sovereignty. Taking on this mission to write 80,000 words on this topic by a specific deadline has been one of the toughest challenges of my career and yet one that has taught me many lessons from how important it is to ask for help, to the need to use all types of mediums to acquire new insights, to the value of celebrating the wins, even the small ones.

Recommended Resources

Finance is constantly evolving, and keeping pace requires learning directly from the ecosystem through industry conferences. To stay at the forefront of the evolving finance ecosystem, I attend 15+ events annually and speak alongside global leaders at staples such as Money20/20 (a 10-year veteran), Fintech Meetup, Open Banking Expo, and the Payments Canada Summit. Beyond the stage, I serve as the president of the OFNC, hosting quarterly events for dedicated open finance innovators, and as a North American curator for the Financial Club.

Another great way to stay close to the conversation is through podcasts. I follow many other industry experts. Some of the voices I've learned the most from include *Fintech Insider* by 11:FS, *One Vision* host Theodora Lau, *Mr. Open Banking* host Eyal Sivan, and *Around the Coin* host Stephen Brent Sargeant. I took the leap to launch my own Spotify podcast, *Step into the Future of Finance*, in fall 2025 to share insights on hot trends with global experts. I hope you have a listen and add it to your playlist. My other recommendation is to spend time building a strong community, as I have found it to be a crucial part of my success not only as an entrepreneur but also throughout my career. My network was built one day at a time over 20 years through LinkedIn connections, over coffee, calls, and meetups. I am lucky to be surrounded by supporters, including my Money 2020 Rise Up and Amplify global community.

It is not easy to keep your ear to the ground on new trends. I recommend subscribing to newsletters such as *Finextra Daily, This Week in Fintech, The Deliveryman*, and *Finavator Finsights*. To ensure the latest updates and insights, there are many webinars worldwide on topics such as fintech, embedded finance, digital currencies, DeFi, AI, blockchain, cybersecurity, and open finance, as well as many free industry meetups. As the world changes in front of all our eyes, I hope this book helps you start to notice how each of these elements touches your life, and it might inspire new and innovative ideas.

I invite you to continue stepping into the future of finance with me. Explore the *Finavator Masterclass*; listen to my podcast, *Step into the Future of Finance*, on Spotify; and connect with me on LinkedIn. Scan the QR code to subscribe to our newsletter and stay ahead of the latest trends in our ever-evolving industry.

Acknowledgments

I wrote this book to simplify the future of finance by drawing on insights from my 20+ years of experience in both corporate and entrepreneurial environments across telecom, loyalty, online shopping, payments, blockchain, and digital identity. I also had the opportunity to travel to 25 countries for either work (speaking engagements, conferences, client meetings) or adventures (living in Australia, traveling in Asia) and, most importantly, family vacations, all while gaining experience on payments from travelers' checks and pre-euro paper money to credit cards, and international payments. Written with the hope of inspiring others to be curious, to learn, and to innovate as they step into the future of finance, it is dedicated to everyone who has shaped my understanding of finance.

Thank you to the remarkable global industry experts, Daniel Kornitzer, Elena Litani, Genvieve Dozier, Sebastien L. Taveau, Panagiotis Kriaris, Frances Zelazny, David Birch, Amber Scott, Carol Grunberg, Eyal Sivan, Emma Todd, Russell Moore, Sue Ennis, Jane Battatt, Malcolm Clarke, Chris Skinner, Professor Michael R. King, and Theodora Lau, who shared their time and wisdom. Your insights brought depth and clarity to these pages.

I want to say a special thank-you to the Money2020 Rise Up & Amplify community of more than 200 leaders worldwide for your friendships, shared passion for dreaming big, and for always supporting one another. Being selected as 1 of 30 in 2019 to join this community has been a great privilege and one of the reasons I took the leap to start my own company, Finavator, that year.

To my clients, supporters, and friends, thank you for your trust, encouragement, and inspiration along the way. I especially acknowledge the inspiration of my late best friend, Shannon Phair, for the impact her life has had on mine.

Thank you to my many mentors, coaches, and industry leaders. You know who you are. I am grateful that you took the time to share your wisdom.

As a first-time author, I can share that this was not an easy process, filled with uncomfortable moments and hours spent writing in parks, cars, planes, hotel rooms, on docks, in my office, and even at my son's soccer practices. Just like any hard task worth doing, the feeling of completion is like stepping offstage and hearing from the audience what they learned and what excites them, which is priceless. I'm thankful to many friends for your early reading comments, including Megha, Elena, Diane, Clare, and Samantha, as well as to my amazing Finavator Team for making this journey fun. A big thank-you to the talented Judy Slack for not only helping turn my vision into words, but also for stepping into the future of finance with me.

And again, to my amazing family, I love all of you. Thank you.

Sources

Introduction

1. https://www.pymnts.com/news/payment-methods/2017/incomm-partners-with-wechat-to-power-digital-payments-for-chinese-tourists-to-japan/
2. https://www.fintechfutures.com/press-releases/fintech-market-size-projected-to-grow-to-882-billion-by-2030-as-advanced-technologies-services-expand

Chapter 1

1. https://www.fintechfutures.com/press-releases/fintech-market-size-projected-to-grow-to-882-billion-by-2030-as-advanced-technologies-services-expand
2. LendingTree – 2025 Credit Card Debt Statistics, August 2025.
3. https://www.mckinsey.com/industries/financial-services/our-insights/global-banking-annual-review
4. https://www.revolut.com/news/revolut_completes_fundraising_process_establishing_75_billion_valuation/
5. https://www.fortunebusinessinsights.com/fintech-market-108641?
6. https://fintechlabs.com/the-397-fintech-unicorns-of-the-21st-century-q3-2025/
7. https://www.mordorintelligence.com/industry-reports/north-america-fintech-mar ket; https://www.sperresearch.com/report-store/united-states-fintech-market.aspx
8. https://www.imarcgroup.com/canada-fintech-market
9. https://fintechlabs.com/the-397-fintech-unicorns-of-the-21st-century-q3-2025/

10. https://www.mordorintelligence.com/industry-reports/united-kingdom-fintech-market; https://www.sperresearch.com/press-release/uk-fintech-technology-market.aspx
11. https://www.imarcgroup.com/brazil-fintech-market
12. https://www.mordorintelligence.com/industry-reports/china-fintech-market
13. CB Insights, State of Fintech 2025, https://www.cbinsights.com/research/report/fintech-trends-2025/, accessed January 2026.

Chapter 2

1. https://www.alliedmarketresearch.com/prepaid-card-market
2. https://www.fdic.gov/household-survey/2023-fdic-national-survey-unbanked-and-underbanked-households-executive-summary
3. https://eqb.investorroom.com/2024-12-04-EQB-reports-record-annual-earnings,-dividend-increase-and-growth-guidance
4. https://www.fintech.ca/2025/10/20/eq-bank-hits-1b-reload-milestone-as-prepaid-cards-redefine-consumer-finance/
5. https://www.grandviewresearch.com/horizon/outlook/banking-as-a-service-market-size/global
6. https://www.shopify.com/balance
7. https://www.spglobal.com/market-intelligence/en/news-insights/research/banking-as-a-service-the-role-of-banks-in-powering-the-fintech-industry
8. https://www.federalreserve.gov/newsevents/pressreleases/enforcement20240614a.html
9. https://www.globenewswire.com/news-release/2025/04/23/3066695/28124/en/Prepaid-Cards-Market-to-Cross-4-Billion-by-2030-as-Consumer-Behavior-Evolves-Market-Gains-from-Increased-Retailer-Acceptance-of-Card-based-Payments.html
10. https://www.mordorintelligence.com/industry-reports/global-banking-as-a-service-market

Chapter 3

1. https://finbold.com/banking-business-starbucks-holds-over-1-8-billion-in-customer-deposits/
2. https://www.mckinsey.com/industries/financial-services/our-insights/the-2023-mckinsey-global-payments-report
3. https://www.bis.org/publ/qtrpdf/r_qt2403c.htm

4. https://fortune.com/2025/06/26/agentic-ai-spending-155-billion-by-2030-cfo-bofa-analysts/
5. https://medium.com/@muniu.dev/the-internet-is-for-bots-why-2026-is-the-year-developers-stop-building-for-humans-0992e53fa02c
6. https://worldpay.com/
7. https://www.juniperresearch.com/press/ecommerce-market-to-reach-440bn-transactions/

Chapter 4

1. https://www.statista.com/statistics/273550/data-breaches-recorded-in-the-united-states-by-number-of-breaches-and-records-exposed/#:~:text=Table_title:%20Annual%20number%20of%20data%20compromises%20and,%7C%20Individuals%20impacted%20in%20millions:%20298.08%20%7C, accessed November 2025.
2. Identity.org on AI and biometrics, https://www.identity.org/the-intersection-of-artificial-intelligence-ai-and-biometrics/, accessed January 2026.
3. https://docs.quickintel.io/crypto-terminology/categories/2.-cryptographic-elements.
4. European Digital Identity Wallet – Security and Privacy features / EU Digital Identity regulation provisions) EU Digital Identity Wallet privacy protections and technical standards. https://ec.europa.eu/digital-building-blocks/sites/spaces/EUDIGITALIDENTITYWALLET/pages/712508927/Security+and+Privacy
5. https://www.bankid.com/en/news-press/press/statistics, accessed January 2026.
6. https://sbs-software.com/insights/digital-id-banking/, accessed November 2025.
7. https://sbs-software.com/insights/digital-id-banking/, accessed November 2025.
8. https://www.business-standard.com/amp/india-news/aadhaar-authentication-hits-2-29-bn-mark-in-june-face-authentications-rise-125070301138_1.html, accessed January 2026.
9. https://stripe.com/payment-method/upi
10. https://gridlines.io/blogs/addressing-aadhaar-card-kyc-security-issues/
11. https://www.apple.com/newsroom/2025/11/apple-introduces-digital-id-a-new-way-to-create-and-present-an-id-in-apple-wallet/

Chapter 5

1. Banco Central do Brasil Open Finance Progress Report, 2025.
2. https://www.ecommerceupdate.org/en/news/o-ano-do-pix-modelo-de-pagamento-processou-42-bilhoes-de-transacoes-e-consolidou-sua-lideranca-no-brasil-com-inovacoes-e-avancos-em-seguranca/

3. https://www.consumerfinance.gov/about-us/newsroom/cfpb-approves-application-from-financial-data-exchange-to-issue-standards-for-open-banking/
4. Mastercard, "The Rise of Open Banking: A Global Roadmap" (2024) and The World Bank, "Open Finance: A Global Overview" (2024); Juniper Research, "Open Banking: Key Opportunities, Vendor Strategies & Market Forecasts 2023–2027" and Statista (2024).
5. BCG, "The Benefits of Data Sharing Now Outweigh the Risks".
6. https://www.mckinsey.com/industries/financial-services/our-insights/financial-data-unbound-the-value-of-open-data-for-individuals-and-institutions

Chapter 6

1. https://www.aaespeakers.com/keynote-speakers/frank-abagnale
2. IBM Security, Cost of a Data Breach Report 2024.
3. https://www.sophos.com/en-us/press/press-releases/2024/04/ransomware-payments-increase-500-last-year-finds-sophos-state
4. https://www.wsj.com/articles/fraudsters-use-ai-to-mimic-ceos-voice-in-unusual-cybercrime-case-11,567,157,402
5. https://www.cisa.gov/sites/default/files/publications/Families%20Cybersecurity%20Presentation.pdf
6. https://www.getcybersafe.gc.ca/en
7. https://www.fool.com/money/research/identity-theft-credit-card-fraud-statistics/
8. Markets and Markets Financial Cybersecurity Report 2024, Gartner IT Security Spending Forecast, IBM Cost of Data Breach Report (Financial Services), McKinsey Cybersecurity in Financial Services.
9. https://www.marketsandmarkets.com/Market-Reports/cyber-security-market-505.html
10. https://www.isc2.org/Insights/2024/10/ISC2–2024-Cybersecurity-Workforce-Study?utm_source = chatgpt.com
11. https://www.isc2.org/Insights/2025/12/2025-ISC2-Cybersecurity-Workforce-Study
12. UNODC World Drug Report.
13. Financial Action Task Force Annual Report 2024.
14. LexisNexis True Cost of AML Compliance 2024.
15. https://sumsub.com/blog/global-digital-id-regulations-and-shifts/, accessed November 2025.
16. CrowdStrike, "Global Threat Report" (2026); Verizon, "Data Breach Investigations Report" (2025).

Chapter 7

1. CSIS interview on "Securing American Leadership on AI," https://www.youtube.com/watch?v=jpZ0dPsnIWw
2. https://home.dartmouth.edu/about/artificial-intelligence-ai-coined-dartmouth
3. https://taktile.com/articles/from-credit-scoring-to-genai
4. https://www.marketsandmarkets.com/Market-Reports/ai-in-finance-market-90,552,286.html
5. https://www.reuters.com/business/finance/us-bank-executives-say-ai-will-boost-productivity-cut-jobs-2025-12-09/
6. Forrester Consumer Banking Survey 2025, Gartner Digital Banking 2025, Accenture 2025.
7. https://iapp.org/news/a/llms-with-retrieval-augmented-generation-good-or-bad-for-privacy-compliance
8. https://www.publishersweekly.com/pw/by-topic/industry-news/publisher-news/article/98544-anthropic-agrees-to-pay-1-5-billion-to-settle-copyright-lawsuit.html
9. https://time.com/6327635/ai-needs-to-be-regulated-like-nuclear-weapons/
10. https://www.mckinsey.com/featured-insights/artificial-intelligence/notes-from-the-ai-frontier-modeling-the-impact-of-ai-on-the-world-economy
11. Council of Europe global treaty on AI https://www.coe.int/en/web/portal/-/council-of-europe-opens-first-ever-global-treaty-on-ai-for-signature
12. Sources: IDC Regional Spending Analysis 2025, Statista AI Market Data 2025, McKinsey Global Banking Report 2025.
13. Banking Interactions (90% by 2027): Gartner: 2026 Tech Predictions & Implications; Asset Management ($16T by 2028): Juniper Research: Mobile Banking Trends & Digital Wallets; Financial Crime Reduction (70% by 2029): Hawk AI: AI Adoption in Financial Crime & Compliance.
14. https://www.mindstudio.ai/blog/enterprises-ai-manage-compliance-policy-documents
15. MarketsandMarkets, AI in Fintech Market Forecast 2030.

Chapter 8

1. https://www.prnewswire.com/news-releases/heifer-international-ethichub-invest-420-000-to-improve-financial-access-for-smallholder-coffee-farmers-in-mexico-301,848,959.html
2. Consensys: The Industrialization of Trust (July 2025).
3. Polygon ID: Verifiable Credentials for Web3 Stablecoins vs. CBDCs 2025.

4. J.P. Morgan: Introducing Kinexys (November 2024).
5. Polygon ID: Verifiable Credentials for Web3 Stablecoins vs. CBDCs 2025.
6. Bitnodes.io.
7. Bitcoin Whitepaper by Satoshi Nakamoto 2008; Ethereum Foundation Technical Documentation 2026; MIT Blockchain Fundamentals 2026.
8. https://chain.link/
9. https://www.prnewswire.com/news-releases/blackrock-usd-institutional-digital-liquidity-fund-buidl-tokenized-by-securitize-surpasses-1b-in-aum-302,401,480.html
10. https://sdk.finance/blog/high-volume-transactions-lessons-from-the-largest-payment-systems/
11. https://www.blockchain-council.org/cryptocurrency/top-10-cryptocurrencies/
12. https://bitwage.com/en-us/blog/how-crypto-invoicing-reduces-transaction-costs-compared-to-traditional-payment-methods
13. https://www.juniperresearch.com/press/blockchain-to-facilitate-savings-of-10bn
14. MEXC News / TekRevol, https://www.mexc.co/news/127459
15. https://www.jpmorgan.com/kinexys/index#:~:text=Proven%20solutions%20to%20automate%20complex,Learn%20more
16. https://etedge-insights.com/technology/fintech/why-defi-is-no-longer-optional-for-the-global-financial-system/
17. DeFiLlama, 2026; Nasscom, 2026 https://defillama.com/
18. PayPal Tech Blog, https://developer.paypal.com/community/blog/pyusd-cross-border-payments/
19. https://ripple.com/ripple-press/global-financial-infrastructure-entering-a-new-era/
20. https://www.broadridge.com/insights/next-gen-markets-the-rise-and-reality-of-tokenization
21. ADB 2026, MDPI 2024, The Asian Banker 2023.
22. MIC Global, https://micglobal.com/insurance-blockchain-oracles/, accessed January 2026.
23. https://etherisc.com/] Etherisc Flight Delay Insurance
24. https://assets.coingecko.com/reports/2024/CoinGecko-2024-Q1-Report.pdf
25. Ethereum Foundation - Ethereum Energy Consumption, https://ethereum.org/en/energy-consumption/ and S&P Global - Assessing the Risks of Blockchain Oracles, https://www.spglobal.com/en/research-insights/special-reports/utility-at-a-cost-assessing-the-risks-of-blockchain-oracles, accessed January 2026.
26. https://www.ziprecruiter.com/Salaries/Blockchain-Software-Engineer-Salary
27. Ethereum Foundation, Layer 2 Scaling Report 2025.
28. https://coin.dance/nodes

29. MarkestandMarkets Blockchain Report 2026, Bitnodes.io Statistics 2026, Chainalysis Market Report 2026, Grand View Research 2026.
30. https://www.forbes.com/sites/boazsobrado/2025/11/11/bolivia-tests-election-tool-on-solana-to-reinforce-democracy/
31. https://www.coindesk.com/coindesk-indices/2025/04/30/ai-crypto-agents-are-ushering-in-a-new-era-of-defai
32. *"The promise and challenges of crypto + AI applications"* https://vitalik.eth.limo/general/2024/01/30/cryptoai.html
33. Gartner, Blockchain Value Add Forecast (via ConsenSys).

Chapter 9

1. River Learn: Can Bitcoin's Hard Cap of 21 million Be Changed? https://river.com/learn/can-bitcoins-hard-cap-of-21-million-be-changed/, accessed January 2026.
2. https://www.investopedia.com/news/what-erc20-and-what-does-it-mean-ethereum/
3. Blockchain website: https://www.blockchain.com/learning-portal/lessons/stablecoins-explained?, accessed January 2026.
4. https://english.www.gov.cn/news/202512/29/content_WS69526d4ec6d00ca5f9a08511.html, accessed January 2026.
5. Central Bank Digital Currency: Lessons from the Bahamas Alliance for Financial Inclusion, https://www.afi-global.org/opinion/central-bank-digital-currency-lessons-from-the-bahamas/, accessed January 2026.
6. https://remittanceprices.worldbank.org/, accessed January 2026.
7. Exploring the Pros and Cons of Wallets vs Exchanges | TheAmberPost. https://theamberpost.com/post/exploring-the-pros-and-cons-of-wallets-vs-exchanges, accessed January 2026.
8. https://buffett.cnbc.com/video/1994/04/25/buffett-you-dont-find-out-whos-been-swimming-naked-until-the-tide-goes-out.html
9. Tonellotto, E. (2019). Unlocking the hype: An analysis of how blockchain technology could affect hospitality culture. https://core.ac.uk/download/334564863.pdf
10. Paxos Transparency Reports, December 2025.
11. Visa, 2025; CoinLaw, https://usa.visa.com/about-visa/newsroom/press-releases.releaseId.21951.html, accessed January 2026; CoinLaw.io, https://coinlaw.io/stablecoin-statistics/, accessed January 2026.
12. RebelFi, https://rebelfi.io/blog/stablecoin-yield-vs-bank-yield-the-real-difference-for-fintech's-and, accessed January 2026; Visa, https://corporate.visa.com/en/sites/visa-perspectives/newsroom/visa-launches-stablecoin-settlement-in-the-united-states.html, accessed January 2026.

13. Bitcoin: A Peer-to-Peer Electronic Cash System, https://visaonchainanalytics.com/
14. Super Achiever Club: How to Make Money in a Crypto Bear Market & Crypto Crash https://www.dailymoss.com/super-achiever-club-how-to-make-money-in-a-crypto-bear-market-crypto-crash/, accessed January 2026.
15. Morgan Stanley – Stablecoins: Modernizing financial infrastructure 2025, https://www.eatonvance.com/insights/articles/modernizing-financial-infrastructure.html, accessed January 2026.
16. World Bank, https://remittanceprices.worldbank.org/, accessed January 2026.
17. BIS – Advancing in Tandem: 2024 CBDC Survey, https://www.bis.org/publ/bppdf/bispap159.pdf, accessed January 2026.
18. The Merge https://ethereum.org/roadmap/merge/, accessed January 2026.
19. Cassels: From Poster Boy to Posting Bail https://cassels.com/insights/from-poster-boy-to-posting-bail-sam-bankman-fried-gets-25-years-for-ftx-scandal/, accessed January 2026.
20. OSC, A Review by Staff of the Ontario Securities Commission https://www.osc.ca/quadrigacxreport/, accessed January 2026.
21. https://www.bis.org/publ/arpdf/ar2023e3.htm
22. Mintlayer "$16–30 Trillion by 2030: Unlocking the RWA Opportunity," https://www.mintlayer.org/blogs/16-30-trillion-by-2030-unlocking-the-rwa-opportunity, accessed January 2026.
23. https://www.mexc.co/en-IN/news/595483
24. https://ieeexplore.ieee.org/document/11170949
25. https://ieg.worldbankgroup.org/evaluations/financial-inclusion-foothold-ladder-toward-prosperity
26. https://www.worldbank.org/en/publication/globalfindex
27. https://www.sc.com/en/news/corporate-investment-banking/rise-digital-assets-finance-mandy-defilippo/

Chapter 10

1. Grand View Research – Banking-as-a-Service Market Size Worth $74.55 Billion by 2030 https://www.prnewswire.com/news-releases/banking-as-a-service-market-size-worth-74-55-billion-by-2030-grand-view-research-inc-301616184.html
2. Globe Newswire – Prepaid Cards Market Intelligence Report 2025–2030 – Global Prepaid Cards Market https://www.globenewswire.com/news-release/2025/12/15/3205332/0/en/Prepaid-Cards-Market-Intelligence-Report-2025-2030-Featuring-200-Companies-Industry-to-Grow-at-10-4-CAGR-Fueled-by-High-Uptake-and-Technological-Progress.html

3. https://mica.io/
4. Juniper Research – Users of Digital Identity Documents to Exceed 6.5 Billion Globally in 2026 https://www.juniperresearch.com/press/users-of-digital-identity-documents-to-exceed/
5. Mastercard introduces Verifiable Intent, co-developed with Google, https://thepaypers.com/payments/news/mastercard-introduces-verifiable-intent-co-developed-with-google
6. eIDAS 2.0 | Updates, Compliance https://www.european-digital-identity-regulation.com/
7. The Danish approach to copyright and deepfakes: A model for the EU? https://www.europarl.europa.eu/RegData/etudes/ATAG/2026/782611/EPRS_ATA(2026)782611_EN.pdf
8. Singpass Singapore's National Digital Identity https://www.mddi.gov.sg/newsroom/singpass-factsheet-02032022/
9. Large Scale Pilot – NOBID https://ec.europa.eu/digital-building-blocks/sites/spaces/EUDIGITALIDENTITYWALLET/pages/924975315/LSP-NOBID
10. ISO 31700-1:2023(en) – https://www.iso.org/obp/ui/en/#iso:std:iso:31700:-1:ed-1:v1:en
11. JP Morgan – PSD3 Builds a regulatory foundation for open banking, cross-border payments, and more https://www.jpmorgan.com/insights/payments/operations-optimization/psd3
12. The Financial Data Access (FiDA) Regulation https://www.financial-data-access.com/
13. UK Parliament – Data Protection and Digital Information Bill https://bills.parliament.uk/bills/3430?__cf_chl_f_tk=IV8VFmtYQN9aE17sO3AX8ssde7U3HxQ5bsl3fIq4euE-1771964402-1.0.1.1-2t0ctTjBlfVqXo9IVlTphPT27LgMsPZ12Y8uqq_I2Fk
14. https://www.prove.com/blog/prove-state-of-identity-report
15. Deep Strike – Cybersecurity Skills Gap Statistics: What the Numbers Reveal https://deepstrike.io/blog/cybersecurity-skills-gap
16. Markets and Markets – AI in Finance https://www.marketsandmarkets.com/Market-Reports/ai-in-finance-market-19033.html
17. Cognizant – How agentic AI is shaping the future of payments https://www.cognizant.com/us/en/insights/insights-blog/impact-of-ai-on-the-payment-ecosystem
18. Center for AI Safety – Statement on AI Risk https://aistatement.com/, accessed January 2026.
19. Goldman Sachs – Gen AI: too much spend, too little benefit? https://www.goldmansachs.com/insights/top-of-mind/gen-ai-too-much-spend-too-little-benefit, accessed January 2026.

20. Transcript IQ – Decentralized Finance (DeFi) Market to Skyrocket: USD 20.5 Billion (2025) to USD 231.2 Billion by 2030, Growing at a 53.7% CAGR https://www.transcript-iq.com/product/decentralized-finance-defi-market-to-skyrocket-usd-20-5-billion-2025-to-usd-231-2-billion-by-2030-growing-at-a-53-7-cagr, accessed January 2026.
21. Grandview Research – Decentralized Finance Market 2026 – 2033 https://www.grandviewresearch.com/industry-analysis/decentralized-finance-market-report, accessed January 2026.
22. BIS – Finternet: the financial system for the future https://www.bis.org/publ/work1178.htm
23. Boston Consulting Group – Relevance of On-chain Asset Tokenization in "Crypto Winter" https://www.bcg.com/publications/2022/relevance-of-on-chain-asset-tokenization
24. Atlantic Council – Central Bank Digital Currency Tracker https://www.atlanticcouncil.org/cbdctracker/
25. Yahoo Finance – Stablecoin Transactions Soared 72% in 2025, Hit $33 T With USDC in Lead https://finance.yahoo.com/news/stablecoin-transactions-soared-72-2025-054951388.html
26. BVNK – Stablecoin Utility Report 2026 https://bvnk.com/utility
27. https://www.prnewswire.com/news-releases/major-financial-institutions-unveil-bank-led-on-chain-money-initiative-302792661.html
28. Forbes – Kraken Financial Becomes First Crypto Bank To Get Fed Master Account
29. SOLID https://solidproject.org/
30. Cloudflare – https://blog.cloudflare.com/state-of-the-post-quantum-Internet-2025/
31. Tracking AI – AI IQ Results https://trackingai.org
32. HAI Stanford – Artificial Intelligence Index Report 2025 https://hai.stanford.edu/research/ai-index-report
33. CertPro – How Does ISO 42001 Align with Global AI Regulations? https://certpro.com/how-does-iso-42001-align-with-global-ai-regulations/
34. World Economic Forum – Stablecoins as a bridge, not a threat: why interoperability will define global finance https://www.weforum.org/stories/2026/01/stablecoins-bridge-not-a-threat-why-interoperability-will-define-future-global-finance/
35. Australian Government – Consumer Data Right: Giving You Choice and Control https://www.cdr.gov.au/
36. MyData Global – Human-Centric Data Ownership: https://mydata.org/
37. Forbes – 10 Best High-Yield Savings Accounts Of March 2026: Up to 5.00% APY https://www.forbes.com/advisor/banking/savings/best-high-yield-savings-accounts/

38. EBANX – Pix to approach 8 billion monthly transactions as it marks five-year milestone https://www.globenewswire.com/news-release/2025/11/14/3188285/0/en/Pix-to-approach-8-billion-monthly-transactions-as-it-marks-five-year-milestone-EBANX-study-finds.html
39. https://www.bis.org/publ/work1178.htm
40. Goldman Sachs – How Will AI Affect the Global Workforce? https://www.goldmansachs.com/insights/articles/how-will-ai-affect-the-global-workforce
41. TECH FUNDING NEWS – 4.8M unfilled roles: Why cybersecurity's talent gap is reshaping the tech workforce https://techfundingnews.com/4-8m-unfilled-roles-why-cybersecuritys-talent-gap-is-reshaping-the-tech-workforce/

About the Author

Michelle Beyo is a fintech and open finance leader, founder and CEO of Finavator, and host of the podcast *Step into the Future of Finance*. With more than 20 years of experience spanning payments, digital identity, open data, loyalty, and telecommunications, Michelle helps organizations navigate digital transformation and build practical, future-ready financial solutions.

A TEDx and global keynote speaker, Michelle has shared her insights on international stages, including Money20/20, Fintech Meet Up, and Open Banking Expo. She is a Money20/20 RiseUp alumna and industry mentor, supporting the next generation of fintech leaders, and creator of a six-hour *Future of Finance Masterclass*, empowering professionals and organizations with actionable strategies for today's rapidly evolving financial landscape.

Michelle also serves as president of Open Finance Network Canada, where she champions open finance, data rights, transparency, and collaboration between traditional institutions and emerging technologies. In addition, she serves on multiple advisory boards, working with founders and financial institutions as they navigate innovation, governance, and ecosystem development.

Her contributions to the industry have been recognized through numerous honors, including the Global Fintech Powerlist (2022), Top 50 Women Leaders of Toronto (2023), Fintech Female Entrepreneur of the Year, North America (2024), and the Powerlist at Open Banking Expo Canada (2025 and 2026). These awards reflect her impact in advancing open finance, driving innovation across financial services, and championing inclusive leadership within the global fintech ecosystem.

Michelle's expertise spans fintech strategy, payments innovation, open finance governance, ecosystem building, and North American market expansion. She is driven by a belief that financial innovation should be inclusive, practical, and human-centered.

Based in Canada and working globally, Michelle is passionate about helping people and organizations confidently step into the future of finance through speaking, teaching, and writing.

Connect

Michelle's LinkedIn: https://www.linkedin.com/in/michellebeyo/

YouTube channel: https://www.youtube.com/@Finavator/videos

Finavator newsletters: https://www.finavator.online/get-free-training

Future of Finance Masterclass: https://finavator.com/#course

Reach out: https://finavator.com/contact/

Step into the Future of Finance podcast: https://open.spotify.com/show/6tfflOY52ClLkLxgJEJSmo?si=e7ef65c49da748c9

Index